KINSHIP AND MARRIAGE
AMONG THE ANLO EWE

LONDON SCHOOL OF ECONOMICS
MONOGRAPHS ON SOCIAL ANTHROPOLOGY

Managing Editor: Anthony Forge

The Monographs on Social Anthropology were established in 1940 and aim to publish results of modern anthropological research of primary interest to specialists.

The continuation of the series was made possible by a grant in aid from the Wenner-Gren Foundation for Anthropological Research, and more recently by a further grant from the Governors of the London School of Economics and Political Science. Income from sales is returned to a revolving fund to assist further publications.

The Monographs are under the direction of an Editorial Board associated with the department of Anthropology of the London School of Economics and Political Science.

Fuŋɔsi, chief priest of the town god at Woe, sitting in front of his shrine

LONDON SCHOOL OF ECONOMICS
MONOGRAPHS ON SOCIAL ANTHROPOLOGY
No. 37

KINSHIP
AND MARRIAGE
AMONG THE
ANLO EWE

BY

G. K. NUKUNYA

UNIVERSITY OF LONDON
THE ATHLONE PRESS
NEW YORK: HUMANITIES PRESS INC.
1969

Published by
THE ATHLONE PRESS
UNIVERSITY OF LONDON
at 2 Gower Street London WCI

Distributed by Tiptree Book Services
Tiptree, Essex

Australia and New Zealand
Melbourne University Press

Canada
Oxford University Press
Toronto

485 19537 2

Library of Congress Catalog Card No. 69–18054

Printed in Great Britain by
WESTERN PRINTING SERVICES LTD
BRISTOL

PREFACE

This work, apart from minor corrections, was approved as a thesis for the Doctor of Philosophy degree in the Faculty of Arts (Anthropology), University of London. The corrections largely concern facts which have become apparent since the submission of the original thesis.

Many people have helped with this study in diverse ways, and as it will be difficult to mention every one individually I take this opportunity to thank them all. Some, however, must be mentioned. My warmest thanks go to all my informants at Anloga, Alakple, Woe and other villages for their co-operation during the period of my fieldwork among them. Their friendliness and desire to help made my stay very enjoyable. I must mention in particular Chief Avudzega III of Alakple for the keen interest he has taken in my work at all stages, especially his efforts to introduce me to those well-informed elders of his town who volunteered much information to me.

To my mother's brother, Mr Kwami Kpodo, I owe a special debt of gratitude, not only for his patronage and financial support throughout my academic career, but also for allowing me to lean so heavily on his vast knowledge of Ewe culture. In fact it was when helping him to copy his radio talks on Ewe customs some ten years ago that my interest in our social institutions was kindled. Since then he has always been a ready storehouse of information for me on these matters. I have no means whatsoever of thanking him – except by writing this book.

In London my academic training, the fieldwork and writing of the thesis were supervised by Professor Lucy Mair of the London School of Economics whose continual encouragement and help enabled me to complete the work on time. Her sensitivity and discernment were a constant source of inspiration for me and under her direction the quality of the work improved greatly. She has also been responsible for most of the arrangements necessary for the publication of the thesis. For all this help so generously given my gratitude is unbounded.

Miss Barbara Ward of the School of Oriental and African Studies, who had earlier made a study of the Ewe, placed all her manuscripts and published works on the Ewe at my disposal. I also benefited considerably from the several discussions I had with her before and after my fieldwork. My great debt to her is evident throughout the book. My sincerest thanks also go to Professor I. Schapera and Dr Jack Goody for reading through the manuscript and making several useful suggestions.

My friend and colleague, Mr Divine Amenumey, formerly of the School of Oriental and African Studies, who has recently completed his research into some aspects of Ewe history, has allowed me to benefit from his results. Of my former colleagues and friends at the L.S.E. I must acknowledge the help and encouragement of Dr George Benneh and Mr S. K. Gaisie. I owe a special debt to Mr Gaisie. Many of my ideas have been influenced by the many stimulating discussions we have had during several years of comradeship. His keen interest in this work has been greatly appreciated.

My thanks also go to Mr P. Kemevor of the Department of Geography, Legon, for kindly drawing the maps and diagrams, to Mr C. K. Davordzie, of the Ghana Academy of Sciences, for taking and printing the photographs and to Mr M. N. Quartey of the Univeristy of Ghana, Legon, for secretarial assistance.

My course at the L.S.E. as well as the fieldwork was financed by the University of Ghana. For this help I am very grateful. Responsibility for all views expressed in the book is, however, entirely mine.

University of Ghana,   G.K.N.
Legon. November 1966

CONTENTS

TABLES

FIGURES

CONTENTS ix

PLATES

Plates 1 and 2 between pages 150 and 151
Plates 3 and 4 between pages 166 and 167

MAPS

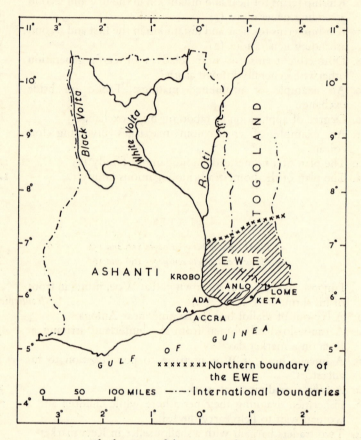

MAP I. The location of the Ewe in Ghana and Togo

I

Introduction

The Ewe-speaking people now number about a million souls.[1] They are a congeries of autonomous kingdoms of varied sizes living in the southern half of what is now the Republic of Togoland, and in south-eastern Ghana, where they form the present Volta Region of the Republic.

The whole Ewe-speaking area, with the exception of its south-western corner, formed part of the former German colony of Togo until after the First World War, when it was divided and transferred to France and Britain.[2] The eastern half was administered by France as a separate unit, while the other half was administered by Britain together with her former colony of the Gold Coast. The Ewe also featured in this division, about half of them going to the French side and the rest to the British side.

Until the arrival of the European powers the Ewe never formed one political unit. They lived in politically autonomous groups. The smallest politically independent units consisted of single villages, while the largest, such as the Anlo, contained many large settlements and covered very wide areas (Maps 1 and 2). Jacob Spieth[3] in 1906 was able to enumerate 120 of these political units, hereafter referred to as tribes.

Language and common traditions of origin formed the most important bases of Ewe unity. The original home of all the Ewe is traced traditionally to Oyo in Western Nigeria, whence they are believed to have migrated into their present country around the seventeenth century.[4] In the linguistic sphere (which is their second unifying factor), however, marked local variations are

[1] The 1960 Ghana Population Census returned a total of 563,005 for the Ewe-speaking districts, while that of Togoland in the same year was 537,000. Census Office, Accra 1962, *1960 Population Census of Ghana* Vol. 1, p. xxiii and *Recensement General de la Population Du Togo 1958–1960* Vol. 2, p. 7.

[2] The Franco-British boundary was fixed by a commission of the League of Nations in 1920–2. [3] 1906, pp. 34–49.

[4] This tradition is generally supported by the traditions of other peoples and identifiable traditional sites. See Wiegrabe, 1938, p. 24, and Ward, 1958, pp. 134–6.

found, which make it difficult for people of one area to understand properly the local dialects[1] of others. Although our knowledge of most of the tribes is still sketchy[2] it is clear that other
cultural traits also differ from place to place. These are most
clearly evidenced in musical forms, dancing, modes of salutation
and facial markings, to mention only a few.

Local differences are also found in the traditional social structure. For instance, while Spieth[3] describes the Ho, an inland tribe,
as strictly patrilineal, Westermann's[4] account of the Glidzi, who
live on the east coast of Togoland, mentions a system of inheritance by which certain portions of personal property pass from a
man to his sister's son. In Anlo, another coastal tribe, and Tongu,
who live along the Volta, there are patrilineal clans and well-
integrated local patrilineages, which, as far as we know, are not
found in many of the other tribes.

Because of these differences, generalizations embracing the
whole Ewe-speaking group are bound to be misleading unless
the sphere or area of their application is clearly delimited. It is only
through detailed studies of the different tribes that the similarities
and differences between them can be established. A useful study
must concentrate on a fairly homogeneous unit, and from its
results comparisons could be made with the studies of other units.

The present study is a step in that direction. The unit chosen
for study is the Kingdom of Anlo, one of the largest of the Ewe
coastal tribes in Ghana. The selection of Anlo is largely determined
by my personal knowledge of the area, being an Anlo myself.
Another point in favour of Anlo is that it is large and fairly
homogeneous compared with the neighbouring tribes, and its
military strength in the past had helped to extend its influence and
social practices. A knowledge of Anlo will therefore be of great
use in understanding the social systems of its neighbours.

I. ANLO COUNTRY: HABITAT AND ECONOMY

Anlo country lies on the coast in the extreme south-eastern corner
of Ghana. It covers and area of 883 square miles,[5] of which about

[1] Ewe is one of the Kwa group of Sudanic languages closely allied to the Akan,
Guang and Ga tongues of Ghana and the Ibo, Ijaw, Yoruba and Nupe of Nigeria.
[2] Of the 120 tribes enumerated by Spieth only Glidzi, Ho, Tongu and Anlo
have been subjected to anthropological study.   [3] *Op. cit.*, *passim.*
[4] 1935, *passim.*   [5] Census Office, Accra, 1962, p. xxiii.

a sixth is covered with lagoons. The 1960 Ghana population census figure for the area was 231,017 inhabitants, giving a density of about 321 persons per square mile.[1] The country is dry, with a moderate rainfall which is very irregular, and never exceeds 30 inches. The Anlo are surrounded on all sides by other Ewe tribes, except in the south, where they are bounded by the sea. In the west live the Tongu, in the north the Ave, and in the east are the Be, Noefe and other small chiefdoms (Map 2). The coast of sand-bars which forms the southern boundary runs approximately north-easterly and is about forty miles long. It is bounded by the constant surf, the spray of which was in the old days thought to be steam and smoke arising from the boiling waters of the torrid zone. This coast, which is fringed with coconut trees, is sand-wiched between the sea in the south and the numerous large lagoons in the north. It is a narrow strip of land, barely exceeding two miles at its widest portions, and only 100 yards wide in certain places. Yet it contains many thickly peopled settlements of varying sizes, lying in continuous streams like beads along a string.

Of these settlements Keta, with its 16,000[2] inhabitants, lying roughly halfway through the belt, is easily the largest, not only in Anlo, but also in all Ewe-speaking Ghana. Besides being a port of call for small cargo ships, it is the commercial and administrative centre of the Anlo district, and has large European stores, several Government offices and two Government secondary schools. It was the first centre of missionary activities, and now has a large Christian community. The Keta market, which, like all others in the area, falls on every fourth day, attracts traders and customers from all over Ghana, Togo, Dahomey and Nigeria. But its importance is now decreasing, due to the increasing menace of sea erosion, from which it has been suffering for a long time.

Twelve miles to the west lies Anloga (pop. 11,000), the traditional and ritual capital of Anlo, which is now rapidly developing at the expense of Keta. It has a large flourishing market, comparable in size to that at Keta; a police station; a teacher training college; a secondary school and several middle schools. It is also hoped that in the very near future Anloga will become a major

[1] *Ibid.*, p. xxiii.
[2] *Ibid.*, p. 183. All population figures are taken from this report unless otherwise stated.

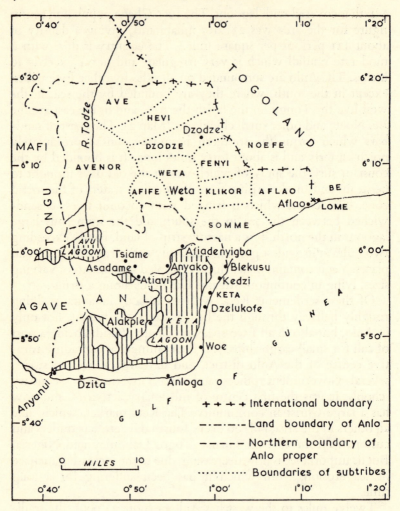

MAP 2. Anlo and their neighbours

industrial centre because of the rich deposit of oil recently discovered there.

Halfway between these two settlements is a cape named St
Paul, on which in 1900 the Gold Coast Government built a lighthouse. About one mile north of the lighthouse, on the shores of
the lagoon, lies the small township of Woe (pop. 3450). It is an

important historic town, whose chief in the past commanded the Right (Dusi) division of the Anlo army. Other important settlements on the littoral are Aflao (pop. 7439), Denu (pop. 1823), Kedzi (pop. 5015), Dzelukofe (pop. 5511), Tegbi (pop. 5924) and Dzita (pop. 1814).

Behind the sandbars stretch the lagoons, fed by numerous creeks and streams. The Keta Lagoon, largest of all, is about twenty miles long and twelve miles wide at its widest areas. It is a brackish water, the coastal fringes of which evaporate during years of scanty rainfall, leaving large incrustations of salt which provide a most important article of trade for the locals. In extremely dry years almost the whole area is dried up. But in years of heavy rainfall, which comes mainly in May and June, the waters of the lagoons rise, flooding the surrounding lands for several months. The lagoon is navigable for boats and large canoes as far as Blekusu, the eastern limit of Anlo proper, and for small canoes as far as Amutinu in Somme country. In the rains canoes ascend to Adafienu, where the lagoon terminates in a swamp which extends almost to Aflao. Despite its 'divisive' nature the Keta Lagoon, because of its navigability, provides a link between the coastal belt and the north. Important settlements on the northern fringes are Anyako (pop. 5097), Afiadenyigba (pop. 4920), Tsiame (pop. 3833) and Atiavi (pop. 2811).

Inland from the lagoons, and stretching northward to the northern boundary, lies a different soil, red laterite alternating with sand. Here the land stretches in an undulating plain, gradually rising until, at a distance of twenty or thirty miles inland, schist and gneiss appear. The monotony of the treeless savannah is only punctuated at irregular intervals by borassus palms and solitary baobab trees.

The population in this area is much more sparse than on the sea coast, the only large towns being Dzodze (pop. 5776), about forty miles north of Keta, and Abor (pop. 2566).

The differing physical features provide a multiplicity of economic activities. The coastal strip sandwiched between the sea and the lagoons is advantageously placed for an important fishing industry. Chapman in his *Our Homeland* Book I[1] refers to the area as 'the home of Gold Coast fishermen', and continues, 'A good deal of the fishing in other parts of the Gold Coast is in the hands

[1] 1943, pp. 98–9.

of these people, and fishermen from Keta and nearby villages are found as far afield as the Ivory Coast, Dahomey, and the Congo, and in Nigeria, Badagri is their centre.' That was in 1943. Twenty years later, in 1963, Polly Hill[1] could still refer to the Anlo coast as 'more heavily fished than any other in West Africa'. These statements give a true picture of the economic scene. In the great majority of towns in this area almost the whole population is engaged in sea-fishing. This is especially true of settlements east of Keta, where the coastal strip is so narrow that there is only enough land for housing purposes. Fishing takes place both in the lagoons and in the sea. Seine fishing is the usual method of sea-fishing, and is on a relatively large scale, each net involving about thirty men for its operations. In the lagoons smaller nets are employed in addition to weir baskets, angling and other traps. The only other occupation of note in these settlements is weaving.

West of Keta many practise some form of subsistence farming in addition to fishing. Common crops are cassava, maize, pepper and vegetables. A flourishing onion-growing industry is carried on along the edge of the Keta Lagoon in the neighbourhood of Anloga, where the effective drainage and the improvement of the heavy clayey soil by admixture with sand and the application of guano and cattle dung help to maintain fertility.

But until the late 1940s, when the Cape St Paul wilt[2] started to kill the coconut trees, and coast erosion washed away thousands of them, the most valuable source of income was copra and coconut oil. Today all settlements on the littoral between Woe and Aflao have been hit in varying degrees by this disease. At Woe and Tegbi all the trees have been destroyed, and the future spells certain gloom for the other settlements.

In the hinterland farming in maize and cassava is the chief occupation. Farming here is usually on a relatively large scale, and the bulk of the farm products are exported to the coastal areas in exchange for fish and vegetables.

Along the northern fringes of the lagoons, and in many inland areas to the north, several handicraft activities supplement farming

[1] 1963, p. 1455.
[2] The disease is named after the area of its origin. The root cause of the disease is not officially known but it is generally attributed to an insect pest, a kind of beetle whose stings are believed to have caused the death of the trees. The disease has wiped out all the trees in the Cape St Paul area and a considerable part eastward of this spot as far as the Togo border.

to Conut, poultry

and fishing. In the 1948 census report[1] 1565 men were described as cloth weavers, 911 of them in Weta alone and 316 in Seva. There were 589 women making pottery, 381 of them in Dzodze. Weaving of mats, mattresses and wicker baskets is also common. In the 1948 census 1907 of these weavers were recorded, of whom 787 were in Atiavi alone. In Dzodze area, where rainfall is somewhat heavier than in other parts of the region, rich palm groves are found, giving rise to a flourishing industry in oil and kernel.

3

But the Anlo, especially those on the coast, are also traditional poultry farmers. As early as 1850 Governor Winnett, the British Governor of the Gold Coast who took over the Danish Fort at Keta, noted his impressions of the industry in his journal. 'Bounteous nature', according to him, 'supplies the natives with an ample share of the necessities of life: turkeys, ducks, fowls, bullocks, sheep, goats, etc. abound along this part of the coast.' Indeed it was from this part of the country 'that nearly all the live-stock consumed by the Europeans and respectable natives'[2] throughout the Gold Coast were supplied. Forty years later, in 1891, Keta was still 'the poultry market' of the Gold Coast, according to an official Government report.[3] Today the position is still largely the same. In every Anlo homestead are reared large numbers of poultry, mainly by women and children, which find their way on each market day to Accra and other large Ghanaian towns. There are also large numbers of goats, sheep and pigs, but even if they had cattle in the past the cattle population in Anlo today is negligible.

These multiple economic activities, and local specialization in certain products, result in an exchange system among the various localities which makes trading an important occupation, especially for women. Indeed Westermann[4] was led to observe that 'there is hardly any woman who does not trade'. Certainly a large number do.

The Anlo thus have a mixed economy, involving mainly fishing and farming, but including weaving, pottery, poultry and trade. It is also worthwhile to mention the small number of blacksmiths, whose profession is the prerogative of certain lineages.

[1] *Gold Coast Census Report, 1948*, p. 4.
[2] Governor Winnett's *Journal*, 30 March 1850. ADM. 1/451, G.N.A. (Ghana National Archives).
[3] *Census Report of the Gold Coast Colony, 1891*, p. 11.
[4] 1949, p. 48.

2. THE ETHNIC COMPOSITION OF THE ANLO KINGDOM

The political boundary of Anlo was in the past very fluid, and the clarity now presented is no doubt a direct result of wars and European administration.

North and East of the Keta Lagoon are certain areas generally regarded as Anlo and included in the Anlo administrative area, which owed no direct allegiance to the Anlo King. Their relation with the Anlo had been due in part to their weakness in the past, which forced their leaders to put their territories under the protection of the Anlo against aggressors. These territories, which include Avenor, Afife, Aflao, Somme, Klikor, Weta, Fenyi and Dzodze are shown on Map 2. Also included in the past were Agave and Mafi.

Anlo hegemony was extended when in 1912, on the recommendation of F. G. Crowther,[1] then Secretary for Native Affairs in the Gold Coast, these areas were amalgamated into one administrative unit named the Anlo State, with the Anlo King the recognized head. Since then they have been administered together with the Anlo as one unit.

It is necessary to make this distinction, because not only do these semi-autonomous groups differ from each other in their social organization, but each exhibits some marked differences from the Anlo. One important difference which needs mention here is in clanship. Whereas everyone in Anlo belongs to one of the fifteen patrilineal clans into which the tribe is divided, the only traces of clanship we have in most of these other areas are from descendants of Anlo immigrants. The Avenor, in fact, have their own clan system, quite separate and different in organization from the Anlo.

However, in many other respects these areas have much closer resemblance to each other and to the Anlo than to any of the other Ewe groups, especially in language, music, dancing and forms of salutation. Nevertheless, in view of the differences referred to, the account which follows refers only to Anlo proper, and not to these other units unless otherwise stated. Anlo proper includes the coastal belt lying between Anyanui on the Volta and Blekusu, four miles east of Keta. North of the Keta Lagoon it extends as far as Abor, about forty miles to the north of Keta (Map 2). Altogether

[1] 1927, pp. 11–53.

it covers an area of about 300 square miles, and had a population of nearly 100,000 at the time of the 1960 Ghana Census. Traditionally the Kingdom was reputed to comprise 36 different towns and villages, but in 1960 no less than 116 localities were shown in the census returns.

3. THE POLITICAL SYSTEM

A detailed account of Anlo political institutions is beyond the scope of this study. What follows contains only a broad general description of their main features.[1]

The traditional political system of the Anlo may be described as 'centralized',[2] since it provides for a constituted executive authority, an administrative machinery and judicial institutions. At the head is the *Awoamefia*, the King who lives in a sacred place made holy by the presence of the gods. Below him are three senior chiefs, who in the past commanded the three military divisions in the traditional Anlo military formation. Next came the town and village chiefs, followed by the ward and lineage heads respectively.

The degree of centralization was however small, and the local settlements (villages and towns) enjoyed considerable autonomy. In the past the central authority was invoked only in time of war and in serious judicial cases such as homicide which were beyond the competence of the village and town chiefs.

The kingship is vested in two royal clans, Adzovia and Bate, whose local segments at Anloga, the traditional capital, alternately provide the *Awoamefia*. The rotary principle is strictly adhered to, but primogeniture is not the rule. Instead, when it is the turn of one clan to provide the King, the elders of the clan meet to select a candidate on the basis of physical appearance, intelligence and character. Usually the various segments of the clan, each presenting its own candidate, compete with one another for some time before a candidate acceptable to all emerges.

Crowther suggested that this alternating rule was established to prevent the assumption of too great a power by one ruling clan. But even if this has been its effect, the rule owes its origin to a historical accident. The stool belonged to the Adzovia clan. The

[1] For more details of the political system see D. E. K. Amenumey, 1964, esp. pp. 51-60.
[2] M. Fortes and E. E. Evans-Pritchard, 1940, p. 5.

Bate clan acquired succession rights only as a reward for a service performed by their apical ancestor Adeladzea for his mother's brother Sri, the first King, owner of the stool and founder of the Adzovia clan.

The King has many attributes of divinity. As mentioned already, he lives in seclusion, in *awɔme*, a sacred place associated with the gods. In the past he always remained indoors and never appeared in public. Consonant with his seclusion from his people was his prerogative of not going to war. By custom he must never fix his gaze upon a corpse. This would spell disaster for his people. He was King and High Priest at the same time, and as such he had to remain at home and perform sacrifices for success in war.

As the King lived in seclusion, matters came before him only through the three senior chiefs, after they had discussed them with the village chiefs under them. The King discussed these matters with the divisional chiefs and the other chiefs. It was usually the affairs of the whole state and appeals that came before him. He was also, as it were, the foreign minister for the state, since all significant foreign happenings were communicated to him before they were referred to the chiefs and people for discussion.

The *Awoamefia* was helped in his deliberations by two councils, the council of elders, representing the fifteen clans in the state, and the military council consisting of the three divisional chiefs. The clan council appears to have been the more active of the two, partly because it represented the people as such, and partly because its members, as clan heads, were all normally resident at Anloga, thereby providing a more regular forum for discussion than the military council. As representatives of the people, the clan leaders occupied an important position in the political structure, since the Anlo believed that the King's power derived from the people. *Du menɔa fia me o. Fiae nɔa du me* (The people do not live with the King. It is the King who lives with the people). The prominence of the people in the political structure was institutionalized in the conditional tone of the oath of allegiance sworn to the King on his installation. They would give him their obedience if he ruled in their interest. But he could be deposed if he lost their confidence.[1]

The clan council advised the King on general matters and those

[1] There was, however, only one case of destoolment of a King in Anlo history, involving one of the earliest Kings: Kofi Adzanu Fiayidziehe who reigned about the end of the eighteenth century.

brought before him by his divisional chiefs. Usually the opinions and views expressed by the *Awoamefia* to the council of divisional chiefs would be the decisions he and his clan council had already arrived at.

The King's court was the last court of appeal. As he did not in theory judge cases in the first instance, those which reached his court were usually cases which had already passed through the courts of the village, town and divisional chiefs. The judicial system provided for capital punishment for those whose presence in the state was not conducive to the public good. This form of punishment was given only with the approval of the King after careful and prolonged deliberations,[1] because it was considered necessary to establish a man's guilt beyond doubt before condemning him to death. Usually first offenders were either pardoned or given fines and warnings. It was only when the criminal did not heed these warnings and light punishments that the death sentence was pronounced.

In the days of the slave-trade it was more profitable to sell into slavery persons condemned to death, for besides getting rid of the criminal this transaction could add substantially to the King's income. Serious offences which received the death sentence were stealing, adultery, indebtedness and dishonesty, while for small offences, such as assault and isolated cases of rape and stealing, fines were imposed.

The fines inflicted on offenders formed an important part of the King's income. He also had stool farms on which he exacted corvee labour from his chiefs and their people. But the greater part of his revenue came from gifts from chiefs and wealthy individuals, especially local and foreign traders operating in his country. The slave-traders were also his favourites, and so long as they enslaved only strangers and not the Anlo their activities had his blessing. Booty obtained as a result of the frequent wars was also shared with him.

Directly below the *Awoamefia* were the three senior or wing chiefs, *Asafohenegāwo*,[2] who captained the military divisions, left, right and centre, in times of war. Though military in origin the

---

[1] See Fiawoo, 1947, *passim*.

[2] The term *Asafohenegā* (sing.) is undoubtedly an Akan word. Its application to the Anlo military wing has given rise to the view that the Anlo military formation was based on the Akan system and was probably borrowed from the Akwamu and the Ashanti. See Amenumey, 1964, p. 57.

divisions came to be incorporated in the traditional system of government. Thus each divisional chief had towns and villages for which he was responsible. No matter could go to the King without first passing through the courts of the local and divisional chiefs respectively. But the chiefs of the left and the right divisions were also chiefs of towns, Whuti and Woe respectively, and in this capacity acted just like any other chief as far as those two towns were concerned. The *Avadada* (lit. War Mother), chief of the centre and most senior of the three, was also the commander-in-chief in time of war, and in this capacity was expected to lead and administer all military operations on behalf of the King. But, unlike his colleagues of the left and the right divisions, the *Avadada* was not a chief of any town, though he normally lived in Anloga to allow easy communication with the *Awoamefia*.

As the leadership of the military divisions needed special fighting qualities it was not traditionally hereditary. The post was given to a chief who had distinguished himself in previous battles and had the necessary qualities of leadership. Since the end of serious inter-tribal wars, however, the posts have remained hereditary within the towns and lineages of the last chiefs to hold them in the period of the wars.

In the government of his division the chief was assisted by a council of chiefs and elders. There were no hard and fast rules about the composition of this council,[1] but it was expected to include all the chiefs of the division, influential individuals and men who had distinguished themselves in the various spheres of life, warriors and wealthy businessmen. There were also no regular meeting times for the council, but the chief was expected to summon it whenever an important matter arose. Regular consultation with his advisers was an essence of good government. Not only did it show that all the essential elements in the division had a say in its affairs, but, as the Anlo always emphasize, one head does not make a council. However, as the division included towns and villages scattered all over the country, frequent meetings were difficult, and only very important matters could bring all the councillors together. For minor cases the chief could rely on his advisers in the divisional capital.

The next political unit was the town, *du*, or village, *kɔfe*, each with its chief, *dufia*, chosen from the lineage of the first settler.

---

[1] *Ibid.*, p. 56.

Here again real power rested with the people, *Duawo*, as opposed to the *Fiahawo*, i.e. the chief and elders of the royal lineage. The *Duawo* had a governing council comprising lineage heads, referred to in this capacity as *dumegãwo*[1] (big men), and leaders of the young men, known as the *Tsyɔfomegãwo*.[2] Though there were no fixed and regular meeting times, the chief was expected to summon the *dumegãwo* whenever any matter came before him. In effect all executive decisions concerning the town and its relations with other towns should have the support of the *Duawo*. The elders of the royal lineage also had important functions in the local government. They were the advisers of the chief, and any position he might take *vis-à-vis* the *Duawo* represented the end result of his discussion with elders of the royal lineage. And since the chiefship was elective within the royal lineage, the elders of this lineage also had the task of choosing a new chief. For though the *Duawo* might disagree with a particular candidate for the chiefship, and could depose an unpopular chief, the selection of the chief was always the prerogative of the royal elders. They had to make the selection first, before seeking the approval of the *Duawo*.

At the town or village level a distinction was always made between the executive and the judiciary (if these terms could be applied to a traditional system). The *Duawo* and the *Fiahawo*, as we have tried to show, jointly constituted the executive authority. The judiciary, however, was composed entirely of the *Fiahawo*, i.e. the chief and the royal elders.[3] The chief's court was the highest in the village or town. It was concerned with the settlement of disputes between villagers, and also with such cases as stealing, adultery and divorce. As indicated earlier, all cases going to the courts of the divisional chiefs and the *Awoamefia* had to pass through the village chief's court.

Mention must also be made of the residential group known as the *to*. All large settlements were territorially divided into sections or wards known as *towo* (sing. *to*). The *to* was a residential, not a

---

[1] The term for lineage head in ordinary usage is *afedo-mega*, but as a political leader at the town or village level he becomes a *dumegã* (pl. *dumegãwo*).

[2] This is another word derived from Akan. In Ashanti military formation the *Twafo* formed the vanguard of the central army. See Busia, 1951, pp. 13–14.

[3] The *dumegãwo* were not entirely without judicial functions. As will be shown later, they were the judges of the respective territorial and social units under their authority within the village.

kinship group, which occupied a portion of the town, but the core usually consisted of members of a single lineage, the descendants of the first settler in that section. To this lineage were added, in time, descendants of later comers, related or unrelated to the first settler. The ward had a head, usually the head of the dominant lineage, who governed the ward with the help of the heads of the various lineages within it.

Forde[1] describes the ward in *Yako* as 'a territorial segment in communities grown too large for convenient organization of secular activities on the basis of interpersonal relations'. This statement is applicable to Anlo settlements in the sense that certain functions were considered to be more effectively performed within the framework of the ward than in that of the whole settlement. In the first place, only large settlements were divided into wards, and even there the number of wards was determined by the size in terms of area and population. Alakple, with a population 1351, had only three, Woe with 3450 had four, while Dzodze, one of the largest towns, had no less than twelve.

The organization and management of funerals of members were among the most important functions performed at ward rather than village or town level. After the kinsfolk of the dead person, ward members of the dead were the most active participants in the funeral. On the day of the burial members of the dead person's ward were forbidden to go to work. From that day until the end of the rites, which might take about a month, the ward had to meet time and again to dance and sing dirges in remembrance of the dead person.

Dances were also organized by the ward. It was only in small villages that they were organized by a whole settlement. In bigger settlements every ward was a dancing group, and it was only on special occasions, such as the death of a chief, that a whole settlement would emerge as a dancing group.

Dancing used to generate great competition and even hostility among the wards in their bid to excel each other. This hostility was vividly manifested in the dance known as *Halo*, in which all the songs and the music of the drums of one ward were framed in insulting language directed against members of another ward who were expected to reciprocate.

But the final, and perhaps the most active, political and judicial

[1] 1950, p. 289.

authority sub-groups were the lineages, under the authority of the lineage heads. A fuller account of the lineage and its organization will be given in the next chapter. Here it is sufficient to point out that the lineage head was responsible for the administration of justice in cases involving members of his lineage.

4. THE LITERATURE ON THE EWE AND THE ANLO

To the English-speaking anthropologist the Ewe are a people about whom very little is known. Since A. B. Ellis wrote his *The Ewe-speaking peoples of the Slave Coast* in 1890 no major study has been made or published on the Ewe in English. For many decades, therefore, this book, which was based on contemporary travel literature, was the sole English work on the Ewe. The book, however, is remarkable only for its deficiency in facts, and what facts it gives refers to customs generally associated with Dahomey. Consequently Ellis as an important source book was dismissed by later students of both the Dahomey and the Ewe. Spieth refers to it as of little value; Herskovits condemns it as containing nothing new; and D. A. Chapman, an Anlo Ewe, describes it as 'useless'.

This dismal picture on the English side was, however, more than compensated for by works in German by missionaries of the Norddeutsche (Bremen) mission in German Togoland, who made studies of specific Ewe areas and some general aspects of Ewe social life. Notable among them was Spieth, already referred to, whose *Die Ewe Stamme*, published in 1906, based largely on the social institutions of the Ho, contains one of the most complete studies ever made of the Ewe. But as a missionary his chief interest was in religion. Besides translating the Bible into Ewe, he also published in 1911 *Die Religion der Eweer in Sud-Togo*, which was also based on the Ho.

Another missionary who worked on the Ewe was Westermann, a more prolific writer, who not only wrote on the social institutions of the Glidzi tribe, but through his wide interests and sympathies also studied the Ewe language and helped a lot towards its development. His chief work, published in 1936, is *Die Glidyi-Ewe in Togo*, in which the main aspects of Glidzi social organization were documented with occasional references to other tribes. He also published the *Evefiala*: an Ewe-English dictionary;

Gbesela Yeye: English-Ewe dictionary; and his *Grammatik der Ewe-Sprache*, translated in 1930 by Bickford Smith as *A study of the Ewe language*, is still the most authoritative reference book for students of the Ewe language.

One quality of these German books is that the investigators had the advantage of working through the Ewe language, and the enormous value of Spieth's great works is that they are largely composed of actual Ewe texts, with parallel German translations.

It was these German publications which later formed the basis of the work of Barbara Ward in her *The Social Organization of the Ewe-speaking People*. Though she describes this work as 'largely descriptive' and as representing 'an English rendering of the German material', many important institutions such as kinship and the family are given modern sociological treatment. As a source book for students of the Ewe the value of the book lies in the fact that it presents in one volume a synoptic account of the main aspects of Ewe society. For this reason it will remain for a long time an authoritative work on the Ewe as a whole.

On the debit side may be mentioned the fact that in an attempt to cover the whole Ewe group at one go Ward had perforce to sacrifice many local variations in order to achieve accurate generalizations. This is largely a limitation in the German works on which she had to depend, because their materials do not give a representative account of the Ewe. Moreover, none of the German works can be accurately described as a sociological treatise. As Ward herself has observed, 'it was not Spieth's fault or that of his contemporaries that they were working before the birth of African Sociology. Full and careful as his work is it is yet a collection of curious customs rather than a source book for sociological study. . . the student who uses his volumes must quarry deeply into the mine of ethnographia if he is to find grains of sociologica, and even when this has been done he finds that he has amassed more questions than answers.'[1] Westermann's work on the Glidzi suffers from the same limitations.

It is also worthy of note that when Spieth published his book in 1906 some Ewe educationists, mainly priests, who realized at that time the limitations of the book, published in Ewe a different and much fuller version of the history and customs of the Ewe. This volume was reprinted in 1938 as *Ewe gbalexexle Akpa enelia*.

[1] Ward, B. E., 1949, p. iv.

All the German works were written mainly on either the Ho or the Glidzi tribes. On the Anlo they gave only hints and impressions, and no detailed systematic account. The only works devoted to the Anlo are by Anlo scholars. Important in this respect are Rev. F. K. Fiawoo's *The Fifth Landing Stage*, an English translation of an Ewe play based on Anlo tradition, which won a prize in the International African Institute's competition in 1933; and D. A. Chapman's *Our Homeland*[1] which gives a somewhat detailed geographical account of the area. Though neither of these works is concerned with a description of Anlo social institutions they nonetheless contain much valuable information. The former describes some customs relating to traditional legal proceedings and marriage, while the latter gives some valuable descriptions of the economic activities of the Anlo.

The most recent, and probably the most reliable, work on the Ewe and the Anlo is Dr D. K. Fiawoo's study of changes in the 'religious concepts and organization'[2] of the Southern Ewe-speaking people of Ghana, mainly the Anlo. As a result of intensive field research, in which oral tradition featured prominently, Dr Fiawoo was able to amass a wealth of material, and tried to indicate the changes now taking place in Anlo religious ideas as a result of Christian missionary activities and formal education.

In its own field the study is both deep and incisive, but though ancestor worship is given a lot of space, the relationship between kinship and religion is not treated in such a way as to be of much use to the student of kinship.[3] This is largely because the author ignored the method of participant observation,[4] a *sine qua non* in modern anthropological fieldwork, and was therefore unable to observe carefully how religion and kinship are closely interlocked. On kinship therefore nothing has been done so far apart from Ward's general work.

5. FIELD WORK AND METHODOLOGY

The fieldwork for this study was done in Anlo country between June, 1962, and April, 1963. A relatively small area was chosen for intensive study, and from this area periodic trips were made further afield for purposes of comparison and to obtain a

[1] 1943.   [2] 1958.   [3] He admits this on p. 89.   [4] *Ibid.*, p. 9.

comprehensive view of the whole field. Two settlements were chosen for study, Woe, a small town on the littoral, and Alakple, an island in the Keta Lagoon (see Map 2).

The two settlements were chosen for their general suitability as field centres; because their populations were of such size as to permit thorough study of kinship and family structure in terms of fieldwork methods and resources; because they are fairly old by Anlo standards and contain substantial traditional flavour, and because, being at a different distance from the main urban centre of Keta, they have had varying degrees of contact with outside influences.

They were, then, not chosen according to rigorous sampling techniques, so, strictly speaking, the conclusions drawn from the study, especially the figures, should not be used as basis for generalizations for the Anlo country as a whole. On the other hand, there is nothing to suggest that these two settlements differ significantly from other Anlo communities. Actually no two settlements, however close they may be in ethnic composition, are absolutely the same in all essential features, and no ethnographer sets out to look for uniformity and monotony in all social practices. However, wherever it was known that significant differences existed in certain localities contrary to our general information, no time was spared in ascertaining the facts.

In the field attempts were made to use all the modern anthropological field techniques we could afford. The questionnaire was designed to include open-end and poll-type questions. But direct interview and personal participant observation were the most important tools.

Illiterate informants were considered more helpful because they were less adulterated in their attitudes and ideas. But no opportunity was lost to get the views of those old Anlo literates who had valuable information to offer. It turned out, moreover, that in giving life histories and autobiographical accounts the memories of the literate were generally clearer than those of the illiterate informants.

The fieldwork was to a large extent an exercise in what may be called auto-ethnography. My prior knowledge of the area gave me certain advantages which made my work in the field much easier than would have been the case if I were a foreign investigator.

First, Ewe is my mother-tongue, and, as I had already spent a large part of my life in the area, I had no problem of familiarization to local conditions. Because I was one of them and not a 'foreign intruder', the fear and suspicion which always lurk in the minds of subjects and informants during social research in general were almost absent. They had confidence in me because they knew I could not 'sell them'. Many a time informants were met who admitted 'this is a thing we normally don't divulge to outsiders, but since it is you we shall give you all the necessary help.'

Also as an auto-ethnographer I was to a point my own informant having fully participated in certain behaviour patterns and practices which were the subjects of my enquiry. But this can also lead to serious difficulties. There is the danger not only of taking certain things for granted but also of regarding certain special personal experiences as representing the general practice in the community.

In fact, for most of the advantages he gets from being a local man there are corresponding difficulties for the local ethnographer. For instance, as a local man he is expected by his informants to be knowledgeable in certain basic things, and certain queries which from an alien may be attributed to a curiosity 'to know things' may be considered irrelevant or even impertinent coming from him. Also in questions concerning personal problems, especially where morals may be involved, some informants gave the impression that by revealing facts about their private lives to me they were in some sense giving themselves away. This looks paradoxical but it is true, because as an insider I might be led, it was thought, to pass the information on to other members of the community who previously had no knowledge of it. But where an outsider is involved his questions can always be attributed to mere curiosity. This problem was really acute when it came to questions on divorce, marriage payments and illegal unions. For example, one thing about which an Anlo woman feels very strongly is to mention that there is no marriage payment on her head – that she was not married properly. I remember one occasion when, after the topic of marriage payment was introduced, the woman protested, 'What sort of question is this? Then I am leaving you.'

Emotional outbursts of this kind and the feelings of 'guilt' which generate them are not altogether unnecessary. One prime element in anthropological approach in research is the unpleasant possibility of getting involved in local values. Into this the local ethnographer will find it much easier to be drawn. His naturally unavoidable sympathies for or disapproval of certain institutions may tend to overshadow his scientific desire for an objective appraisal of every situation. This is a weakness which militates against detachment and objectivity unless conscious efforts are made to overcome it. I therefore find it rather difficult to agree with local ethnographers or 'culture-bearer anthropologists' who think 'growing up' in a society and 'being emotionally involved with cultural values and biases'[1] as they do, will necessarily give them an advantage over foreigners. In my view the most important single asset in fieldwork is proper training in research methods. This alone can alleviate the disadvantages which emotional involvement in cutural values entails.

In writing up the findings of my research, therefore, I shall do my best to report as an anthropologist and not as a culture-bearer of Anlo society.

[1] Cf. Uchendu, 1965, p. 9.

see p. 153

for chapter 2

2

The Kinship System

I. THE CLAN

The key to Anlo kinship is patrilineal descent. This is based on a lineage system which is generalized at a higher level in clanship. Every Anlo belongs to one of the fifteen patrilineal clans around which the society is organized. The Anlo term for clan is *hlɔ̃*, and this may be defined as a group of people, male and female, who are believed to have descended in the male line from a common putative ancestor and who share the same totemic and other observances.

Membership of the clan is obtained by birth, but strangers and slaves were sometimes incorporated into the clans of their masters, and were accorded almost full membership status, except that when their foreign origins are remembered today they are refused succession rights. Strangers who were not specifically attached to any particular Anlo were grouped into one special clan created for strangers only. The reason for the creation of this strangers' clan, whose descendants are now known as the Blu,[1] will be seen later.

The clans are dispersed throughout the entire tribe in such a way

---

[1] The name of this strangers' clan, Blu, is of some historical significance. 'Blu' is the Anlo term for the Ashanti and other Akan tribes, and the naming of this clan after the Akans may be a result of the strength of the activity between these two peoples in the past. Today many members of the Blu clan are able to trace their ancestry to Akan settlers. But the clan also includes people from other neighbouring tribes like Krobo, Ga and some other Adangbe tribes. In fact it appears from the ancestries of many Blu that the Krobo and Adangbe members outnumber the Akan, and referring to them as Akans rather than Adangbes might have been caused not necessarily by a greater number of Akans among them but by the fact that Anlo had more intercourse with the Ashanti than any of their neighbours. The Ashanti had always been the allies of the Anlo, whereas the Ga and Adangbe, though nearer territorially, have always been their enemies.

Since members of this clan descended from strangers of different tribes, that part of the above definition of the clan referring to common ancestry does not apply to them. However, they have totems, taboos and all other attributes common to all the other clans.

that every large settlement has a branch of most of the clans living in it. The fifteen clans are Lafe, Amlade, Adzovia, Bate, Like, Bamee, Klevi, Tovi, Tsiame, Agave, Amɛ, Dzevi, Uifeme, Xetsofe, and Blu.[1]

Westermann explained that some clans, due to their weakness in numbers, placed themselves under the protection of others and thus lost their independence. It seems the conflicting statements as to the correct number of Anlo clans are due to the recognition sometimes of these accessory groups as separate clans. The official list[2] does not give them clan status, and in both their structure and functions they lack most of the qualities of a clan. We shall therefore restrict the use of the term clan to the fifteen mentioned, and treat these accessory groups in the general context of the localized segments of the clan which we shall discuss later.

Though a dispersed group the clan has many characteristics of corporateness. Land, palm groves and fishing creeks are owned by clans.[3] They have appointed leaders in whom are vested legal and ritual powers. They also meet occasionally to discuss matters of common interest. This last aspect of corporateness is still seen today. For instance, in 1962, when the South Anlo Local Council wanted to acquire a piece of land at Anloga belonging to the Bamee clan for building a new market place, branches of the clan throughout the entire tribe were invited to Anloga to discuss the matter. In the same year I met people collecting taxes on Lafe clan lands on behalf of the Lafe clan head.

All clans except the Xetsofe have their ancestral shrines at Anloga, the traditional capital. The Xetsofe have theirs at Tsiame across the Keta Lagoon. Every year clansmen from all over the tribe make pilgrimages to these shrines. In the past these pilgrim-

[1] This list was given according to the seniority of the clans, based on the history of their migration and settlement in their present country. The Lafe are said to have led the groups during the period of migration. This was before the establishment of Anlo as a Kingdom. The ancestors of some of the clans are believed to have descended from other clans.

[2] The official list was the one given by the King's court at a durbar on 8 December 1962, during the Anlo Migration Festival at Anloga.

[3] Clan property is what is believed to have been acquired by the ancestors of the clan, as opposed to what was acquired by the founders of the lineages. The latter belongs to the lineage of the founding ancestor, not to the whole clan. The former, however, belongs to the whole clan. Thus the head of the Lafe clan, who owns land in many parts of the tribe, still collects taxes on all Lafe lands which are under use. Both clan members and members of other clans using the land are taxed. It will be shown later that clan land is not cultivated by clansmen only.

ages were made for specific ritual and ceremonial purposes. Apart
from the usual offerings and prayers, children were brought to the
shrine to be washed in the *agbametsi*, the clan's ritual water, and
'inducted into full membership of the clan', as one writer puts it.[1]
It was also at these ceremonies that facial marks were made.
Today, although prayers are offered during these visits, they are
more sightseeing excursions than religious pilgrimages.

In the past vengeance was effected through the clan. An offender
would have his clansmen taken or killed if he ran away or somehow evaded the punishment applicable to the offence committed.
Likewise an offended party was entitled to help from his fellow
clansmen. In fact *hlɔ̃*, clan, literally means 'vengeance'; the phrase
do hlɔ̃ (lit. to commit the clan) is the term for 'to commit an
offence punishable by death or sale into slavery'; and *bia hlɔ̃* (lit.
ask the clan) means 'to retaliate by death'. Informants maintained
that it was for this collective responsibility of the clan for the conduct of its members that it was found necessary to make strangers
answerable for the conduct of their fellow strangers by grouping
them into a clan of their own. In the context of a centralized
political organization, the only implication of this rule is that the
clan was answerable to the political authority for the conduct of
its members.

Ward appears to have found a contradiction in a dispersed clan
having characteristics of corporateness, when she writes 'two of
the properties recorded by Westermann as characteristics of the
hlɔ̃ seem incompatible: *hlɔ̃*, he says, are not localized groups though
they have traditions of origin from certain places. . . each *hlɔ̃* has
an appointed head in whom political, legal and ritual authority is
vested. . .'[2] I think the above explanations and examples may
serve to dispel these doubts. The Anlo case is moreover not unique.
The Yako *lejima*, matriclan, for instance is a dispersed group with
corresponding characteristics.[3]

There are no aristocratic clans in Anlo. All are equal in status,
but they perform different functions in the settlements and the
tribe at large. For instance the paramount stool belongs to the
Adzovia and Bate clans, who alternately provide the King; the
Lafe are the Kingmakers; and the Lafe together with the Amlade
are the hereditary priests in each settlement and at the national

[1] Kodzo-Vordoagu, 1959, p. 41.   [2] Ward, B. E., 1949, pp. 74-5.
[3] Forde, 1950, p. 306.

level, while the Dzevi provide the chief priest for the War God, the Nyigbla.[1] But in each settlement the clan which is dominant in terms of numbers, or was the first to settle there, provides the chief. Thus the Alakple stool belongs to the Amɛ clan, the first settlers, while the Woe stool belongs to a Blu lineage, the largest in the town.

Membership of a clan carries with it many distinguishing marks. Among these are names, food taboos, avoidances and injunctions and the possession of a clan cult. For instance every clan has a pair of names, one for men and the other for women.[2] Each also has its own totems, associated with stories about the clan and its origin or referring to some exploit of the founding ancestor. Each clan has its own funeral rites and ceremonies.

Membership of a particular clan is believed to imply certain personal qualities. Members of a particular clan may be spoken of as being addicted to certain practices or as being notably wicked, even-tempered, violent or even fecund. These qualities are imputed not to a particular group of agnates but to all the members of the clan.

Because of its dispersed character the clan is not exogamous. In fact in the past, and today in some remote villages, marriages are encouraged among clansfolk whose genealogical connections could not be traced, but there was no rule of clan endogamy.

The relation between clansmen is characterized by friendliness and mutual help in general terms. Of greatest importance from the individual standpoint is perhaps the help a man may receive from clansmen outside his own settlement. An Anlo traveller stranded in any part of the country would only have to trace his fellow clansmen there to be assured of the utmost hospitality. For

[1] This point on distribution of religious functions needs clarification. Each Anlo village has a god (trɔ̃). In addition there is a national God, the Nyigbla, whose priests as stated, are provided by the Dzevi clan. The priest of the village trɔ̃ however need not necessarily be Amlade or Lafe. However whether or not the village priest is Amlade or Lafe, these two clans have a joint hereditary right to perform certain ritual functions especially rituals concerned with the land and political ceremonies. Thus at the beginning of any public meeting the leaders of the localized segments of the two clans in the village have to give joint prayers to, and ask blessings from, the ancestors and the land. This ritual position was conferred on the two clans because they are believed to be the oldest clans and the first two to have settled in Anlo. They are therefore believed to have some ritual association with the land. The rituals involving these two clans are also performed at the national level.

[2] Kpodo, 1944, pp. 4–5. See also Appendix II.

the belief is that members of the same clan, wherever they might be living, have a common patrilineal ancestor a long time ago, though genealogical connections between them may be difficult or impossible to establish. It is the recognition of this belief that keeps clansmen together and makes mutual help an integral part of their relationship. In this way the clan system provides for the application of kinship categories over a social field much more extensive than known kinship.

But as a dispersed group the clan is not an important unit for regular and frequent social interaction. Although clan membership defines a person's status and citizenship in Anlo and provides him with the rules which regulate his behaviour in everyday life and in times of crises, it is at the local level in the settlement that these agnatic ties are clearly brought into play.

2. THE LINEAGE

All large settlements have segments of many clans living in them. The members of these local segments who trace common descent from a known ancestor form what we may call the lineage. There are in some settlements more than one lineage of the same clan.

Earlier students of the Ewe seem to have had some difficulty in finding an appropriate Anlo term for the lineage. This is probably because the Anlo themselves are not always definite about it and refer to it by various terms. Following Westermann, Ward,[1] Manoukian[2] and Fiawoo[3] all refer to the local patrilineage as 'fome'. Thus Ward wrote 'the term hlɔ, like the Ashanti abusua, applies to both the clan and the lineage, though it appears from Westermann's pages that the Anlo often use fome to distinguish the latter'.[4] As we shall see later, the Anlo word 'fome' means multilateral kinship and refers to a 'kindred'. When, however, it is necessary for the Anlo to distinguish the lineage from other kin groups with bilateral connotations the terms kpɔnu, entrance; afeme, house; or more commonly, afedo, ancestral home, is used for the former. For instance, the lineal ancestors are called afedo-me-ŋɔliwo as opposed to tɔgbe-ŋɔliwo, the ancestors in general; the ancestral rites are called afedo-nu; and the lineage members are called afedo-ɖeka-me-tɔwo. In trying to present our material in

[1] 1949, p. 71.   [2] 1952, p. 22.   [3] 1958, p. 91.   [4] Ward, B. E., 1949, p. 91.

Anlo kinship categories, therefore, the term *afedo* will be used for the lineage.

The *afedo* may be defined as that branch of a clan found in a settlement which comprises all those persons, male and female, who are able to trace relationship by a series of accepted genealogical steps through the male line to a known or putative male ancestor and theoretically to each other. The genealogical depth of the lineage is about eight to ten generations. The lineage, unlike the clan, is exogamous.

Every lineage is named after its founding ancestor and has as symbols of interest and unity a stool or *zikpui*, an ancestral shrine, a lineage cult or *trɔ*, a lineage head, and an interest in common property.

Within the lineage members are entitled to a number of rights and privileges. By his membership every man has a plot of land to cultivate, a creek to fish in, a place to live and a group to care for him in time of difficulty. With these rights and privileges go duties and obligations such as helping needy members, working towards maintenance of the lineage's good name, promotion of its unity, reverence to the wishes of his lineal ancestors and obedience to the lineage head and other older members.

The lineage head is usually its oldest surviving member in terms both of generation and age. Where age and generation conflict, the latter takes precedence, for the office has to run completely through each generation before descending to the next. The lineage head is often identified with the ancestors because of his age. He knows more about them than the other living members. Indeed, the older he is the more venerable are his ritual powers held to be, and only extreme incapacity or senility will necessitate the transfer of his office to the next in line of succession while he is still alive. His duties are as many as they are varied. He administers lineage land and other property, and no transaction concerning this or other lineage interests can take place without his consent. He judges disputes involving the lineage members and is the lineage's representative on the ward's governing body. He is normally always consulted about any major undertaking in an individual member's life such as marriage, joining of a cult group and today joining one of the Christian denominations.

Yet though his office commands deference and great respect, and his position is almost inviolable unless he is extremely arbitrary, few major decisions concerning the lineage will be taken without the advice and approval of the elders from the several segments which together form an informal council of the lineage.

The lineage head's functions are not only secular. He is also, so to speak, the chief priest of the lineage. He is believed to be the link between the living and the dead, and the only one who can speak with sufficient authority to the understanding of the ancestors. All offerings made to the dead are presented to them by him on behalf of the lineage.

Ancestor worship plays an important part in the life of the lineage. There is a great belief in the efficacy and power of the ancestral spirits in the lives of their living descendants, and the doctrine of reincarnation, whereby some ancestors are reborn into their earthly kin-groups, is also given credence. The dead are believed to live somewhere in the world of spirits, *Tsiefe*, from where they watch their living descendants in the earthly world, *Kodzogbe*. They are believed to possess supernatural powers of one sort or another coupled with a kindly interest in their descendants, as well as the ability to do them harm if the latter neglect them. It is said that nothing is nearer to the hearts of the dead than to know that their descendants live in peace and unity. They are believed to punish quarrelling among kinsmen, adultery and incest, the possible disruptive forces within the lineage. Such punishments take the form of serious sickness, and the wrath of the ancestors is made known through divination. Ancestor worship, therefore, provides powerful sanctions for accepted social behaviour, and generates a series of reciprocal rights and duties among lineage members that are essential factors in the corporate unity and solidarity of the lineage, and the preservation of its existing structure.

The fear and worship of the dead are expressed in several ways, the most important being offerings of food and drink which the living members make both individually and in a body. The practice of putting the first morsel of food, the first drop of water or alcohol on the ground before satisfying oneself is one of the many ways by which individuals express belief in the ever-watchful presence of the ancestors, while the lineage in a group do so in the periodic ancestral or stool festivals, *afedo-nu* or *zikpui-nu*. The *Zikpuinu* was formerly an annual affair, but, as D. K. Fiawoo[1] has pointed out, it is circumstances which now determine the

[1] 1958, p. 63.

performance of such festivals. Widespread misfortune within the lineage or continued bonanza in farming or fishing may lead to their performance. If nothing remarkable happens there may be three or four years between festivals. The rite itself entails the slaughter of animals, especially sheep or goats, and the offering of drinks, with supplications to the ancestors to pardon sins committed against their persons and wishes, and ends with prayers for the long life and prosperity of the living members.

Despite their importance in the religious lives of the Anlo, neither the lineage nor the clan is coterminous with the religious unit. In addition to ancestor worship and lineage and clan cults, individuals may make their own personal cult affiliations by joining one or more public cults, whose membership cuts across lineage and kinship lines.

The lineage is largely a residential unit. As will be seen later, while all the lineage members do not live in the area which bears its name, a lineage is almost always confined to a single section of a ward. In this section the houses of the lineage members occupy a continuous stretch of land, divided from each other only by walls of palm-leaves or reeds. The original site of the house of the founding ancestor, which normally lies in the centre of the lineage houses, is given pride of place. There one finds the ancestral shrine which houses the stool. It is a small mud house roofed with thatch or reed. This is where the lineage gathers when its members meet in a body. It also forms the burial ground for the dead, and even now that burial normally takes place in the public cemetery of the settlement every dead person's *luvɔ* (lit. soul), comprising the finger nails and hair, is still buried here. When a dead body is buried outside its home town or in a foreign land, the *luvɔ* is always brought home for burial in the ancestral home.

Not all lineage members live in the area around the ancestral home. Demographic and economic factors often make this impossible. The *afedo* may be overcrowded, and the lineage head may advise a number of the younger members to move away and build their houses in the bush land outside the original residential area. This is not often difficult, as many lineages have uncleared bush land in different parts of the settlement. This new settlement is called *kɔfe*, hamlet, as opposed to the *afedo-me*, the ancestral home, and is named after the first to settle there. In many settlements the *kɔfe* dwelling areas have now grown much bigger than the original residential areas. Anloga and Woe are typical examples of this development.

It also happens that a lineage becomes too large to be supported by the farms and other resources at its disposal, in which case the only remedy is emigration to other parts of Ghana as labourers on cocoa farms, or to fishing centres in Ivory Coast, Sierra Leone or Nigeria. The effect of scarcity of resources on the present generation is shown in the fact that in 1961 over thirty per cent of the adult population of Woe and Alakple (excluding the literates) were away from home. This is a direct result of the high density of population in the area, 321 per square mile.

Wherever they may be, whether they live in the *afedome* or *kɔfe* or have emigrated, all lineage members are regarded and treated as full members. Nor does the movement of sections of the lineage to *kɔfe* dwellings result in fission. This is partly because the movements to *kɔfe* do not necessarily follow genealogical lines (as those who occupy the new *kɔfe* may be drawn from different segments of the lineage while others remain in the *afedome*) and partly because of the strength of the pull towards the ancestral home. For instance, funerals of all lineage members, including those living in the *kɔfe*, take place in the *afedome*; *kɔfe* residents are expected to attend all functions arranged by the lineage in the *afedome*, and all lineage meetings, including those directly concerned with or initiated by *kɔfe* dwellers, as a rule take place in the ancestral home. Another factor helping the unity of the lineage is the fact that there is no hierarchy of ancestral shrines, and therefore in matters of lineage worship only one head matters.

Before leaving the discussion of the lineage as a whole one important aspect of its unity may be mentioned here. This is the relationship between land, *anyigba* (lit. earth), and the lineage. Land as a unifying force is based on the belief that it belongs to the dead, who do not expect the living to divide or alienate it by selling. The ancestors are called *anyigba-tɔwo*, owners of the earth, and are believed to come to the land every night to do their own cultivation; because of this, work on the land at night by the living is forbidden.[1] The reverence for the ancestors already mentioned

---

[1] *Anyigba* is also used for reptiles, and it is believed that one may be bitten by a reptile when hoeing at night. But there does not seem to be any express relationship between reptiles and the dead. It seems that reptiles are identified with the earth because they crawl on it.

is further illustrated by the seriousness with which the beliefs connecting them with the land are respected. There is no earth cult as such, but any major use of virgin land, either for cultivation or building, is preceded by prayers and offerings to the dead. The right of the lineage members in the land is therefore purely usu-fructuary, under the administration of the lineage head, and it is this quality of the land which keeps the lineage together as people with interest in common property. Ideally, therefore, the lineage land cannot be sold. But in the event of some particularly severe economic crisis affecting the whole lineage, part of the land can be sold provided the consent of all is obtained.

At this point it will be necessary to digress a little and consider very briefly how clanship, as opposed to the lineage principle, operates at the local level. Though agnatic relations at the local level are usually seen and described in terms of lineages, it is more convenient even here to speak of the clan rather than the lineage in certain social situations, especially in cases of taboos and life crisis rituals. Thus what a person may or may not eat, what he must do on certain specific occasions, and the funeral rites to be performed on his death, all these are governed by clan, not lineage rules. This is not as confusing as it appears at first sight. It is true that, as the lineage is a sub-division of the clan, the principles governing the latter apply *ipso facto* to the former. But in the social situations mentioned the Anlo speak and think in terms of clans and not lineages, even at the local level. Several reasons may be adduced for this. In the first place, the taboos and practices concerned with these occasions are common to the whole clan. Secondly, clansfolk from nearby settlements are always invited to these functions, and as these visitors by definition share the same observances and could participate fully in the ceremonies, local sentiments are submerged in favour of clan solidarity. Besides, it even happens sometimes that suitable persons cannot be found among the lineage members for the performance of certain rituals, and visiting clansfolk have to be called upon. Also, in the case of funerals, any death occurring outside the home town of the deceased is the responsibility of his clansfolk in the vicinity.

Thus in planning funerals and visits to funeral ceremonies one of the first questions which come to mind concerns the clan affiliations of the deceased. A knowledge of this will determine the sort of people the principal actors at the function would be, the specific rites to be performed, and the dates when the principal ceremonies would take place.

Taboos and rites of passage are the domains of clanship as such, which cut across agnatic relations at the local level. They are therefore important means of furthering the interests of the clan as opposed to those of its local segments. In the absence of frequent social interaction amongst members of the clan, common taboos and observances and belief in the inter-dependence of clansfolk wherever they might be at times of life crisis, these and the belief in common origin serve to enhance the solidarity of the clan. The solidarity of the lineage, on the other hand, lies on a different plane. It is based on permanent co-residence and co-activity and is therefore concerned more with the material aspects of everyday life.

Returning to the lineage, it is important to add that it is not an undifferentiated mass of agnates united by land, lineage head, a name and an ancestral home. Nor are the rights and duties of the members uniformly distributed. It is true that theoretically the structural distance[1] between members, both in terms of residence and degree of social interaction, is correlated with their relative positions on the genealogical chart: the nearer they are the closer the relationship. Yet this correlation does not in practice radiate symmetrically from the nearest to the remotest agnates. Rather, every individual has some closer ones with whom he identifies himself in the co-operation of everyday life. With others he only comes into contact in times of crisis and during ancestral rites, funerals, and other occasions when the lineage as a whole meets in a body. These two sets of agnates may be described as close and distant relatives respectively.

This dividing line is the result of the general cleavage which governs the authority structure and internal organization of the lineage. The group we call close agnates is three to four generations in depth, and is itself divided into smaller segments. The smallest unit within the lineage is the hut, $x\jmath$ (lit. room), the home of a wife and her young children. The Anlo practise polygyny, though less than forty per cent of the married men have more than one wife. A wife either has her own separate hut for herself and

[1] The term 'structural distance' is used here as defined by Evans-Pritchard (1940, p. 110), as 'the distance between groups of persons in a social system, expressed in terms of values'.

her children or shares an apartment in a large common hut with her husband. In a polygynous household it is usual for each wife to have her own kitchen, granaries and hut. We shall in a later chapter discuss more fully the structure and composition of households. It is sufficient here to point out that the huts of one husband form a distinct compound, separate from those of related families and surrounded by its own walls. The term used for the compound in its literal and social senses is *afe*, house, and it is the home of a man, his wife or wives and their unmarried children, the adult sons on marriage building their own *afe* nearby while the married daughters leave for their husbands'. Every man is master in his own compound, administering its affairs without interference from anyone.

These compounds are usually grouped into larger residential units, which may be called 'clusters of families' (Figs. 2 and 3). A cluster consists, in the main, of the compounds of full and half brothers, and sometimes parallel first cousins, under the authority of their eldest living member. The family cluster is not a static group. It undergoes a cycle of growth and segmentation, and sometimes even decline and fusion with others within the lineage. It rarely includes agnates whose common ancestor is more than four or five generations removed. But whatever its size it is defined by the possession of an elder. He is responsible for the settlement of minor disputes within the cluster, for not all cases are referred to the head of the whole lineage. The cluster is therefore an identifiable unit in the intergroup relationship within the lineage, and in many cases the structural distance between the clusters is shown in the spatial distribution of their compounds, which is only prevented in some other cases by lack of suitable land for settlement.

In function and structure the cluster is modelled on the lineage at large, and the functioning of its authority may be explained by comparison between the lineage and the ancestors. Just as the lineage head is the link between the lineage and the ancestors, so is the head of the cluster the link between his group and the lineage as a whole. This relationship is based on Anlo principles of seniority. A man is generally considered a minor as long as his father lives. During meetings of the lineage, for instance, when the heads of all the various clusters together with the rank and file are present, a man is not expected to speak or to perform any major task while his father is around. It does not, however, necessarily follow that a younger man who loses his father attains social maturity earlier than an older man whose father lives. The principle does not revolve solely around the father-son relationship. On the contrary, age is an important consideration, and it is this which results in the fusion of close groups of family clusters. A man usually assumes jural responsibility for his younger brothers and the children of a dead brother.

The point we want to emphasize here is that the social relations between members of the same family cluster are much closer and more intimate than those between members of different clusters. Members of the lineage are expected to be friendly and to help one another in general terms. A man looks to them for hospitality and support in times of serious trouble. But it is on the members of the family cluster that he relies most. These people advise and help him in all his problems and undertakings. They assist him in work and such duties as housebuilding or fencing his house. His more distant agnates, unless they are actual neighbours, seldom figure prominently in his life.

We shall try, with the help of Fig. 1, to illustrate the relationship between the family cluster and the lineage by certain events in the life of a section of the Amelor lineage of Woe. This is a fairly large lineage, and, unlike most of those in the area, it has not lost any members by emigration. In many respects it may be taken as a fair approximation to the past. This is largely because they have sufficient fertile land to support them, and they are all onion farmers, with the exception of Samuel (No. 31), who is a carpenter, and Ame (No. 23), who is a bricklayer. The lineage head is Adzɔ (No. 7), who at about 70 years old in 1962 was one of my principal informants.

One important index of social relations within the lineage was the conduct of the funeral of Amedɔme (No. 24), who died in August 1962. Adzɔ (No. 7), as the lineage head, was officially announced as the chief mourner, though the effective administration of the funeral was done by Amedzi (No. 9), father of the dead man.

Before analysing the facts brought out by the death, it may be necessary to say a few words about how funerals are conducted in Anlo. It must be mentioned at once that local variations occur in detail, and the following description refers only to Woe.

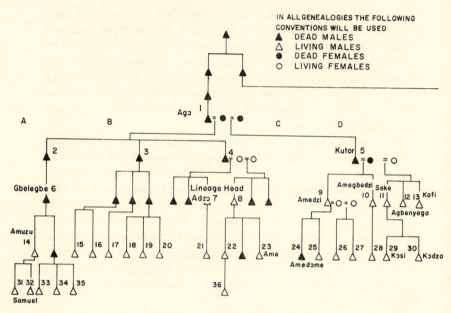

FI G. I. Family clusters within a section of the Amelor lineage of Woe excluding women and children

Nowadays the major funeral rites and ceremonies take about a month to complete. The important events connected with the death fall on the following days:

1. *Ameḍigbe:* The day of the burial.

2. *Ŋdinamegbe:* The day following the burial, when the chief mourners receive greetings from sympathisers.

3. *Ŋudᴐgbe:* The day for wake-keeping. This falls on the fourth or sixth day after the burial, depending on the clan of the dead man.[1] In this case it was the fourth day.

4. *Yᴐfogbe:* The day following wake-keeping, when lineage rituals are performed in memory of the dead person. On the same day the mourners begin to receive donations from the public.

5. *Akᴐŋtawᴐgbe:* Three days after the lineage rituals, when donations are assembled.

---

[1] As has been said already, every clan has its own funeral rites. Each clan also has its date for the lineage rituals, which are preceded the night before by wake-keeping. There are two main dates for the lineage rituals, the fifth or eighth day after the burial. See Appendix III.

6. *Xɔmefewɔgbe:* About one week later (there is no fixed time) when donations and expenditure are made public.

The sixth event is the last public activity connected with any death. But for the relatives of the dead man there is another meeting called *xɔwoxɔme*, when discussion takes place on ways and means of raising money to pay for the expenditure if the public donations are not sufficient for this. In this case there was a debt of £24.[1]

The first six occasions listed are public functions, involving the whole settlement and relatives and friends from other settlements. One important aspect of Anlo funerals, however, is that, though these dates are strictly adhered to, there is a continuous stream of sympathisers and donors flowing in every day between the date of the burial and the last ceremony. There are also relatives from distant settlements coming to spend several days at the funeral. For these reasons it is incumbent on the chief mourners and close relatives to come to the ancestral home to receive donors and sympathisers, and to help perform the various pieces of work that might be necessary.

Now subtracting the six public days, there are nine days left between the day of the burial and the last public occasion, *xɔmefewɔgbe*, when the public do not turn up in a body. It was the attendance of lineage members from the various clusters at the funeral during these nine days which became crucial in showing the degree of social interaction in the Amelor lineage.

It is significant that in addition to the six public ceremonies which all the lineage members also attended, Amedzi (9), the father of the dead man, his brother Amegbedzi (10) and all the four children of these two spent every day at the funeral till *xɔmefewɔgbe*. So did Seke (11) and Agbenyega (12). Kofi (13) was there on three occasions, and Kɔsi and Kodzo only twice.

The attendance of people from family clusters A, B, and C was even more irregular. Adzɔ, the lineage head, was the most regular of them all, failing to turn up only twice. Nearly half the lot, fairly equally distributed among the three clusters, never

[1] Funerals cost a lot in Anlo. Apart from the coffin and the clothes in which the dead are buried, there is expenditure on the entertainment of guests. All the important dates mentioned are marked by public dancing, in which ward members and sometimes other members of the settlement take part. The dancers are lavishly treated to alcohol. The visitors from distant villages are also given food. Amedome's funeral cost £107 while the donations reached only £83.

turned up at all. One of these was Amuzu, an eighty-year-old whose absence might be excused on account of his age. But of those who turned up none was there on more than three occasions.

Decision concerning the settlement of the debt was also not without interest. At the meeting on this issue it was revealed that money towards the funeral expenditure was advanced by Amedzi's brother, Amegbedzi (10) a fairly rich man by Anlo standards. It was decided that all members of D except Amedzi (9) should contribute £2 each, and Amedzi (9) the remaining £4.

When I asked why Adzɔ (7), the lineage head, did not have to pay anything, Seke (11) told me it was because he was not one of them. Adzɔ's own explanation was that his 'duty as lineage head was to see that the debt was fairly distributed among the chief mourners'. I am, however, inclined to agree with Seke. If the death had occurred in cluster C, Adzɔ's own cluster, he would certainly have had a share of the debt, as Seke indicated. Actually it would be a drain on Adzɔ's pocket if his status as lineage head obliged him to involve himself in financial matters concerning all segments of the lineage.

This example, though somewhat hackneyed, shows clearly a progressive lack of interest in each other's affairs which corresponds closely to the relative distance of the lineage members on the genealogical chart. It is events of this kind which helped in our grouping of the four family clusters. It may therefore be used to illustrate the factors which govern segmentation of the lineage into these clusters. The break of cluster D from the others stems from the difference in maternal origin of Kutor (5) and Agɔ's (1) other three children. That the Kutor segment has not yet segmented is due primarily to the fact that Kutor was an only son, so that his segment is smaller than the others.

There is also the conflict between age and generation within the segments, especially between A and D. Amuzu (14) at 80 is much older than Adzɔ (7), the head of the lineage, and Kofi (13), who is in his early forties, is of the same generation as Amuzu's father Gbelegbe (6). This, as Seke (11) told me, was because Seke's father's mother was married by Agɔ (1) in his old age.

Even in cluster D there is already a sign of cleavage, as shown by the rather irregular attendance of the descendants of Kutor's second wife at Amedɔme's funeral.

There is, therefore, a continuous proliferation of family clusters within the lineage, in which the degree of social intercourse and identification are a function of the relative distance on the genealogical chart of those involved. Every generation produces men who are potential branching points of the genealogical tree in a process described by Professor Barnes[1] as chronic segmentation. Before two brothers are born it is fairly certain that their descendants will sooner or later segment.

The role of the lineage head as link between the various segments and as symbol of unity is shown by the activities of Adzɔ. Though a member of a different family cluster, his status as lineage head places him above sectional interests in the performance of his duties.

Another point of interest illustrated by the Amelor lineage is the role of the ancestral rites in maintaining or at least expressing the unity of the lineage. The fact that there is no hierarchy of lineage shrines corresponding to the various branching points on the genealogical chart concentrates all ritual power of the lineage in the lineage head.

Nevertheless, the influence of genealogical distance on social relations is reflected in certain ceremonies. For instance, at one of the annual stool festivals of the Amelor lineage which I witnessed there was not a single absentee. This was in connection with a ritual concerning the founding ancestor of the lineage, an occasion on which the whole lineage was expected to emerge in a body. It was therefore not surprising that every member was present. When, however, on another occasion diviners asked Seke (11) to sacrifice to the ancestral stool because of the illness of his son, this being a minor occasion, there were no less than six absentees from clusters A, B, C. It may be argued that the importance attached to the annual festivals made it imperative for all to attend whereas Seke's sacrifice was a minor one. But the fact that the absentees belong to A, B, C, and none to D, Seke's own cluster, is no doubt a result of the relationships involved.

The development and spatial segmentation of the lineage can be seen by comparing the sites of their compounds in 1912 and 1962. This shows how in fifty years one cluster has segmented into four (Figs. 2 and 3).

These few facts about the Amelor lineage give some idea about the factors influencing interpersonal relations within the lineage.

[1] 1962, p. 8.

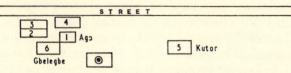

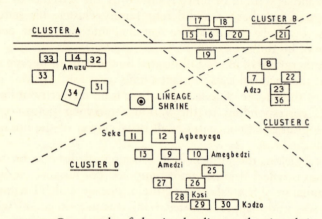

FIG. 2. Compounds of the Amelor lineage, 1912 (not according to scale). Compounds of matrilateral kin not included. Numbers refer to persons in Fig. 1

FIG. 3. Compounds of the Amelor lineage showing their grouping into family clusters 1962. Same site as 1912

To say that the lineage emerges as a corporate group on major occasions concerning its members is to tell only part of the story. Occasions for the attendance of all members are very few, and are limited to the periodic ancestral rites and meetings called for the discussion of lineage property. In most cases it is the cluster which emerges as the most effective unit. It is equally important to remember that every generation sees the proliferation of the lineage into a bigger and less solidary unit. This in turn increases the number of effective sub-units within the lineage.

3. THE BASIC BEHAVIOUR PATTERNS AMONG AGNATES

The basic pattern for interpersonal relations within the lineage is governed by three main factors: the opposition of adjacent generations within the nuclear family, epitomized by the father-son relationship; the residence pattern, which results in co-residence and habitual co-operation of agnates; and patrilineal inheritance, which makes agnates common owners of lineage property.

As in many patrilineal societies, the father-son relationship is characterized by the authority and superordination of the father and the total dependence and subordination of the son. Though it is recognized that a strong affection should develop between father and son through co-residence and co-operation in work, the disciplinary role of the father is not easily reconcilable with any free association between them. The relationship is developed in the son's childhood when he is learning from his father, and perfected in his adulthood, when he prepares to take over from him.

In the household the father as head is the most important person. He is the *afetɔ*, owner of the house and everything within it. So long as he lives all his property, including any that he has given to his son, remains in his name, because 'a living person's property is never inherited'. Only a dead man's is.

A son is expected to be deferential and submissive to his father. On no occasion should he address him by name, but always by the kinship terms applicable to a father, *fofo* or *tɔnye*. He is expected not to stand before his father while talking to him. He should squat on the floor unless asked by the father to sit down. It is improper for a son to sit on a seat vacated by his father. If he does, he will be accused of wishing the latter's death in order to replace him. At meal times he should not start eating before his father does, nor eat any fish or meat in the soup until his father tells him to. Talking at table, especially by boys, is taboo.

The duty and respect due to a father continues up to the son's adulthood. Though a man is expected to establish his own compound after he is married, he remains almost at the beck and call of his father, and is master only in his own compound. After his son's marriage a father gives part of his own land, or the uncleared bush adjoining it, to his son for his own use, but at sowing, hoeing or weeding times the father still has a claim on the son's labour. In fact his demands take precedence over the son's own needs. Thus the establishment of a separate household by the son does not in itself establish his independence of his father. Indeed he builds his compound at a place chosen for him by the father, usually not far from his own compound, so that the son can be of help to

him whenever he needs him. A further index of his authority is
the fact that the son cannot start building his new house until the
father has ritually laid out the groundwork for it.

A good son is one who obeys his father, is gentle, and models
himself on his father's life. The greatest compliment to a boy is,
Ðevi sia tsɔ fofoa fe kɔ, 'this boy follows his father's footsteps'. A
bad son on the other hand is one who is disobedient, avoids his
father, and is always running from him to seek refuge in his
mother's kitchen.

One may speak then of an institutionalized inequality and even
antagonism between father and son. The saying that one does not
inherit the property of a living man, and some of the other usages
associated with the relationship, are expressive of the hidden
unwillingness with which the father concedes responsibility and
authority to his son.

The father-daughter relationship is not different in general
principles, but as there are limits to their co-activity in everyday
life due to sexual division of labour, the preceding discussion must
be considered less relevant to daughters. But in spite of this, or
rather because of it, it is said that a daughter must be even more
respectful towards her father, because of the general subservience
of women to men.

The relationship between a man and his father's brother, who
in Ewe is also called father (big or small according to his age
relative to the father's) is similar. It is said that because this relationship lacks the intimacy of the real father-son relationship the
paternal uncle is feared and is even more respected than the father
himself. It is further said that there is an inherent hatred between
them, stemming from the belief that the paternal uncle regards
the brother's son as a rival to his own son in relation to paternal
property. However, though he can ask for his help in performance
of various tasks he has not as direct a demand on his brother's son's
labour as on his own sons'.

A father's sister commands even greater respect than her male
siblings. Owing to virilocal residence, when women marry they
leave their parental homes and their male agnates behind, though
links with them are never severed. Subject to the relative distance
of her new home from her male siblings' there is lacking between
her and her brother's sons the frequent social intercourse amongst
male agnates which co-residence entails. But the relationship is

formalized in specific terms with deep mystical overtones. The
father's sister's curse is believed to be most dreaded. In fact this is
the only relationship in Anlo which is expressed in terms of curs-
ing. It is also believed that when a man is not successful in life it is
for his father's sister to offer special sacrifices on his behalf. Her
carelessness too can sometimes affect the health of her brother's
children, because of the belief that if, when she is preparing porridge, some of the flour falls into the fire, they will have swellings,
dzodzoŋgui, on their bodies. Another belief is that in the past,
when Anlo disliked people growing abnormally tall, the father's
sister was the person who could stop this by making an incision
at the back of her brother's son's knee. These prerogatives of the
father's sister make her a very important person in the life of every
Anlo, and it is said that a person's one important life-long consideration is not to offend his father's sister.

When we move from members of adjacent generations to
agnates of the same generation, we at the same time travel from
the realm of inequality to that of equality and comradeship. The
relationship of agnates of the same generation is distinguishable
from the previous one by lack of formality. Siblingship in general
is discussed below. Here we are only concerned with agnatic
siblingship.

Comradeship and co-operation characterize the relationship of
children of the same father or of brothers, though potential rivalry
and hostility are also recognized. Paternal half-siblings and ortho-
cousins are regarded much in the same way as brothers and sisters,
and, growing up together as they do in the same neighbourhood,
they are usually playmates in childhood. Adult brothers and ortho-
cousins help each other in farm tasks and have first claim to the
use of land formerly held by their fathers. For, though the administration of the lineage land as a whole is in the hands of the lineage
head, a person's rights of usufruct are inherited on his death by his
own sons and daughters. The position of daughters and their
children in the inheritance system will be discussed later.

A man regards his brothers and patrilineal cousins, especially
those in the same family cluster, as important advisers. He would
not decide such important matters as his own marriage or the
marriage of his children without consulting them. These people
advise and help him in all his problems, and, as members of his
own generation and generally of his own age group, he is on

much more intimate and freer terms with them than with his father and his siblings.

Due to lineage exogamy ortho-cousins cannot marry, and they are taught from an early age that sex relations between them are forbidden. But daughters and sons of brothers do not avoid each other, they are often seen playing together. Yet within this framework of habitual co-operation and collective rights, there are sometimes jealousies and disputes, especially among male ortho-cousins, owing to rival claims to unused land and other properties, and the arbitrary exercise of authority.

We turn finally to a consideration of the relationship between relatives of alternate generations. As Ward[1] has observed among other Ewe tribes, the principle of merging of alternate generations certainly operates in the minds of the people themselves. Grandchildren are frequently named after their grandparents and addressed as such, and the relation between the two is exceptionally free. This is a time when both are on the fringes of useful social life, one generation being in their extreme youth and the other in their old age. Few responsibilities in the day-to-day management of the compound are theirs. As a result a pleasant, free and easy relationship can obtain between them.

Though no distinction is made in language between maternal and paternal grandparents, it is with the latter that children are more intimately acquainted. But they too do not normally live in the same household, and are therefore free from the disciplinary associations which mark the relation of adjacent generations. The Anlo child, therefore, like those in many other societies, looks to its grandparents for especially kindly treatment, for gifts, endearments and general spoiling.

4. NON-AGNATIC KINSHIP

So far we have been concerned solely with a description of pure agnatic kinship, without reference to the other ties which join people of different lineages. This procedure is useful as a way of giving an unadulterated picture of the lineage, its structure and its internal organization. But in a sense this picture is both artificial and unreal, because the social horizon of every person extends beyond the limits of clan and lineage. In short, the lineage does

[1] 1949, p. 50.

not exist in isolation. As women marry they create new ties with other lineages in the community, which have important influences on members of their own lineages as well as those of their husbands. The children of these women too retain rights and duties in the lineages of their mothers. As the Anlo themselves put it, by marriage a woman *do fome* (lit. joins kinship) with other lineages. The importance of ties through women is always stressed by the Anlo, and runs through all their kinship values. In support of this it is said *Vi le tɔfe le nɔfe, ame ɖeka memlɔa anyi dzia vi o*, 'a child belongs to the father's and the mother's huts, because it does not take one but two persons to produce a child'.

Of all a person's non-agnatic ties the most important are those which connect him with his mother's patrilineage. The social and economic relations springing from association with the mother's patrilineage are second in importance only to those derived from his own. Generally speaking the difference between the two is one of degree and not of kind, and it is difficult to make a clear-cut distinction in their spheres of application. It is true that patriliny takes precedence over non-agnatic kinship, especially in respect of political rank, land usage, the inheritance of transferable wealth, residence rights, funerals and ritual allegiance. Nevertheless, as we shall see, these rights and obligations which characterize the patrilineage can be conferred upon an individual by his mother's patrilineage.

One important field in which this is clearly demonstrated is inheritance. We have already indicated that in the inheritance of a dead person's property the daughters are never left out.[1] The portion allocated to the daughters does not pass after their death to their brothers but to their children. This practice applies equally to both lineage property and personal property acquired by a man.[2] As far as daughters are concerned it is to be emphasized that, though no fixed proportion is allocated to them by law,

[1] Goody (1962, p. 315) describes systems of this kind as 'diverging transmission'.
[2] Actually what becomes lineage property after a number of generations almost invariably starts as personal property. For a long time after their settlement in their present country it was not necessary to divide a dead person's land or creek every generation, since there was always enough land for all without the application of rigid laws of ownership and inheritance. Thus group ownership of land was preserved; what the ancestors used became over the generations the property of their surviving children. As the pressure on the land increased, especially during the last two generations, it became necessary to allot specific portions to each member of the land-owning group.

their share is usually smaller than those of the male offspring.[1] But
the important thing is not the size of the share but the principles
which govern the distribution. Thus usufructuary rights in land
and other properties are enjoyed by both agnatic and matrilateral
relatives of the original owner.

The cumulative effects of this dual approach to inheritance are
that:

1. An individual potentially has links with several lineages apart
from his own, to whose land and other properties he has claims,
and many people actually do utilize these matrilateral claims.

2. In every succeeding generation an increased portion of
lineage land falls into the hands of matrilateral relatives, though it
nominally remains in the name of the lineage. This is the reason
why a land standing in the name of a lineage or clan invariably
has among its cultivators many who do not answer to this name.

Ideally there is little difference between the rights of lineage
inheritors and those of non-lineage kin, since both are governed
by the belief in the inalienable nature of the land, so that nobody
can have more than usufruct.

There is however one relationship between the land and the
lineage members from which non-agnates are debarred. Since
succession to leadership is through lineal descent, no outsider to
the lineage can become the head of the land-owning group, and
since sacrifices to the land and its dead owners are made by the
lineage owning the land, no non-lineage user can perform these.
Any non-agnatic user of the lineage land who wants to make such

[1] A man is expected to get about twice as much as a woman. But in practice he
usually gets much more. In one case a man with five sons and five daughters left
a total of 230 onion beds as his main heritable property. Each of his sons received
30 beds and the daughters 10. The eldest daughter's son (i.e. the grandson of the
deceased) also received 30 beds, partly because, it was argued, he spent all his life
on this farm with the deceased, and partly because he himself had no paternal
property suitable for his training as an onion farmer. In another case each daughter
had 18 as against 36 for the sons. In yet another the ratio was about 4 to 1 in favour
of the sons, and in another about 5 to 4. With these examples in mind it is only
safe to say that both sons and daughters have rights of inheritance in the system
but the women get smaller shares than the men. The reason why the women
receive less is, of course, that their children will receive more from their paternal
side. It often happens that a piece of land is too small to be divided individually
amongst the claimants. In this case the land, or whatever property it is, may be
divided into the number of women who had children by the owner, each group
of full siblings receiving a share proportionate to their number. Such land will be
entrusted to the care of one of the siblings.

a sacrifice must do so through the lineage head. As will be shown later, a man can make sacrifices to ancestors of lineages other than his own, but these have to pass through the lineal descendants of the ancestor in question. By enjoying the land or property of a lineage not his own a person indirectly places himself under the authority of the land-owning lineage and their ancestors.

The above are the main principles which govern the inheritance of lineage property. How the system works in practice, however, depends in each case on the relationship of demographic factors to available land and the reasonableness of the various claimants. For instance, a man whose own lineage has a large area may not find it necessary to utilize his matrilateral claims elsewhere. In other cases large portions of land have been given to non-agnatic relatives.

Related to this system of inheritance is the development of an identifiable group of relatives, which may be called *dzidzimeviwo* (lit. offspring), a group comprising all the lineal descendants of an ancestor and his descendants through all other lines. This is a group the members of which in every generation have rights of one kind or another in their ancestor's property. Within this group agnates are differentiated from matrilateral kin, *srɔnyiviwo* both in name and in rights. The agnates are the nominal holders of the group's property, the observers of its taboos, the bearers of its name and the successors to its titles. They include not only males but also their sisters, who form the originating points of the non-agnatic members. As marriage is virilocal, the non-agnatic members do not form a residential group with the agnates, and they do not often utilize their rights in the property of the group, except where, as we have seen, their own agnatic group has not sufficient land. Moreover, unlike agnatic ties, the links of non-agnatic kinship do not go on ad infinitum. After a few generations the matrilateral relationship (especially if it has not been attached to property) becomes lost, if not to recognition, at least to active participation. Therefore it is the nearness of the links with the agnatic group which determines the intensity of their privileges and active participation with it and the nearer one's generation to the matrilateral ancestors who utilized these claims the greater one's chances of remembering the links.

Claims through women therefore provide a subsidiary source of income and capital for people whose lineages have insufficient property. Thus in Anlo a man can turn with greater confidence than in many patrilineal societies to groups outside his own lineage for support.

The extent to which people actually utilize non-agnatic claims is indicated by a case study of 120 farms at Woe.[1] Of this number 49, about 40 per cent were being used by lineal descendants of the original owners. The remaining 71 were in the hands of non-agnatic descendants of the original owners. On the majority of the farms the plots in the sample were only one of the two or more plots they had in different parts of the village. In fact there were only 19 – about 16 per cent who had no land other than that of their lineage, and all of these belonged to lineages who are fairly rich in farm land.

Personal property follows almost the same line as lineage property, except that objects exclusively used by men, such as guns, men's clothes, hand-looms or fishing nets, pass to sons, while women's clothes, beads, and gold and silver ornaments go to daughters. The importance of these last items can be very great in view of the great value placed on ancient beads and clothes, and some sisters prefer to leave them indivisible for use in their entirety in turns by the siblings and other uterine kin. Thus, like the Yako,[2] the Anlo have, in addition to patrilineal inheritance, a set of proprietary rights transmitted matrilineally. But there is no such corresponding corporate matrilineal descent group as the Yako *lejima*. The Anlo matrilineal property-owning group has no name, does not meet, has no shrine and no elected leader. It is only a group of female users of property and has no male members as do matrilineal descent groups. Related to this matrilineal succession may be mentioned witchcraft which is also believed to be inherited through the female line. The inheritance of witchcraft however includes both male and female uterine kin.

It should be mentioned here that Westermann's view, later developed by Ward,[3] that personal property among the Anlo is transmitted matrilineally from a man to his sister's son, has no foundation in oral tradition or genealogical history. However it sometimes happens (and there are several instances) that a sister's

---

[1] This did not include farms mortgaged to or bought by those in the sample. Certain farms were originally acquired by women, in which case ownership was traced to the oldest man to have used them.

[2] Forde, 1950, p. 306.　　[3] Ward, B. E., 1955, pp. 3–5.

son lives with, and serves, his mother's brother and is given part of the latter's property. Also, in view of the fact that daughters have rights in their father's property and the possible intervention of demographic factors it is not surprising that certain properties are traced to ancestors other than lineal forbears. However, I think the term 'mixed descent', suggested by Ward, is an apt description of the system[1] because of the flexibility of the lineal principle.

The dual aspect of the kinship system is also shown in residence. In Woe and Alakple the local agnatic incidence (adult males only, excluding those living on land they had bought) was just 75 per cent in 1962. This incidence appears relatively high, but it shows nonetheless that no less than 25 per cent of adult men have to utilize matrilateral claims for residence purposes.

The principle is further illustrated in ward membership. Though a person normally belongs to his father's ward, he can if he likes choose his mother's. Moreover, though every ward is territorially identified with the section of the settlement which the members usually occupy, to the Anlo themselves it is participation in the ward's activities, not residence, which determines membership. A man whose parents belong to different wards, and who prefers, for instance, the songs of his mother's ward to those of his father's, may choose the former. Thus it happens that a person may live in the quarter of his lineage and ward and yet be counted as a member of another ward. But in many cases it is residence in the mother's ward which leads to his choosing to participate in its activities. An example may help here. Amɛ and Husunugbo belong to different wards although they are full brothers. The reason given for this is that Amɛ spent his childhood with his mother's brothers and grew to like their activities. He still lives there, and does not participate in the activities of his father's ward. He is not on the register of his father's ward and does not regard himself as a member of it. He himself told me that, when he dies, 'It is my mother's ward, not my father's, who will bury me, because that is where I belong'.

It has also been pointed out that Anlo attribute immortality to their ancestors through their belief in the doctrine of reincarnation which they call amedzɔdzɔ. Among the Yoruba,[2] who also adhere to this doctrine, the dead are believed to return into their own lineages. In Anlo, however, owing to the importance attached to

[1] Ibid. [2] Schwab, 1955, p. 352.

'both sides', the dead person is reincarnated as a member either of his or her own lineage or of his or her descending kindred or 'personal kindred', *fome*, of a younger generation.[1] This is further emphasized by the belief that some dead persons return in two forms, one in their own lineages and the other among their non-agnatic kin.

We round off the general discussion of non-agnatic kinship by a further look at ancestor-worship. This subject has been treated purely from the point of view of the lineage. Here we must see how non-agnates fit into the picture.

The principles governing the relationship between living and dead resemble in some respects those of the Lugbara. There, as Middleton[2] reports, lineal as well as matrilateral ancestors make certain demands on their living kindred, and the latter in turn expect guidance and help from both. The difference between the two systems in this respect is that, unlike the Lugbara, the Anlo do not make matrilateral shrines, but pray or sacrifice to the matri-lateral ancestors in question through the ancestors' lineage shrine and lineage head. An Anlo individual is then linked ritually with many other lineages apart from his own. And because of the interest of the ancestors in their cognatic descendants, all known cognatic descendants are invited to and do attend the lineage's ancestral rituals.

Non-agnatic kinship is, thus, given emphasis in some of the important aspects of Anlo social life. This we have tried to show by considering the part played by it in inheritance, ancestor wor-ship and other aspects of the social system. One important effect of the extra-lineage ties, especially those deriving from the inheri-tance system, is to widen the cleavages, when they occur, within the lineage. This happens particularly in lineages which are poor, and whose members have to look towards their different matri-lateral kinsmen for support.

5. THE BASIC BEHAVIOUR PATTERNS IN MATRILATERAL KINSHIP

Perhaps the most significant feature of non-agnatic kinship is that it is not the basis of any corporate group. Since residence is viri-local and lineage exogamy the rule, non-agnatic relatives must be

---

[1] A child's antecedent ancestor is known by divination.   [2] 1960, pp. 57–61,

distributed among the different patrilineal territories of a settlement. Also, matrilateral ties are ego-oriented, and the circle of
kinsfolk is distinct for each group of full siblings. It is for this
reason that some authorities, notably Fortes,[1] prefer to call this set
of relationships 'personal kinship'. Because of their dispersal,
persons linked by these ties are not subject to such friction as
characterizes agnates with their permanent co-residence and co-
activity. Hence from the personal point of view the non-agnatic
bond is held to be stronger and more affectionate than that of
agnatic kinship. That the absence of shared residence among matrilateral kinsmen is a strong factor in the maintenance of these
affective ties is realized by the Anlo themselves, and is expressed
in several proverbs and maxims. 'Adzɔge nɔvie nya wɔna', says one
maxim, 'kinsfolk are at peace when they live apart'. In other
words, co-residence is known to cause friction. Little wonder,
therefore, that at the level of interpersonal relations, agnatic kinship is less strong than non-agnatic.

The basic behaviour patterns among non-agnatic kinsfolk
radiate from the relationships within the nuclear family. From the
Anlo point of view, the strongest ties of affection are not those
between spouses, but those between parent and child and between
siblings. Of the parents the mother is considered much closer and
more intimate. The mother-child relationship, as the strongest of
all ties, is created in the first place by the child's physical dependence on the mother and the close bodily contact between the
two in the child's formative years. She fondles and tends it, and
carries it around on her back until it is weaned after two years.
Compared with this the father's relationship with his child is almost
negligible. The rules forbidding him to sleep with his wife till the
child is weaned, and his outdoor activities during the day, keep him
away from mother and child, thus preventing him from giving the
child any care at this time comparable to that of its mother.

As the child grows its psychological attachment to the mother
grows, while the attitude to the father does not improve. The
hardness, authority and disciplinary functions of the father have
already been described. Between these and the child the mother
serves as a buffer. She tempers the father's wrath whenever it is
aroused, while her own relationship with the child is characterized
by softness and indulgence.

[1] 1949, p. 37.

Apart from the mutual trust between mother and child in childhood, it seems that the effects of travail on the mother also introduce a special relationship between her and her child which the father-child bond lacks. This is expressed in the concept of *vidzika-fe-amefotsotso*, i.e. the feelings aroused in a mother bringing to mind the time of travail. These emotions are aroused when her child is either in pain or in trouble of any kind. A mother meditating one day on the sad plight of her son ended thus: *Vinye la! Gbemagbea nenye miafe me mawuwoe melɔ o la ne nu bubu dzɔ*, 'my child! – that day if it were not for the help of our lineage gods a different thing might have happened – I would have died.' Often when a father is beating a child one can hear the mother pleading, 'but he is only a child. Please leave him.' Many mothers told me that it is the recalling of that day – the day of travail, which generates this sympathetic attitude.

It has been said that because of the sexual division of labour in everyday life a father has more to do with his son than his daughter. A mother for the same reason is more closely linked with her daughter, and it is a mark of the affection of the mother that this co-operation, which also involves some degree of discipline, does not result in antagonism. Moreover, there is a recognized preference among Anlo women for their first born to be female (as it is among men for sons). A daughter will help the mother tend the younger children and assist in the housework. At the same time the economic importance of the son is also emphasized. He takes charge of the father's estate and is looked to by his mother for support in her old age. The lack of frequent contact which results from the difference of sex is compensated by their permanent co-residence, which the daughter does not share. The result is a free permanent relationship of affection.

The affective free and informal ties of mother-child relationship also extend to the mother's siblings. A mother's sister is called mother. When travelling outside the settlement a mother prefers to leave her children with her sister rather than with her co-wife, even if this would mean taking them to a different section of the village. When a child loses its mother it is more usual for its mother's sister than its father's sister to assume responsibility for it.

The familiar pattern described for many patrilineal societies,[1] of the informal, intimate relation between a man and his sister's

[1] Radcliffe-Brown, 1952, pp. 15–31; Goody, 1959, pp. 61–6.

son is also found in Anlo. A mother's brother's house is the second home of every Anlo. A sister's son may take certain liberties in his mother's brother's house: he may help himself to food and take anything at all that he likes, because 'your mother's brother, *nyrui*, is like a mother to you. He will not be stern with you.' There is also a very high frequency of children, especially boys, living with their mother's brothers, as will be seen in Chapter 4.

Something has already been said about siblingship in an agnatic context. Here we consider the relationship in a uterine context. The absence of primogeniture eliminates one important element of potential hostility among uterine siblings, since the paternal estate is equally divided among brothers on one hand and among sisters on the other. But the same is not true of succession to titles within the patrilineage and the family clusters within it. There, as has been seen already, seniority is given great emphasis, and a man cannot hope to be a head so long as his elder brother lives. There are sometimes grumblings here and there about an elder brother, as lineage head, taking the lion's share of the sacrificial objects or taking arbitrary decisions, but on the whole these tensions occur within the general agnatic framework of the lineage, where full siblings usually side together against their opposite numbers. Seniority within the sibling group, therefore, though given expression in language and general behaviour among siblings, does not cause conflicts as in the agnatic group at large. Siblings, therefore, form a very closely knit group, among whom there is mutual trust and confidence.

There does not seem to be any special alignment by sex among siblings. However, the ties between sisters are remarkable for lack of tension. Though they change domicile after marriage their relationship is maintained by frequent visits. Brothers and sisters too grow very fond of each other. Before women marry they grow up in close contact with their brothers, and talk freely with them about all their interests. A young man often discusses his love affairs with his sister, who is undoubtedly placed in a position to know much about other girls, and she may approach the girl in whom he is interested on his behalf. There is no privacy between them. They can see each other's nakedness without remorse. But they may not have sexual relations. This is taboo, and violation may result in serious sickness for both. Brother and sister maintain close ties after they have married. However long the distance between them, frequent visits are exchanged. A sister may pay long visits to her brother, which he has to reciprocate. These links are further strengthened by personal interest in each other's children, who are often taken to spend several days with their parents' siblings, some even living with them permanently.

It is undoubtedly because of the importance attached to full siblingship that special mystical sanctions are associated with permanent disputes among them. It is believed that when siblings quarrel and remain unreconciled, the ancestors will intervene by bringing sickness on them or their children. Such a sickness can be cured only after the parties have been ritually purified.[1] Siblings do quarrel, but they are expected to be reconciled as soon as possible. The same applies to half-siblings, but it is full siblingship which is always emphasized.

One other fact which underlines the unity of the sibling group is the belief already mentioned that full siblings share the same witchcraft ancestry through the female line. If someone is accused of witchcraft it follows that the accusation applies equally to the whole sibling group. Witchcraft is not a serious social problem in Anlo, but association with it carries grave social stigma, and accusations are fiercely resented by those involved.

The above considerations serve to unite the sibling group and to foster great affection among them. Hence the uterine relationship is the one on which all other kinship ties are modelled. Accordingly the term nɔvi, mother's child, which is the normal term used to describe full siblings, is often used to refer to anyone else with whom one has close kinship, or to differentiate a very close relative from among a class.

The cross-cousin relationship is also close and cordial, but rests on a different plane because of the sex element in it. Cross-cousins are expected to associate freely on terms of great intimacy and love. They are regarded as the most suitable mates. Even if they do not marry, or are of the same sex, they are entitled to be familiar. If they are of opposite sexes one often hears their parents referring to them as potential spouses. This relationship is symmetrical between cross-cousins on both sides.

In addition to the special cases described, the relationship between classificatory siblings of all sorts is recognized as widely as genealogical connections are known. In all cases the relationship is

[1] The specialist in this rite is always a man from the Ame clan. See Appendix I.

characterized by mutual help and friendly behaviour. The strength of the tie in each case, apart from the distinctions made, is dependent on relative genealogical closeness.

6. THE LANGUAGE OF KINSHIP

One important way by which kinship behaviour patterns can be studied is through the terms used to address or speak of different categories of kinsfolk, usually referred to as kinship terminology. This is because there is always some relation between the kinship system and the kinship terminology. According to Radcliffe-Brown,[1] 'In the actual study of a kinship system the nomenclature is of the utmost importance. It affords the best possible approach to the investigation and analysis of the kinship system as a whole. This, of course, it could not do if there were no real relations of interdependence between the terminology and the rest of the system. It will be borne out. . . by any anthropologist who has made a thorough field study of a kinship system.' The central problem, then, for the student of kinship is 'to see his kinship terminologies as a definite part of the dynamism of kinship relations, to determine how far the separation and combination of relatives under linguistic labels can be correlated with other sociological phenomena.'[2]

The first step in this exercise is to discover what terms are used and how they are used. We shall then consider these terms in relation to the whole system of social relations.

Anlo kinship terms are a combination of classifactory and descriptive terms, though the former are more common in ordinary usage. In its classificatory aspect the kinship terminology shows many of the social categories in observed behaviour. The basic pattern is set by the terms used within the family, for the distinction of kin in ordinary terms of reference and address, apart from individual description in detail, does not go further back than the second ascending generation, that is, the grandparent level.

Parents are distinguished according to sex. Father is *fofo* or *tɔ* and mother is *dada* or *da*. Children can also be distinguished according to sex, a son being *vi-ŋutsu* and a daughter *vi-nyɔnu*, but the common term for both is simply *vi*, child, or *vinye*, my child. The general term for a sibling is *nɔvi*, mother's child in the literal

---

[1] 1952, p. 62. [2] Firth, 1957, p. 247.

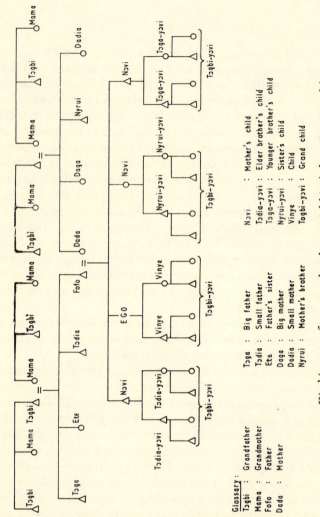

Glossary:

Tɔgbi	:	Grandfather	
Mama	:	Grandmother	
Fofo	:	Father	
Dada	:	Mother	

Tɔga	:	Big father
Tɔdia	:	Small father
Ete	:	Father's sister
Daga	:	Big mother
Dadia	:	Small mother
Nyrui	:	Mother's brother

Nɔvi	:	Mother's child
Tɔdia-yɔvi	:	Elder brother's child
Tɔga-yɔvi	:	Younger brother's child
Nyrui-yɔvi	:	Sister's child
Vinye	:	Child
Tɔgbi-yɔvi	:	Grand child

FIG. 4. Kinship terms for paternal and maternal kin (where Ego is male)

sense. However, it is an important principle of traditional etiquette that while a younger relative may be called by a personal name, an older one should always be addressed and called by the appropriate term of seniority. In these terms of seniority sex is clearly shown. Older male *nɔvi* are called *efo*, elder brother, and older female *nɔvi* are *daa*, elder sister. Grandparents are distinguished by sex only, and no distinction is made between the father's parents and those of the mother. The general term for a grandfather is *tɔgbi* and for a grandmother *mama*. These basic terms are generally extended to all relatives outside the family according to generation, with some modifications in detail. In the first ascending generation the father's siblings are clearly distinguished from the mother's. The terms for father's male siblings all have the root *tɔ*, and those for mother's female siblings all have the root *da*, but the appropriate distinctions are made for relative seniority. Father's elder brother is *tɔgã*, big father, and father's younger brother is *tɔḓia*, small father, but a father's sister of whatever age is *etɛ*, female father. Similarly mother's elder sister is *da-gã*, and her younger sister is *da-ḓia*, but any mother's brother, irrespective of age, is *nyrui*, male mother. Thus, where the sibling is of the same sex as the parent in question, the sibling's relative age is indicated in the term, while relative age is not indicated in the case of a sibling of the opposite sex.

These terms are also used for ortho-cousins and matrilateral cousins of the parents, and in fact for every relative of the parents' generation to whom consanguineous relation can be traced. One remarkable feature of the terminology is that in the classificatory usages of the terms lineage kin of the parents are not distinguished from non-lineage kin, even on the paternal side. The principle of equivalence of siblings is so extensively applied that any kinsman or kinswoman of a parent is seen as a sibling, regardless of the nature of the ties which connect him or her to the parent in question. Thus the father's full sister is called *etɛ* and is classified by the same term with the father's mother's sister's daughter. In the same way mother's full elder sister is called *dagã* (*daḓia* for the younger one). The same term is applied to the mother's mother's sister's daughter who is older than ego's mother and to all maternal female relatives of this generation. Also the father's elder brother is called *tɔga*, the term used for the father's father's sister's son and for all male paternal relatives of this generation. (See Figs. 6 and 7.)

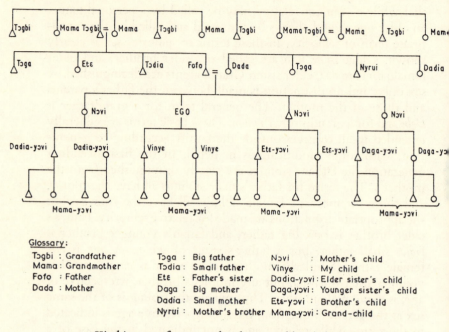

Glossary:

Tɔgbi : Grandfather	Tɔga : Big father	Nɔvi : Mother's child
Mama : Grandmother	Tɔdia : Small father	Vinyɛ : My child
Fofo : Father	Etɛ : Father's sister	Dadia-yɔvi: Elder sister's child
Dada : Mother	Daga : Big mother	Daga-yɔvi : Younger sister's child
	Dadia : Small mother	Etɛ-yɔvi : Brother's child
	Nyrui : Mother's brother	Mama-yɔvi : Grand-child

FIG. 5. Kinship terms for paternal and maternal kin (where Ego is female)

What is important to ego in the term he uses for a particular person is not the actual relationship between this person and the parent, but simply that he is either a paternal or maternal relative. All paternal relatives of this generation, of whatever degree, are called by the same terms as the full siblings of the father, with the appropriate distinctions of sex. Similarly all maternal relatives of this generation, of whatever degree, are called by the same terms as the full siblings of the mother. (Figs. 6 and 7.) Ego's main concern is with the parent to whom the person is related, and not with the details of the genealogical relationship.

As already noted, the general term for full siblings is *nɔvi*. This term is extended to all relatives of ego's generation. But within this category there are important differences expressed terminologically, and the addition of suffixes to denote sex and age has been noticed. Other important distinctions are those between full siblings and paternal half-siblings and between full siblings and

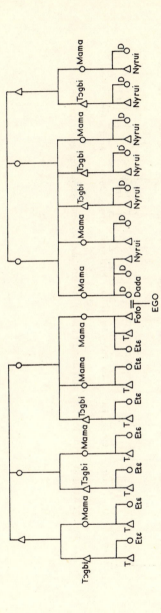

Glossary:

Tɔgbi : Grandfather   Foto : Father
Mama : Grandmother   Dada : Mother
Etɛ   : Father's Sister   Nyrui : Mother's Brother

T. stands for Tɔga, father's elder brother
   or Tɔdia, father's younger brother
   (Lit. Big father and small father respectively)

D. stands for Daga, mother's elder sister
   or Dadia, mother's younger sister
   (Lit. Big mother and small mother respectively)

FIG. 6. Kinship terms for near and distant kin in the first and second ascending generations (I)

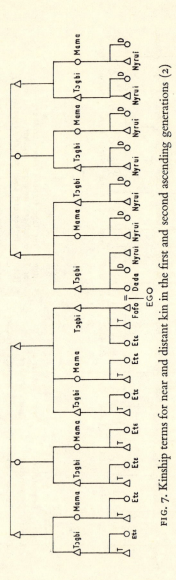

FIG. 7. Kinship terms for near and distant kin in the first and second ascending generations (2)

maternal half-siblings. Paternal half-siblings are distinguished from full siblings by the term *fofovi* and maternal half-siblings by *dadavi*, 'father's child' and 'mother's child' respectively. *Fofovi* and *dadavi* are not terms of address. As terms of reference *fofovi* is used only in contradistinction to *dadavi* to emphasize that the relationship is not that of full siblingship. Another distinction is that between cross-cousins and parallel cousins. The term for cross-cousins is *tasivinyruivi*, i.e. children of siblings of opposite sexes; for ortho-cousins, *fofovi* or *tɔgatɔɖi*, i.e. children of brothers; and for maternal parallel cousins, *dadavi* or *dagadaɖi*, i.e. children of sisters. Here again actual genealogical ties are not meticulously distinguished. For instance, though the term *dagadaɖi*, 'children of sisters', refers to the common maternal origin of the children's mothers, it is

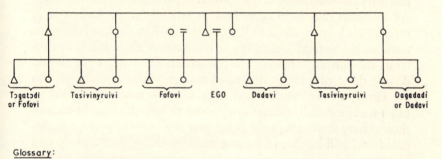

| Tɔgatɔdi or Fofovi | Tasivinyruivi | Fofovi | EGO | Dadavi | Tasivinyruivi | Dagadadi or Dadavi |

Glossary:

Tɔgatɔdi : Children of father's brother
Tasivinyruivi : Children of father's sister/ mother's brother

Fofovi : Paternal half-sibling children of father's brother
Dadavi : Full sibling maternal half sibling children of full sisters

FIG. 8. Distinctive terms for near relatives of Ego's generation otherwise known as Nɔvi

also used for children whose mothers are related by agnatic kin-ship. In other words, ego and the children of any woman ego calls *daɖia* or *dagã* (mother's sister) are in *dagã-dadi* relationship whether or not the mothers are real siblings. What is important in determining the usage is that the mothers are related, and as such are 'sisters'. In the same way the term *tɔgãtɔɖi*, children of brothers, can be applied to the children of male cross-cousins, because as cross-cousins they are 'brothers', though the term literally applies to children of male agnates. These terms, *tasivinyruivi*, *tɔgãtɔɖi*, and *dagãdaɖi* are only terms of reference and not of address. *Nɔvi* is the general term of address among them, and to this further indices of 'precision'[1] for age and sex may be added as described for siblings.

Subject to these distinctions the general term for full, half, and classificatory siblings is *nɔvi* .This clearly illustrates further the principle of the social equivalence of siblings. There are of course important observable differences in general behaviour, which may not be covered by the classificatory principle. Moreover, the strength of the affection between persons in *nɔvi* relationship is not uniformly diffused. In each situation the special bonds of uterine kinship, the frictions among agnates, and, most important of all, the relative position on the genealogical scale of those involved, are important considerations. Nevertheless, *nɔvi* does form a category which may be recognized by their behaviour both mutually and to outsiders. Actually the term *nɔvi*, as Ward[2] has pointed out, can only be understood in the context of particular social situations. An example may help here. Distant relatives from Alakple may refer to each other when in Keta as *nɔvi*. In Alakple itself the same term would be used to distinguish members of the ward or lineage from the others, while inside this group the same term would denote those of a closer degree of consanguinity. Finally, within the family group, *nɔvi* would refer to what might be called its exact meaning, full siblings as opposed to half-siblings. In each of these different situations the behaviour towards the persons designated *nɔvi* will be that of uterine siblings, that is mutual help and identification. It is an important description of uterine kinship that the term *nɔvi*, mother's child, is used in all these contexts, as well as in other situations where people appeal to good kinship behaviour. This is because the full-sibling bond is the prototype, for the Anlo as for many other societies, of the strongest possible bond.

In the first descending generation the commonest term is *vi*, child, which is used by any person for his or her own children, for the children of siblings and for other consanguineous relatives of one's children's generation. No distinction is made between children of agnates and non-agnates, nor between children of female and male siblings. But in many social situations the term *vi* with its indices of precision does not give sufficient meaning to relationships outside the nuclear family. It is usual in these cases to add the reciprocal *yɔvi* to the terms used by persons of the first descending generation. For instance, the term for mother's brother is *nyrui*, and ego may refer to the sister's son either as *vi*, my child

[1] Firth, 1957, p. 261.   [2] 1949, p. 48.

or *nyrui-yɔvi*, sister's child (lit. the child who calls me mother's brother) – so we have *tɔgã-yɔvi*, younger brother's child or the child who calls me *tɔga* or great father; *tɔɖia-yɔvi*, elder brother's child or the child who calls me *tɔɖia* or small father; *dagã-yɔvi* younger sister's child or child who calls me *dagã* or big mother.

In the second ascending generation paternal and maternal relatives are merged, but sex is distinguished. Father's father and mother's father are both *tɔgbi*, grandfather, and father's mother and mother's mother are both *mama*, grandmother. The only terms for a child of the second descending generation are descriptive, *tɔgbi-yɔvi*, grandchild (lit. the child who calls me *tɔgbi*, grandfather, if I am a man) and *mamayɔvi*, grandchild (lit. the child who calls me *mama*, grandmother, if I am a woman). But a grandchild is usually addressed by name or merely called *vinye*, my child, like the speaker's own child. (Figs. 4 and 5.)

These are the main principles governing Anlo kinship nomenclature. It appears from the utterances of the Anlo themselves that relatives who are grouped under the same linguistic labels form distinct social categories *vis-à-vis* ego. That is, identical behaviour patterns are expected from persons covered by the same linguistic labels. This is clearly in evidence when social relationships are idealized in such remarks as 'A father's sister is an important relative'; 'an elder brother must be respected', etc. There are indeed important cases where relatives to whom different patterns of behaviour apply are also called by different terms. The parent-child relation, which forms the basis of all terms between adjacent generations, is always characterized by respect on the part of the younger generation and superordination on the older. In this same generation further distinctions are made which correspond to observable behaviour. Mother's brothers and mother's sisters, who are considered more affectionate, have different terms from father's brothers and father's sisters, who are identified with the father's discipline and relative formality. Equally true are the age differences among siblings and classificatory siblings, which are expressed both terminologically by terms like *efo*, elder brother, and *daa*, elder sister, and in the respect shown to them.

It is also worthy of note that, though agnates and matrilateral relatives of each parent are lumped together terminologically, a general distinction is made nonetheless between maternal and paternal relatives of the parent's generation. Thus all the mother's male relatives of this generation are *nyrui* and all father's female relatives are *etɛ*. This distinction, I think, is crucial in emphasizing the principle of the social equivalence of siblings. It has been observed already that ego's relations with the father's sister and father's brother are framed in as formal terms as those with the father himself. This is completely different from relations with the mother's brother and mother's sister who, like the mother, are affectionately disposed towards their sister's child. The terms for relatives of this generation therefore exemplify correspondence between verbal and social categories.

On the other hand the same term is sometimes used to denote persons who are structurally differently related to ego. Two of such terms are *tɔgã*, father's elder brother, and *tɔɖia*, father's younger brother, which, as we have seen, apply in their classificatory usages to both agnatic and matrilateral kinsmen of the father.

The same kinship term is also used for people with whom marriage and sexual relations are forbidden and for those who may be married. One such term is *nɔvi*, sibling, which in the classificatory sense applies to cross-cousins, between whom marriage is allowed, and to ortho-cousins, between whom marriage is taboo. Another term is *tɔgãtɔɖiviwo* (pl.), children of brothers, a term primarily used for agnates, between whom marriage is forbidden, but in its classificatory usage also for children of male cross-cousins.

In this regard it may be pointed out that the Anlo material does not fully support the view that 'the terminology of relationship is rigorously determined by social conditions',[1] especially marriage, though in many instances there is clear correspondence between the verbal and the social categories.

[1] Rivers, 1914, p. 1.

3

Marriage

General accounts of the marriage customs of some Ewe tribes have been given by Spieth[1] in his book on the Ho, Westermann[2] in his account on the Glidzi, and Ward.[3] Of the Anlo in particular these books give only hints and impressions and no systematic description. But the available evidence on Anlo traditional marriage shows that there were not many striking differences between the Anlo customs and those of the Glidzi and Ho. In rural areas there has been very little change in these customs, though greater latitude is nowadays allowed in their observance. The most important changes have been in the ceremonies which conclude the marriage, and in the substitution of money payments for bride-service. The rules regulating the choice of partners have, however, remained largely intact. We start our discussion with an account of prohibitions on marriage and incest.

I. MARRIAGE PROHIBITIONS

Apart from being expressed in behaviour patterns and in language, kinship affects sexual relations. The Anlo, like many other peoples, prohibit marriage and cohabitation between relatives of certain categories; they also approve and even encourage the marriage of relatives of other categories.

By a 'marriage' I mean here a union in which the man and woman, having passed through the approved customary procedures, are legally recognized as husband and wife, and are therefore subject to all the rights, duties and obligations such a relationship entails.

The selection of spouses is one of the first important considerations in any discussion of marriage. Accordingly we shall begin by discussing the rules which govern the choice of partners. There are several categories of kin and affines between whom marriage is

[1] 1906, pp. 183–99.   [2] 1935, pp. 51–84.   [3] 1949, pp. 106–50.

forbidden. Stated in general terms, lineage exogamy and the prohibition of marriage between uterine kin and between affines are the most important restrictions.

A man may not marry a member of his own lineage. This rule is enforced and observed with meticulous rigidity. Its importance to the Anlo is seen in the fact that youths and girls are taught not to look towards agnatic relatives for sex matters as soon as they begin to think in terms of sex. The adults do not discuss it at all. I never heard of any breaches, and constant enquires led to the conclusion that they are always prevented. Through exogamy a series of kinship ties and mutual interests are established between hitherto unrelated lineages. These ties are of much value in the settlement of inter-lineage disputes. When there is a dispute between lineages joined by marriage, it is said that a member of one lineage who has mother's brothers and other matrilateral relatives in the other is usually the mediator. It also appears that one of the reasons for the lack of interest in inter-ward *halo* (inter-ward hostilities expressed in songs) in these days is probably not that the present generation does not like *halo* but that more inter-ward marriages are taking place now than in the past, with the result that many lineages have affines and matrilateral relatives in other wards of the settlement.

Another prohibition is that against marriage between uterine kin. The feeling of personal and close intimacy in the relationship of *dagādaɖiviwo* or uterine kin is best illustrated by the Anlo attitude to sexual relations between them. It is considered incestuous for two persons to have sexual relations if their uterine connection is known, however distant the relationship, and marriage between them is of course forbidden. It is like incest between full siblings, because it is said, 'Your mother's sister's child is like your own mother's child'. However, because of the residence pattern, uterine kin are dispersed, so that remote ties are easily forgotten, and even closer ones sometimes escape the attention of many. Consequently this rule is not strictly observed, especially where those involved are only distantly related.

Lineage exogamy and the prohibition of marriage between uterine kin represent the only restrictions based on kinship *per se*, though these are by no means the only relationships covered by rules prohibiting marriage. Added to them are a long list of affines. In this regard one of the most striking features about marriage

regulations is the taboo on bride exchange. A man may not marry
a close affine. For instance, marriage between a man and his sister's
husband's sister is forbidden. Anlo say that such a union is bad
because it is like an exchange of spouses by two lineages or kin
groups. It also spoils relationships between kinsmen by transform-
ing kinship relations into affinal ones.

It is clear that such a union may bring confusion into kinship
statuses and in-law relationships. It will also affect kinship terms,
as informants pointed out. For how will the children of couple A
address children of couple B if both parents marry the siblings of
their own siblings' spouses? (Fig. 9.) And it will certainly bring

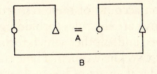

FIG. 9. An example of prohibited matings:
taboo on bride exchange

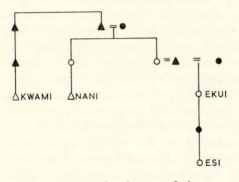

FIG. 10. Degree of application of taboo on
bride exchange

confusion into the role expectations of the children of the marriages.

This rule is rarely violated. Informants could remember only
one instance some thirty years ago, when one of the husbands,
who insisted on marrying the sister of his own sister's husband,

died suddenly, and his death was attributed to the violation of this rule.

The prohibition is extended to all close cognates of the spouses to about the degree of third cousin. Thus in 1962, when Nani wanted to marry Esi, her mother's mother Ekui objected on the ground that Nani's mother's sister was married to Esi's great grandfather, and suggested that Kwami, a more distant relative of Nani, would have been a more agreeable suitor (Fig. 10).

A rule of this kind sometimes brings frustrations to young lovers, especially in these days, when pre-marital friendship is increasingly becoming a necessary prerequisite for marriage, and when both youths and girls are having more say in their choice of partners. Many a time it happens that marriages contemplated by lovers are stopped on account of these restrictions.

Related to the above are the rules forbidding marriage between a man and two sisters, and another which forbids two kinsmen to marry two sisters or two kinswomen. These rules are based on the fact that Anlo consider it an act of benevolence for one kin group to give its daughter in marriage to another. It is therefore regarded as improper for more than one man from the same kin group to enjoy this benevolence from a single other kin group. This will mean a group of relatives enjoying undue benevolence from one lineage or kin group. The only exception to this rule was the case of liberated female slave kinswomen, who were in the past sometimes married into the kin groups of their captors or owners irrespective of the latter's genealogical connections. Reference is frequently made to this practice today when proposals considered to be within this prohibited category are rejected, with the question, 'Ðe wofle mía?' 'Have they bought us?'

Another argument for this prohibition is the belief that the jealousies of co-wives will spoil the love of sisters or kinswomen. This reasoning, though often advanced, runs counter to that given in favour of sororal polygyny in many parts of Africa, where a man is encouraged to marry a sister or kinswoman of his wife in order to reduce co-wife jealousies.

In the past these prohibitions extended as far as third cousins of whatever line. That is, it was forbidden for a man to marry two women who were third cousins. In 1962 the marriages of two second cross-cousins to two sisters provoked much discussion concerning the closeness of the relationship. The gossips maintained that the girls' parents were opportunists and fortune hunters, *nugãdzilawo*, who were trying to exploit the good looks of their children to enrich themselves. Actually the girls were very attractive and the cousins comparatively rich.

Beyond the degree of second-cousin the rule could now be disregarded without much criticism. The death of one of the spouses may, however, bring some alterations into the situation, making it possible for the surviving spouse to remarry a sibling or other kinsman of the deceased.

In making enquiries into marriage prohibitions in Anlo, one difficulty that the investigator frequently encounters is the problem which results from the use of the same kinship terms for kinsmen who are differently related to ego. Of special interest here are terms like *dagãdadiviwo*, uterine kin, and *fofoviwo*, agnates or children of 'brothers'. As we have tried to show in the last chapter, persons in these relationships are forbidden to marry, yet many couples maintained that they were so related. The difficulty can be resolved by referring back to what we said about kinship terms. The fact that two persons are terminologically the 'children of sisters' i.e. *dagãdadiviwo*, does not mean that their female forbears are matrilineally related. What the terminology denotes is that their mothers are relatives. The mothers might even have been agnates, and by this fact alone their children have become children of sisters. Thus it may be necessary to emphasize here once more that in the application of the rules regulating marriage, only *dagãdadiviwo*, uterine kin, and *fofoviwo*, agnates in the strict lineal terms, are covered. It is genealogical connections, not groupings by language, which count in placing bars on particular matings.

2. INCEST AND ADULTERY

The rules which prohibit sexual intercourse between certain categories of kin are directly related to those which prohibit marriage. This is because sexual intercourse is regarded as the prerogative of married life, and whenever it occurs before or outside marriage the reaction to it depends on the question whether it can lead to matrimony. In short, though all sexual intercourse outside marriage is wrong, the gravity of the wrong is determined by the relationship between those involved. Where marriage is forbidden between two persons, sex play is considered a sin rather than a

mere legal offence. For persons between whom marriage is per-
mitted, however, sex play is only an offence. Adultery is also
viewed in relation to the rules governing marriage, and, like
ordinary affairs, is classified accordingly into 'sin' and 'offence'.

'Sin' and 'offence' are governed by religious and legal sanctions
respectively, and are clearly differentiated in Ewe verbal categories. Sin is expressed by the Ewe word *Nuvɔ*. Here there may or
may not be penal sanctions against the culprits, but mystical retribution is believed to follow automatically. An offence is represented in Ewe by *sedzidada* (lit. violating the law). It is the former
that, following the sanctions applied and the verbal categories of
the actors themselves, I designate incest, here represented by the
Ewe term *nuvɔ*, sin.

Nuvɔ is a term applied generally to immoral behaviour of a
serious kind, behaviour so serious as to be followed by inevitable
supernatural punishment, and to violations of tribal and religious
prohibitions which normal persons take for granted. Thus for a
youth to beat his father's father, for instance (to take an extreme
example), whatever his reasons, or for someone deliberately to kill
his totem animal, would be considered unpardonable behaviour
for which mystical retribution will be incurred as a matter of
course. They are *nuvɔ*. Incest is classed with such behaviour. Compared with this, adultery and fornication by persons between
whom marriage is allowed are mere sexual peccadilloes.

Incest in Anlo therefore includes sex relations with lineage
members, close affines and uterine kin.

The closeness, love and intimacy of the mother-child relationship make copulation between a man and his mother the most
serious of all forms of incest. It is actually quite rare. I heard of only
one instance. The boy was ill and was taken to a diviner, where he
confessed, after being warned that his recovery depended on confession of some heinous sin. He recovered, but the mother died
soon afterwards, and her death was attributed to the sin. I also
heard of one case of incest between full siblings, but of none
between a man and his own daughter. In fact, incest in one form
or another occurs occasionally in every village or town. It soon
leaks out, and is remembered with contempt for many years.

Not all cases of incest provoke serious reactions. The closer the
genealogical tie the greater the horror. Incest between a woman
and her husband's third cousin, for instance, will not receive the

same serious reprobation as an affair with her husband's brother. I witnessed a case involving a boy and his father's brother's daughter. The girl was ravished by the boy on her way home from a trading expedition in a nearby village via the hamlet of her father's brother, who was the boy's father. On returning home she reported the matter to her mother. So great was the commotion that the boy was forced to leave the village immediately for a fishing expedition abroad.

That incest is viewed in terms of prohibitions on marriage is shown further by the Anlo attitude to premarital affairs between cross-cousins. When I asked what would happen in such a case the usual reply was that a man is a potential husband of his female cross-cousin. When I pressed the point further by insisting that since premarital or extramarital intercourse in all forms was immoral in the Anlo world view, I was told that as cross-cousins they might eventually be married. This however does not mean that there is licence for prenuptial sexual intercourse between cross-cousins. It only reveals that the gravity with which the Anlo regard fornication is directly related to their rules regulating marriage.

But in a sense sexual relations between persons outside the incest rule are not completely devoid of supernatural sanctions. If any two men have an affair with the same woman these two men have 'mixed their blood' *wo tɔtɔ*, and are therefore liable to *alɔkpli*, a fatal pulmonary disease. *Alɔkpli* is likely to result when the two men in question come into contact with each other under certain conditions: if one is sick and receives a visit from the other the sickness worsens into *alɔkpli*; if one is dead and the other either looks at the dead body or drinks at the funeral he gets *alɔkpli*; and if one eats food placed on a seat or bed previously used by the other he gets *alɔkpli*.

Theoretically the effects of *alɔkpli* extend beyond the boundaries of kinship. This lends support to the earlier point that all sexual affairs outside marriage are considered improper. Nevertheless since the sickness does not follow automatically from the sexual activity *per se*, but rather from subsequent contacts between the actors, persons who are in danger of *alɔkpli* must be those between whom there exists some form of social interaction. In other words *alɔkpli* can only affect persons who interact, under conditions which bring about this sickness.

Aləkpli is therefore most dangerous for kinsfolk and neighbours, because they are easily involved in the activities causing it. Visiting a sick relative, for instance, is one of the most binding obligations in Anlo. In fact exchange of visits between relatives is the greatest expression of kinship obligation. It is when one visits a relative that one knows how the relative is faring. Hence the Anlo saying that *Nɔvikpɔkpɔe nye nɔviwɔwɔ* – visiting kinsfolk is the essence of kinship.

Accordingly Anlo are very careful to avoid 'mixing their blood' with relatives, neighbours and other close associates. When a man plans a clandestine affair with a woman he immediately warns all his associates who might be interested to keep away from her. The man gives a further warning after he has had the affair. If, however, even after these precautions two men have *tɔtɔ* and are aware that they are so 'mixed', they may try to avoid coming into contact with each other under the conditions leading to *aləkpli*.

It is said that a man must be on the look out for *aləkpli* even if the husband or lover of his partner is already dead. Thus in the past, when burials used to take place in the dead man's house, the lover or husband of the widow could not eat or drink there because of the fear of *aləkpli*.

Today it is possible to forestall *aləkpli* by means of antidotes and charms, but their efficacy is still in doubt. To many people avoidance still remains the best remedy.

It follows from the above that the sickness of *aləkpli* could arise either through a deliberate attempt of one of two persons who know that they have *tɔtɔ* to injure the other, or through the ignorance of two men of their relations with one woman, or through the carelessness of one or both men who are aware of their involvement. Usually it is through ignorance or carelessness that *aləkpli* is contacted. When the two involved are still alive, only a mean person will knowingly create a situation likely to cause *aləkpli* to the other.

The incidence of *aləkpli* is difficult to ascertain as it is almost impossible to know the cause of every death or sickness in a community. But one still hears now and then of someone dying of *aləkpli*.

A sex offence of a more general kind which falls outside incest is adultery by a wife. Since Anlo marriage is potentially polygynous, a man's adultery does not provoke any unfavourable reaction from the community unless his partner is married. If it is an affair with an unmarried woman the man can say he wants to marry her and get away with it. Adultery by a woman, however, is considered very serious, and it is not surprising that it is covered by legal as well as religious sanctions. A wife's adultery is believed to cause her own death and even that of her husband, and there is also the belief that a sick man nursed by an unfaithful wife will die. Sometimes, it is believed, confession by the adulteress may save life, since Anlo claim to have special remedies for such ailments. Two deaths at Alakple in 1962 were believed to have been caused by the infidelity of wives. In one case a woman died less than two months after her husband because, it was thought, she refused to make the necessary confession demanded for her recovery. Sometimes adultery is believed to make childbirth difficult, and unless confession is made the adulteress may die with the child.

Anlo men know well the risk to their lives of the infidelity of their wives. To prevent these misfortunes many men have charms which help to strike terror in wives with adulterous intentions. The commonest and most effective of these is *dema* (lit. palm leaf), which consists of a mixture of several occult herbs, *egbe*, which a man buries in his house. A wife who commits adultery and enters the house through the main door is believed to become mad. Two mad women at Woe in 1962 were believed to be suffering from *dema*.[1]

3. PREFERENTIAL MARRIAGES

Though marriage prohibitions cover a wide range of relatives, marriages between certain categories of kin are favoured. The Anlo consider that marriage between persons not bound by any ties of kinship is not likely to be stable, because it is believed that besides being spouses, couples who are relatives regard themselves also in terms of kinship obligations and behave towards each other accordingly. Because of this fact, Anlo parents from the outset

---

[1] The efficacy of *dema* extends beyond protection against a wife's adultery. In a general sense *dema* protects its owner and all members of his household against any misfortunes or dangers that might threaten them. Almost all houses accommodating the ancestral shrines at Woe and Alakple are believed to have it. Houses in possession are designated *afegãwo* (lit. Big Houses). They have taboos on whistling and sweeping at night, among others which are believed to be necessary for its efficacy.

take a special interest in the marriages of their children, and themselves take the initiative to find them suitable spouses, sometimes even before the children are born.

This marriage, called *fomesrɔ* or 'kinship marriage', is still popular with parents. Seventy-one per cent of all first marriages in Woe and Alakple in 1962 were *fomesrɔ*, in that the couples were related to each other by at least one known genealogical connection. In 50 per cent of all first marriages the initiative in arranging the match was taken by the parents.

It may be very easy to over-emphasize this point. Because of interlineage marriages, which result from the rule of lineage exogamy, all lineages are interwoven through several links, so that in any settlement everyone is related through one tie or another to someone in most of the lineages outside his or her own. This is especially the case with small villages where almost everyone is related to everyone else. In this situation it is difficult to find someone outside one's lineage who is not a relative. Since 94 per cent of the marriages in the two settlements were between local people it is natural to find such a high percentage of kinship marriages. Moreover, although other factors, such as good character and economic considerations, may be responsible for favouring one man rather than another, it is easy and more plausible to attribute the reason for his choice, as marriage partner, to kinship.

Implicit in this attitude is the importance of kinship in Anlo inter-personal relations. Kinship exerts peacefulness on social relations, and is therefore considered necessary to perfect even the matrimonial bond. The legal joining of a man and woman is not considered enough for the full realization of the perfect union. Kinship considerations add something extra, the need for spouses to extend to each other all the essential attributes of kinship behaviour.

By far the commonest *fomesrɔ* is *tasivinyruivisrɔ* (lit. marriage of children of brother and sister), or cross-cousin marriage. The Anlo do not make any verbal distinction between matrilateral and patrilateral cross-cousin marriage, but figures show that the former exceeded the latter by a ratio of four to one. Of the *fomesrɔ* recorded 89 per cent were cross-cousin marriages.

The closest kin who can be married without violating any of the rules of incest are first cross-cousins. First cross-cousin marriages occur fairly frequently. Eight per cent of all marriages recorded were between full first cross-cousins, while 21 per cent were between persons whose parents were half-siblings. The majority of the kinship marriages and of the cross-cousin marriages were between more remote cousins. It is therefore clear that Anlo actually prefer the marriage of children of half-siblings and remoter cousins to that of first cousins. In fact, when the Anlo speak of *tasivinyruivisɔ*, they do not always refer to marriages of first cousins. Many informants even maintained that the first cross-cousin relationship is now too close for marriage. Case histories of older members of the population show, however, that it was much more common in the past. Today many youths and girls are averse to this form of marriage because, they say, it lays them open to undue interference in their marital affairs by over-enthusiastic aunts and uncles who are also their parents-in-law. Nevertheless cross-cousin marriage remains an important Anlo institution.

The importance attached to cross-cousin marriage may be further illustrated by the fact that it is not affected by the rules forbidding marriage between close affines. That is, marriage between two cross-cousins is not considered a bar to marriages between their other relatives, so long as the subsequent couples are neither agnates nor uterine kin.[1] This exception was explained in this way. The aim of the rule forbidding marriage between affines is, first, to prevent the direct exchange of spouses between two kin groups, and secondly, to prevent two women from one kin group marrying into another. Now if, after a marriage between cross-cousins, their own cousins, who are also cross-cousins, are married to each other, this will be an advantage to no one, because the four belong to the same kin group though not to the same lineage. Let us look at Fig. 11. In this diagram Adzotɔ and

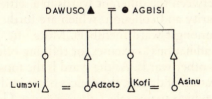

FIG. 11. An example of cross cousin marriages
involving four cousins

[1] Nevertheless the rule forbidding two brothers from marrying two sisters is an absolute prohibition which is not included in this exception.

Lumɔvi are not affines to Kofi and Asinu, but rather first cousins, because both are related to them as first cousins, being all grand-children of Dawuso and Agbisi, and therefore the reasons given against marriage between affines cannot be legitimately applied to them.

Marriage between members of the same clan is also favoured. Of all marriages recorded, 28·7 per cent were between members of the same clan. This represents a lower percentage than cross-cousin marriage. There are two reasons for this relatively low percentage. First, as there is a tendency for people to choose spouses from their own settlements, in a settlement where there is only one lineage of the same clan (and there are many such settlements) members will be forced to look to lineages of other clans for their spouses. Secondly, since no actual clan endogamy exists, not even clans with many lineages in a settlement can marry all their members into their own clans. In fact, as the local segment of a clan in most cases consists of a single lineage, it is only in rare cases that several lineages of the same clan are found together in one settle-ment. In this case the figures for intra-clan marriages in Alakple and Woe must be considered relatively high, and this has been confirmed by visits to other settlements. The high figure for Alakple and Woe is largely due to the presence in each of them of one or two large clans with many lineages. In Alakple, where the percentage of intra-clan marriages was 33·8 per cent, the seven lineages of Dzevi and Amɛ clans account for more than 50 per cent of the total population, and in Woe, Amɛ, the largest single clan in the town, has no less than four exogamous lineages.

The importance of the ward in social life has already been described. Here, however, it is necessary to mention again that the competition between the different wards in a settlement increases in-group solidarity and cohesion, which are further strengthened by marriages amongst ward members. More often than not girls use their ward affiliations as excuses for refusing offers of marriage from suitors of other wards. As the ward is the most effective unit for the organization of dances, the dances organized by youths and girls, through which many select their spouses (described in the next section) also help to increase the tendency towards marriage within the ward. In Woe and Alakple marriages between mem-bers of the same ward accounted for 63 per cent of all marriages.

It will be seen from the discussion so far that though very close

cognates, such as first cross-cousins, are allowed to marry, and prenuptial intercourse between them may be overlooked, rigid rules,
sometimes backed by religious sanctions, are applied to those who
fall within the area of marriage prohibitions, however far apart
they may be on the genealogical chart. The rules taken as a whole
amount to this. A youth looking for a wife has a wide range of
kinswomen to apply for so long as they are neither his lineage
mates, close affines, nor uterine kin, and as he is born and brought
up in a circle of kin which normally embraces the people of his
immediate neighbourhood, people with whom he has been playmates from early childhood, he is generally well placed from the
outset to get acquainted with potential wives.

This social interaction of youths and girls, helped by the fluid
residence pattern, one way or the other accounts for the tendency
of the Anlo to marry in their own localities, because youths and
girls between whom there are no prohibitions are neighbours at a
time when they are looking for spouses.[1]

These considerations of personal relations between youths and
the immediate relatives of their parents can help to account for
cross-cousin marriages, because both the paternal aunt and the
maternal uncle exert great influence on the selection. For it is to be
remembered that though contiguity facilitates marriage between
neighbours and relatives, the initiative is usually taken by parents.
Many Anlo feel it an obligation to give at least one of their children in marriage to a sibling's child. We have already seen that the
maternal uncle's house is the second home of every Anlo youth.
During his frequent visits he is encouraged by the mother's
brother to get interested in the latter's daughters. Even if the
nephew does not develop any special love for uncle's daughters or
vice versa, the maternal uncle makes the union easier by taking
the initiative himself, with the co-operation of his sister, knowing
well that the offer will not be turned down. If this point is established and accepted we may suggest that preference for matrilateral cross-cousin marriages is another manifestation of the love
and intimacy between a man and his maternal uncle. This fact is
enforced by the Anlo belief that 'there is nothing nearer a man's

[1] Anlo marriage is ideally virilocal but many women remain in their parental
homes after marriage and with them their children. A number of children also
live with their maternal uncles and grandparents so that the local agnatic incidence
is never 100 per cent. Moreover in a ward the houses of different exogamous
lineages are only a stone's throw from each other.

heart than to see his daughters married to men he himself loves.'
Yet the impression must not be given that the parental initiative
in these matters always comes from men. On the contrary, women
are very active match-makers, but their position is affected by two
considerations. First, women have more influence on their
daughters than on their sons. Secondly, the special relationship of
formality between a woman and her brothers' children limits the
chances of intimacy necessary for discussion of this kind. As our
figures have shown, it appears that men prefer to have daughters
marrying their sisters' sons rather than sons marrying the sisters'
daughters.

But perhaps the most significant consideration on this subject is
how cross-cousin marriage fits into the Anlo special inheritance
system, whereby daughters and their children are entitled to a
portion of a person's estate. In a patrilineal society the tensions
likely to arise when non-agnatic relatives use lineage land may be
greatly alleviated through kinship marriages. Thus it happens that
in many cases where a man from a poor lineage has to fall back
on his mother's brothers for economic help, he is also advised to
marry one of the mother's brother's daughters. In the same way a
woman from a rich lineage may ask her daughters to marry her
brothers' children.

Of the 120 farmers interviewed at Woe in connection with the
utilization of matrilateral claims on land, 28 were actually married
to their first cousins. All these were among the 71 who were farming matrilateral lands. Of the 19 farmers who had no farms apart
from their lineage lands, only six were married to close kinswomen, none of whom was a first cousin.

It is possible that in some of these cases the primary motive for
the marriage is not property. The relationship between men
farming land claimed through their mothers with their maternal
uncles and their families is likely to be close. In some cases the use
of property inherited through a woman results either in, or from,
settlement near maternal uncles, which increases the chances of
meeting with cross-cousins. Nevertheless, many of these marriages
originate from the desire of parents to keep inheritance rights within as narrow a range as possible.

This limiting of the range of inheritance rights is also the effect
of intra-clan marriages, so that both lineage inheritors of a lineage
property and the non-lineage inheritors belong to the same clan.

4. SELECTION OF PARTNERS AND RELATIONS BETWEEN THE SEXES BEFORE MARRIAGE

Marriage in Anlo, as in many other African societies, is an alliance between lineages, and the particular interests of these groups are clearly shown in the marriage negotiations, in the offering and receipt of the marriage payments, in their participation in the rites that institute the marriage, and above all in their active participation in the selection of partners for their members of marriageable age. The active interest of the kin group in the selection of a spouse is an index of the individual's lack of independence in his own choice. But the Anlo, like other peoples, know that marriage is also a union between a particular man and a particular woman, and each one's assessment of the life-long partner is also considered. Today this individual aspect is steadily increasing in importance. In the following sections an attempt will be made to describe how the kin group's interest is reconciled with that of the individuals directly concerned in the contract.

Older people say that, in the past, first marriages were arranged by parents without consultation with the young people. The young men, however, certainly managed to know that marriage negotiations on their behalf were under way, and there is no evidence that any *man* was ever forced into marriage against his will, though in some cases his own choice might have been vetoed by his parents. Older *women*, however, claimed that they were given little chance of studying the character of the partners chosen for them. Some of them even maintained that they were compelled to marry against their will – in some instances they wished to marry young men of their own choice, in others they disliked the young men chosen for them or rebelled at the thought of being a second or third wife. Willy nilly they were married. Others said they persisted in refusing to live with the husband chosen for them and succeeded in forcing their parents to relent. Others were said to have eventually given up the struggle.

Despite these examples it is probable that many women were willing enough to accept men chosen for them, and those betrothed before puberty certainly knew whom they were to marry long before the marriage took place. In fact, as Spieth[1] points out, immediately after puberty the betrothed girl would undergo an

[1] 1906, p. 183.

intensive indoctrination for the acceptance of the man chosen for her. Moreover, since parents worked generally for stable unions, they usually had no reason to persist in negotiating a union where incompatibility or mutual dislike gave promise of quarrels and eventual separation.[1]

It is usually the girl's parents who are most careful about her future partner. The important things considered are the characters of the youth and his parents and the success which the latters' marriage attained, because it is believed that the home may affect the youth's behaviour. This means that when negotiating a marriage the parents work against a background of considerable knowledge about the characters of possible candidates. They are concerned to choose those considered to have the qualities necessary for a spouse: a man who has learned the work expected of him, who is courteous, shows no disposition to engage in quarrelling or other improper actions, and is industrious.

There was, and still is, some tendency for those who had risen to positions of leadership and economic importance within a neighbourhood, such as successful fishermen and farmers, to intermarry with other families of importance. But for most Anlo there is still little variation in material goods or prestige that makes for much weighting of choice in selection of spouses. Marriages between slaves and free persons were fully accepted, and today the descendants of slaves suffer no discrimination as marriage partners.

At present, there appears to be a gradual change from the old position of parental control over the choice of spouses towards a new position where those directly concerned are given some latitude in making their own selection. Many prospective couples now plan almost everything about their intended union before the youth tells his parents to approach the girl's parents on his behalf. Nevertheless, the parental veto is far from dead, and it is no exaggeration to say that the final word still lies with the parents, as this case will show.

Case No. 1

In 1960 Danu, a carpenter, fell in love with Aku. With her consent he asked his father, a distant maternal relative of her father, to approach her parents. Aku's father readily consented to the match,

[1] Fiawoo, 1943, pp. 68–73.

but her mother refused on the ground that Aku's other sisters
married to kinsmen of their father were not experiencing successful marriages. Aku should therefore be married to a maternal
relative. Accordingly Aku was forced to marry a distant cousin on
her mother's side.

This case not only shows the veto retained by parents, it also
illustrates the possibility of disagreement between parents. Many
a time parents and relatives are divided among themselves as to the
correct choice for their children.

5. COURTING

Traditionally every Anlo girl who reached puberty went through
a ceremony known as *nudodo* or *lekewɔwɔ*.[1] The girl was paraded
through the village dressed in rich beads and clothes. *Lekewɔwɔ*
showed that she had grown old enough for marriage. For girls
who were already betrothed, preparations for the conclusion of
the marriage would start immediately after this ceremony. For
those who were still unattached it gave their suitors the opportunity to make their proposals openly. Today no puberty ceremony is performed. Instead youths may begin to court girls as
soon as the latter are known to be of age.

When a youth is interested in a girl the usual method he adopts
is to tell a close friend to take him to her house in the late evening –
this time being most convenient because by then she has finished
the most important household duties which end with the evening
bath. There the visitors are offered seats, and after exchanging
greetings with members of the household they call the girl and
tell her that they are 'visiting her'. '*X gbɔwoe míe va*', 'X we have
come to see you' is the usual introduction.

No appointments are necessary, but youths who are able to see
their girls previously arrange dates. Whether the girl is interested
or not, tradition and good form demand that at first she simulate
indifference and even surprise or dislike. She reluctantly approaches
her suitors and sits down facing them. The suitor's friend then
introduces the reason for the visit, which she herself has already
surmised, for all such visits have only one aim, courting.

Several visits are necessary before the girl will give a decisive
answer, but the youths say they can read the direction of the wind
after only a few. If they gather that things might not end well,

[1] Kpodo, 1954, p. 15.

some withdraw honourably, but others persist. Persistence, even in the light of apparent failure, is necessary, because it is said that 'a woman does not say yes to a suitor's first proposal', *nyɔnu melɔa ŋgɔgbe nya o*. It sometimes takes several months, or even years, before a girl's consent is finally won.

Wooing in Anlo is an arduous business. A youth must not only be witty and ready to flatter the girl effusively, he must also be ready to answer and counter any questions she may ask. Girls are never willing to succumb without testing the ability of the youth as a person well versed in wooing tactics, *ahiadzidzi*. Some girls say they try to be impossible only to pull the legs of youths they find to be inexperienced. Others say they would be considered cheap if they gave in readily, but they also consider that should they become too difficult their suitors might leave them and look for other girls, so that although they are neither easy with their virtue nor give straight answers to proposals, they can do their best to make it known to a youth that they are not altogether averse to him. This is usually done by polite prevarications and tricky evasions.

Both words and actions are needed during the period of wooing. Besides being generous to his sweetheart, a youth must appear neat and responsible. Adolescence is an important time in the life of both boys and girls. At this time of his life a youth models himself on the accepted pattern of what a young man should do to win the approbation of his girl in particular and the regard of girls generally. There is some consciousness in him that girls are watching him. He pays great attention to his appearance, and takes every opportunity to excel in feats of courage and endurance. At dances he shows that he is a good dancer and singer. On the beach during fishing seasons he tries his best to make his presence felt. Every opportunity is seized to display his newest clothes. When going to the market place at Keta, Anloga or Dzodze or any other big market town he puts on his best clothes, always making sure that a neat towel is around his neck, for he needs it to wipe his face continuously to make it free of sweat. All this a youth does because his mind at this stage is set on girls and marriage, and he is always careful because the girls are the arbiters of decorum, and the severest sanction of breach of good form is their disapproval. Not only is the shame of this disapproval a sanction for etiquette, it is also an important influence in making a youth generous, brave, respectful, and dutiful to his parents, kinsmen and the community at large.

The girls on their side are anxious to earn the good opinion of the youths through correct behaviour in and outside the home. At this time they begin to put on blouses, cover their breasts, tie their hair, cover their heads with kerchiefs and seize the least chance to show their newest dresses.

A youth must be particularly generous to his sweetheart. If he is a fisherman she must enjoy presents of the choicest of the catch. A young farmer also has special obligations to his sweetheart at harvest time. Fruits and vegetables are lavishly poured on her. When a girl begins to bring home such gifts, her parents realize what is happening, if they have so far been ignorant of her associations.

Occasionally a girl herself proposes love to a boy. If she likes a boy who has not been able to talk to her, she finds an opportunity to corner him somewhere and tells him plainly that she loves him. '*Ɖekakpuivi medze ahia wò hɛ!*' 'Young man! I love you' is the usual call, and it is customary for the boy to reply, '*Metre wò dzedze*', 'I loved you first'. This bold step is sometimes taken by youths also. It also happens at public places such as dances and market places. Many such approaches end in serious unions, but others are taken as jokes.

Visits of youths to their girls' houses give opportunity to the girls' parents to know the suitors of their daughters, and the reactions of the parents are not at all difficult to discern. Visits by a suitor whom they favour are condoned and even encouraged. An informant claimed that when he was courting his wife, who was no close relative, he normally visited her house every other evening. On each occasion, the girl's mother used to rebuke her if she appeared slow in entertaining him. The mother also would question him if he failed to keep his usual date.

On the other hand, a suitor disliked by the girl's parents faces many obstacles. I hear that such a man, especially someone disliked by the mother, might not even be offered a seat during his visits, and, should the girl draw nearer towards him, their conversation would be interrupted by frequent calls to her to go on with her household duties. The mother, and sometimes the sisters too, may start making loud and offensive remarks about him. A rather extreme manifestation of disapproval from a girl's mother was mentioned to me. It is clear from the report that, in spite of the mother's disapproval of the boy, the girl herself was interested in him. The mother was, however, determined to strike a final blow, and on one of the boy's visits, she approached him and the girl with an *akpleɖaze*, 'porridge pot', full of *akpletsi*,[1] water, and on reaching him dropped the pot on him 'accidentally'.

But the intention was clear. Many parents do not go so far. When they are dissatisfied with a daughter's boy the normal practice is to advise her against the dangers ahead. Some parents even forestall the hopes of a lover they dislike by betrothing the girl to a youth of their own choice.

Youths have several other occasions for meeting the girls they fancy. These include dances, dance practices, fishing expeditions and market places. Dances form an important recognized occasion for boys and girls to meet in public. At fairly regular intervals of about five years the youths and adolescent girls of a ward, helped by a few adults, organize a dance, as it appears, to commemorate their coming of age. For about three months before the actual dancing season commences, both youths and girls gather each night for several hours in the house of the ward's chief composer to learn the newest songs. Before and after the dancing practices, *hakpa*, the youths seize every available opportunity to make love to the girls. These adolescent dances give both sexes the opportunity not only of meeting their future partners but also of displaying their talents in dancing and singing, and of showing the newest clothes they have bought. Unattached boys and girls do their utmost to catch the eye of someone who can be a suitable partner. After each dancing season, which lasts just about a month, it is usual to hear of several engagements.

Despite these opportunities for getting acquainted, girls who have not been betrothed before puberty must still take their parents' reaction seriously. '*Nya sia nya le fofonye si*', 'my father has the last word', is the usual reply from girls, even from those who have accepted their suitors' offer.

The veto retained by parents, and the free pre-marital association of the sexes, bring great discord into many marriage negotiations. A girl sometimes finds some other boy more congenial than

---

[1] *Akple*, cooked with a mixture of cassava dough and corn flour, is the staple food of the Anlo. After preparation the pot usually becomes burnt at the bottom and is filled with water to make cleaning easy the following day.

the one to whom she has been betrothed. If she takes an active interest in him, her dissatisfaction and resentment at parental intervention may lead to unfortunate incidents. Moreover, parents are not always cognizant of all the love affairs of their children. Sometimes lovers reach a stage in their affairs where intervention of the parents is difficult to accept without a struggle.

Many a time, love magic, *ahiakɛ*, of which the Anlo have different kinds, is used by youths to solicit love. It is believed that when it is applied to a girl she falls so madly in love with the applicant as to make it almost impossible for anyone else, even her parents, to persuade her against him. The most serious kind of *ahiakɛ*, called *sibisaba*, is even believed to take the victim to the point of actual madness, and it is said to have a lasting effect on her uprightness. An informant described it in this way:

When applying *sibisaba* it is not necessary to propose love to the girl personally. *Sibisaba* itself will do that for you. It is sufficient to prepare the herbs, recite the necessary incantations and the girl herself will seek you wherever you may be. If she does not find you, her heart will not rest. Sometimes *sibisaba* miscarries, partly because the girl's 'soul' (*ŋɔlime, gbɔgbɔ*) is too strong to yield or partly because of a mistake in the incantations. In such a case the youth will be in danger, for instead of sending the girl to him, it maddens her, and she parades through the whole village singing at the top of her voice and calling his name. But if it succeeds, and the girl is sent to the boy, it happens that later on in her life, say three years after she is married to the *sibisaba* man, she comes back to her senses. That is why marriages based on love magic alone do not last.

I once witnessed an incident believed to have been caused by the miscarriage of *sibisaba*. It happened in one of the farm villages of Woe, some one and a half miles away from where I was living at the time. Within a matter of minutes the news reached our area, and many people headed towards the market place, *asime*, because such occasions attract the entire population. The girl, aged about nineteen, was apparently not in her right senses. Running all over the place, she cried, shouted, swore and cursed the boy while we ran after her. Later on medicine men were brought to cool her down. Meanwhile the boy himself had fled from the town. It is not advisable for him to show his face in such circumstances, for the use of *sibisaba* is illegal, and he would have to face both legal proceedings and serious public recriminations.

Love magic, *sibisaba* in particular, is a social evil the unmarried
girl fears most. Girls try as much as possible to avoid the company
of those known or suspected of having it. It is used by men who
could not trust their own techniques, skills or abilities to convince
girls, and those who have not got the personal charm to attract
attention. Sometimes also other evil minded men use it when they
are likely to meet unsurmountable competition. A beautiful girl
with several suitors is in danger of being a victim of love magic, for
men intent on doing havoc do not stop their malicious practices
even after the girl has been married to someone else. The unsuccessful suitor may inflict all sorts of supernatural harm on the girl,
I was told. She may suffer from all sorts of ailments, be barren or
not bear live children. Many such misfortunes are attributed to
ahiadzilawo (suitors), i.e. the unsuccessful ones.

It occasionally happens that a girl becomes pregnant before
betrothal or marriage. In such an event, if the young man who has
impregnated her is responsible and respectful and liked by the
girl's parents, he is asked to make the necessary payments to legal-
ize their relationship. This payment is generally smaller than the
usual amount described below. On the other hand, if the boy is
not in favour with the parents, she may be given to another man
after the birth, or be asked to look for a better man.

Any youth who has a girl betrothed to him owes services to her
parents even before the marriage takes place. He must help repair
their house and the mother-in-law's kitchen whenever the roofs
are old. He must be ready to do any work for which the girl's
parents may need him. Above all he must be generous with gifts
of fish whenever he goes fishing, and with farm products at
harvest time. On her side the girl pays frequent visits to her future
parents-in-law and participates freely in any household work
under way. She also helps during harvest time, and assists her
mother-in-law in the preparation of fish if the latter is a fishwife.

Persons who have early betrothals therefore start services to
their future parents-in-law much earlier than those who have to
fend for themselves.

It is claimed that the Anlo married in the past at a later age than
they do at present. It is said that men used to marry between the
ages of twenty-five and thirty, by which time they had learned
everything necessary for a married man.[1] Women married earlier,

---

[1] See Adzomada, Rev. P.F.K., 1950, p. 24.

because in the ideal mating the husband was expected to be older than the wife by about five years. My own investigations, based on comparison of the ages of older members of the population and those of their first born children, show that the age of marriage for men in the last three generations was between twenty and twenty-five. Men now normally marry at or before twenty-two. For women there seems to be very little difference between past and present. As negotiations and preparations for marriage start immediately after puberty, which is at about fifteen, both past and present marriages occur some two or three years later, between seventeen and eighteen or a little later, and there seems to be a tendency for youths and girls to be married earlier if they have been betrothed before puberty.

The preceding paragraphs have been devoted to a description of the choice of marriage partner and premarital relations between the sexes. We conclude by emphasizing that, though courtship and romance are recognized in Anlo, they are not always allowed to determine the selection of partners by the young people themselves. The important limiting factors are the influence of parents and other relatives of the prospective spouses and the characters of the youths. It must also be mentioned that though marriage is the purpose implicit in many a romance, courtship has not yet become a necessary prelude to marriage. It is true that, even if a girl is betrothed, the boy still finds it necessary to have opportunities to discuss love with her, but it is equally true that sometimes, even between lineages not linked by any matrilateral ties, a man asks for the hand of a girl to whom he has never previously proposed love.

6. THE MARRIAGE CEREMONIES

(a) *The preliminary arrangements*

The informal relations between lovers, and the comments of their parents, are given an emphatic stamp of seriousness and permanence by a ceremonial known as *vɔfofo*, or knocking. The bridegroom's parents send his father's sister and his mother's sister to the bride's parents to ask formally for the hand of the bride. On their arrival at the girl's house, her parents enquire the reason for the deputation, and, after hearing it, send them away for about a week while they, the bride's parents, consider the matter. The reason for postponing the reply is that customarily Anlo do not give an immediate reply to any question of major importance. The postponement also gives the bride's parents time to make enquiries about the youth and his parents, if they have not done so already, because not only must a young man be able to support his wife in the manner to which she has been accustomed, it is even more important that he should come from a good stock, from a family free of hereditary defects, witchcraft and criminal mentality. If the bride's people are satisfied on all these counts, and the girl also agrees to the proposal, the bridegroom's deputation are informed on their second call that their request has been considered and accepted. For this information two bottles of imported or locally brewed gin are offered by the deputation in appreciation. This payment is known as *vɔlenu* or knocking fee.

bride price

As soon as the bridegroom's people learn of the acceptance of their request, preparations start in full swing for raising the marriage payments. Though it is the groom himself who should raise the necessary money, his father and mother's brother would help him if he had difficulty. In many cases he will have saved it up in anticipation of the outcome of the negotiations.

It is usually the bridegroom's people who decide what payment they wish to give, though the bride's parents reserve the right to reject an amount they consider insufficient.

When the payment is ready the bridegroom's paternal and maternal aunts carry it to the bride's parents' home either in a large trunk or wooden box, or in a large pan, called *fovi*, the container forming part of the payment. There it is inspected by the bride's parents and when accepted is left there. If it is considered insufficient the whole load is carried back. Interestingly enough, I have never heard of any complaint that a payment was too high. On many occasions the load has to be carried back several times because it is considered too small. In kinship marriages of close relatives there is little haggling. The closer the kinship tie the less fastidious are the bride's parents about the value of the payment.

(b) *The ceremonies*

Anlo marriage is concluded by the giving of marriage payment and by a series of elaborate ceremonies, each of which is considered necessary for the establishment of a legal union. The important ceremonies are the formal handing over of the bride to the bridegroom's parents, or *dedeasi*; the powdering of the bride or *togbagba*; the consummation, or *ɖoɖoabadzi* and the seclusion, *dedexɔ*.

It is the payment, *srɔnu* or *tabianu*, which starts the ceremonies. It is necessary that it be made in full before the major ceremonies commence.[1]

The formal handing over of the bride, which takes place in her father's house, is a short ceremony. It begins by both parents giving advice to the couple, followed by a declaration by both of their willingness to marry. The responsibilities of each to the other are then meticulously enumerated. The occasion is concluded by a short prayer to the ancestors. The significance of the handing-over ceremony seems to be the provisional transference of sexual rights to the groom, but, as we shall see later, he is not expected to have intercourse with her until after the powdering.

The two parties now fix a date for the wedding. The day chosen must be a good day, *asinyuigbe*, that is it must be the day before or after a market day.[2] The ceremonies take place in the evening, during either the third or last quarter of the moon, when the evenings are dark. On the appointed date the groom's father sends his own and his wife's sisters to bring the bride for the rites, which by tradition take place in the bridegroom's father's house.

Meanwhile the bride herself, in preparation for the ceremony, has been bathed and anointed with sweet-smelling ointments and dressed in her most beautiful clothes. On being released by her parents, she is accompanied to the groom's place by her own father's sister and mother's sister, together with those who have come to fetch her. A young girl follows them with the trousseau. The groom and his relatives are at this time gathered in his father's lounge awaiting their arrival. In the bedroom, the *srɔɖeba*, the consummation bed, has already been laid, covered with white bedsheet. For the purposes of the ceremony the groom buys two yards of imported cloth, a yard of silk headkerchief, *seda-taku*, and a stool, *atizikpui*.

Now when they arrive at the bridegroom's father's house, those

---

[1] The practice of the Glidzi, who, according to Westermann and Ward, give the payments after the consummation, appears most unusual. As Ward points out this procedure may ensure pre-marital chastity, since virginity means higher payment. In Anlo the payment for virginity is made after the consummation. This can have the same effect on pre-marital chastity, however.

[2] For details on market days see Appendix IV.

bringing the bride, through their spokesmen, her father's sister, hand her over to the groom's father with these words: 'The parents of the bride have given her to us to bring to you in response to your request. From now on responsibility for her maintenance lies with you. She must be well fed. You must take good care of her when she is sick. We do not quarrel in our house and we do not want her to quarrel in your house.' The groom's father receives the bride and thanks the messengers. Then follow several admonitory speeches by those present, notably the groom's father and mother's brother. Their speeches are mainly concerned with the basic necessities of happy married life: patience, tolerance, understanding of each other's point of view, and above all hard work and co-operation in economic and household activities are all stressed. This done, the bridegroom's lineage head[1] pours libation to the ancestors, addressing them in this way:

Today is an important day for us, the living, and it is fitting that we call you also, our ancestors, grandfathers and grandmothers, to come and join us on this occasion. The reason for our appeal is a good one (ɖagbee). Your own son X has asked Y to be his partner and this evening we shall have the consummation and the seclusion ceremonies. Successful marriage is realized in good health, fertility and prosperity. We therefore ask for our new couple long life. Let them live till 'grey hairs appear on their teeth'[2] and have as many children as possible. In commemoration of these requests we offer you alcohol and cool water, for all of you to drink. You know everything. You can see the invisible. Perish our enemies and let our benefactors flourish.[3] Once more here is water. We call all of you to come and drink.

The bride at this time, on her first visit to her future home, is thought to be very shy, and is aptly called, throughout the duration of the ceremonies, ŋukpetɔ or ŋugbetɔ, 'the shy one'.

The consummation ceremony is performed by a mistress of ceremonies who is usually a father's sister of the groom, and is known to have experienced a successful marriage and herself been fecund, the belief being that the bride will follow in her footsteps.

[1] Since prayers to the ancestors are not said by women among the Ewe in general, Westermann's (1935, p. 59) statement that it is the M.C. who makes this prayer may be peculiar to the Glidzi, because the Glidzi M.C. is also a woman. I was however not able to check this in Glidzi.
[2] This is a very literal translation of the Ewe expression woanɔ agbe afo wɔɖe aɖu ŋuti. . . It is the commonest expression for wishing anyone long life and prosperity.
[3] In Anlo religion there is no blessing for one's enemies.

She holds the *ŋukpetɔ* by the hand and leads her to the door of the bedroom. On opening the door she makes the *ŋukpetɔ* look into the room three times, then cross the doorstep to and fro six times. The seventh time she is taken inside. (It is believed that if the *ŋukpetɔ's* feet touch the doorstep when she is being led into the room, she will not be a good wife.) There she is stripped naked, and her old clothes are replaced by the new two-yard cloth bought by the groom. She is then seated on the new stool, where she is rubbed with powder from a rare tree called *eto*, followed by this address from the M.C. 'I have rubbed you with this powder. From today you have become the wife of X. Henceforth you are not to sit on any seat offered you by any man other than your own husband.'[1] With these words she is helped from the stool on to the bed, where she is joined by the bridegroom. They are made to embrace each other, while the M.C. addresses both of them, 'You are now *atsu kple asi*, man and wife, breed as much as you can'. Her duty done, the M.C. closes the door and returns to join those waiting next door.

Custom demands that the *ŋukpetɔ* should refuse coitus for several minutes, though both of them know well that this is only a formality and part of the proceedings.

Meanwhile those waiting in the lounge continue their conversation and revelling. After a long time has elapsed the M.C. knocks at the bedroom door. The groom opens it. The M.C. goes into the room to examine the white bedsheet. If it is bloodstained, there is great jubilation. The girl is led away to the bathroom, where she is washed in a hot bath, again by the M.C.

The original idea behind the consummation is the public declaration of the *ŋukpetɔ's* virginity, for the groom must make an additional payment if she is a virgin. Establishment of virginity is a matter of great pride for both the bride and her parents. In addition to establishing her unblemished reputation, it entitles her to the use of *blitsikpi*, golden bangles (bracelets), and *atsibla*,[2] after her seclusion period, and more gifts await her when she goes

[1] The Anlo's disapproval of adultery is here given a ceremonial expression. As explained later the elaboration of the ceremonial serves to portray the importance of the occasion to the couple and their relatives.

[2] *Atsibla* is a kind of under-garment for women worn immediately above the buttocks, and is made by tying several pieces of cloth around the back end of the waist-line beads. It has the effect of hiding the actual shape of the buttocks by making the protruberance of the rumps more pronounced.

round later to greet her relatives. Her parents also rejoice, because her virginity shows they have performed their parental duties. In addition her mother receives from the bridegroom a bar of soap and present of twelve shillings, 'to wash the bedsheet which has been stained'.

For the girl who has had pre-marital intercourse or 'has not been seen at home',[1] as the Anlo put it, more than personal disgrace is involved. At the discretion of her own parents she may be forced to name her seducer or seducers, who will also be charged and fined for fornication. Her outdooring ceremony too will be less elaborate.

The day of the wedding and consummation is a time of much activity and great joy. In the bride's homestead the news of her virginity is celebrated with merry-making. The groom's homestead is also full of relatives and friends, the former mostly occupied with drinking and conversations of all kind while the latter continue to sing far into the night. On the following day a fowl is slaughtered for the ŋukpetɔ by her mother.

After the consummation the bride remains in seclusion in the groom's house, her new home, for a period of between four and eight months. The actual duration in each particular case depends on the wish and income resources of the husband, for the seclusion is a fairly expensive business. The bride is expected to eat, so long as she remains there, only the choicest dishes, fresh meat, corned-beef, rice, etc., and only men with ample means can afford to keep their brides in seclusion for long periods.

Necessities for a bride in seclusion are kpakuru, a strongly-scented spice for toilet; three dishes, one for porridge, the remaining two for akple and soup, the main meal of the day; one kente cloth (locally woven) for covering the head when going out for toilet; and ketsi (bulrush) for weaving baskets. All these must be provided by the groom.

During the seclusion period the bride's sisters bring her food from their homestead, while the groom's mother continues to cook his food. The bride always remains in her room, going out only for toilet, and even this she must do surreptitiously so as to avoid meeting anyone. Throughout the day her time is occupied

[1] A bride whose virginity has been established at the consummation is said to have been 'seen at home', wokpɔe afe; one who had sex previously 'has not been seen at home', wo mekpɔe afe o.

with weaving baskets or other handicrafts, but mostly with friends and relatives, who entertain her to indoor games and pastimes. The relatives also, especially her own parents and grandparents, continue to advise her on the prerequisites of successful family life.

But the main idea behind the seculsion is to emphasize from the onset the husband's monopoly over her sexual services. Many a time the bride comes out of the seclusion with a big belly; in fact, she is expected to get pregnant before coming out because this gives hope of a successful union, children being considered a most powerful stabilizing influence on marriage.

The end of the seclusion period is marked by another ceremony of thanksgiving to the dead, for no Anlo undertaking is complete without the participation of the ancestors. After this, the bride, dressed in her richest clothes and ornaments and accompanied by two younger girls similarly attired, goes about the town to visit relatives. The relatives show their appreciation of her by lavishing gifts on her, particularly if 'she was seen at home'. If her pregnancy has reached an advanced stage before her outdooring, these courtesy calls are postponed, and later combined with a similar call made after the out-dooring of the first child. The gifts are brought home by the two young girls. With this the marriage ceremonies are concluded.

From this brief account it is clear that the traditional marriage ceremonies are very elaborate. As such they help to bring home to the couple and their relatives the importance of their undertaking. Most of the splendour and ceremony surrounding traditional Anlo marriage are fast disappearing. There is evidence to indicate that up to some fifty years ago nearly all couples at their first marriage went through the processes described. Today, however, the manifold changes brought about by the impact of formal education and Christianity have introduced a good deal of flexibility into the marriage procedure. The seclusion is now considered a luxury no one is able or willing to enjoy. The rubbing with *eto* as symbol of legality is being rapidly replaced by the giving of a ring, while the consummation ceremony has lost its main function because of the increasing laxity of attitude towards virginity.

(c) The Marriage Payment

It has been seen that each stage of the proceedings is marked by the bridegroom buying or supplying specific articles, both in the form of gifts and as necessary objects for the performance of particular rites. During the formal handing over of the bride, for instance, drinks are provided, and for the seclusion several things are bought for the bride's use. Important though these are, and despite their necessary connection with the ceremony, they are not part of the marriage payment, srɔnu (lit. marriage goods). The marriage payment is a special payment given as such, regardless of anything the groom may have paid for other purposes.

The following list contains what are expected to be the ideal load of srɔnu.

1 trunk or wooden box containing:
2 Kente (Keta)[1] cloths for the bride;
1 Kente cloth for the bride's mother, also known as dɔkpavɔ, the cloth for the womb;
4 imported cloths (garments) or vumeɖui – half piece each;
4 silk headkerchiefs, seda-taku;
1 piece of red cloth, goduivɔ, used as under-skirt;
£5 in cash;
12 bottles of assorted drinks;
£1 1s. 0d. for the parents.

Though this is the ideal payment there is much variation in practice. Indeed, out of twenty lists collected, no two were identical. A man may give dɔkpavɔ but no other cloth for the bride. Dzatugbi for instance received only £1 1s in cash in addition to the other 'things', while Eʋi's payment consisted only of £5 in cash and five bottles of gin. Both marriages took place during the first decade of this century. These differences in the actual amount of the payment make meaningful the rather far-fetched remarks by some informants that the 'choice and amount of payment depend on individual taste and ability'. What we can legitimately say, however, is that though there is an ideal list of items, individuals try to approximate their payments to it in various ways, since the ideal payment is not insisted on in practice. This is largely

[1] This is a hand-woven cloth made in the vicinity of Keta.

the reason for the haggling which usually precedes the payment.

The coming of Christianity and literacy has brought some changes into the items composing the marriage payment. With the steady disappearance of the *eto* rubbing and the seclusion, the use of the ring, *asigɛ*, as a symbol of proper marriage is increasingly coming into vogue. The use of the ring is essentially Christian, but it is not peculiar to Christian converts. Both pagans and Christians now use it with almost equal frequency. Its use by pagans is not strange because one interesting fact about Christianity in Anlo has been the imitation of Christian attitudes, practices and habits not only by the converts but also by those who are still unconverted to the Christian faith. In other words, many Anlo borrow the non-religious aspects of Christianity and utilize them without necessarily accepting the beliefs. This is possible partly because of the importance of the educated class in Anlo as leaders of fashion, and partly because conversion to Christianity is a necessary accompaniment of education.

Other later additions to the items of the marriage payment are *gagba* – large metal cans for carrying loads of all kind. These range from *gbaglavi* in the early nineteen forties to *kpolu* in the early fifties and now *fovi*. *Kente* cloths are no longer considered necessary, though many still give them.

The overall effect of these changes has been the introduction of further flexibility into the items making up the payment. This in turn has resulted in the division of the payment into two, namely *tabianu* (engagement items) and *srɔnu* (the marriage payments proper). As the engagement became part and parcel of the marriage system, the *tabianu* replaced the *srɔnu* as the payment necessary for the commencement of the ceremonies, the *srɔnu* being paid during the course of the ceremonies or even after their conclusion. The items making up the *tabianu* are: ring; twelve bottles of drinks (assorted); 21s and a Holy Bible if Christian.

One further indication of laxity in the system has been the refusal of some to pay the *srɔnu* without much pressure once the ceremonies have been concluded. Another has been the tendency in recent years to combine the *tabianu* and the *srɔnu*, which is increasingly becoming the general practice. The payment given in 1962 by Kwakuvi for the hand of Kwasiwɔ is a typical combined payment. It comprises the following:

	£	s	d
Ring	3	10	0
2 headkerchiefs, *seda-taku*		10	6
1 *Fovi* (pan) and 1 *Gagbevi* (small pan)	3	2	6
3 bottles of spirits (½ pint of Gordon's Gin and 2 bottles *Kele*, local gin)	2	6	6
2 bottles beer		5	6
4 bottles coca-cola		5	0
2 half pieces of cloth, popularly known as Garment (*vumeɖui*)	4	0	0
Cash for the bride	10	0	0
Cash for the mother	1	1	0
1 headkerchief around which cash was tied		5	0
Total	£25	6	0

Generally speaking the items may be divided into two, those for the use of the bride and those for her relatives. Apart from the drinks, the *dɔkpavɔ* and the one guinea for the mother, all the articles fall into the first group. They comprise some of the basic things a bride needs during the early part of her married life, and their inclusion in the marriage payment emphasizes the view that the general material well-being of a wife is the responsibility of her husband. But this does not mean that all the bride's trousseau is included in the marriage payment or provided by the groom. On the contrary every Anlo girl and her parents try to make her as little dependent as possible on her husband. Anlo women have a remarkable fancy for good clothes, and they take great pride in providing their own clothing. Not only is a woman's dependence on her husband for clothes a constant subject of abuse for her during quarrels among co-wives and between spouses, it is also indicative of her own economic failings. In short a woman must work to provide her own basic needs. As the Anlo put it, 'a husband does not have to give money to his wife for pepper and salt'. Petty trading is one of the commonest occupations of women which provides them with reasonable independent incomes. It is only through this type of independent occupation that she is respected.

Nevertheless, however independent a wife may be in the provision of basic necessities, she needs capital for her trading or whatever occupation she takes up, and for this she must look to her husband and to a lesser extent to her parents. Thus, although a woman's hard work is cherished, the husband's help in his wife's economic activities explains the importance of the money payments. With this money the young wife starts life as a *bligbala*, baker, *layiyila*, fishwife, or *asitsala*, trader.

The recent introduction of the *kpolu* can[1] in the Keta area as the most important 'glamorous' item on the list is also of special significance. Women do most of the unskilled labour on onion farms, such as carrying sand on to the water-logged onion beds after the rains and transporting the harvest home. In the fishing industry too the services of the women are enlisted in the transportation. Head-loading is still the essential means of transport over short distances, and *kpolu* is the standard unit for carriage. Its inclusion in the list of items is therefore not without economic significance. Indeed for many women the *kpolu* they use on these occasions is what they got as marriage payment.

Other items, especially the ring, are of a rather symbolic value, and, in view of what has been said about them, clothes also must fall within this category. Clothes received as marriage payment are used, it is true, but many prefer to regard them as life-long possessions to which they can point with pride to friends and immediate posterity; for, despite their material value, a woman has some sentimental attachment to her marriage clothes. They confer prestige and respect. Receipt of marriage payment means maturity before marriage, premarital moral behaviour and above all proper marriage. Hence the special value placed on them.

The remaining items, including the *dɔkpavɔ* and the drinks, go to the parents and relatives of the bride. Actually only the drinks are shared among relatives outside the nuclear family, because the *dɔkpavɔ* is the bride's mother's exclusive property, and the one guinea is also hers. As a rule all the bride's relatives on both the paternal and maternal sides must have a share of the marriage drinks. The taking of the drinks by relatives outside the nuclear family is their final expression of interest in the union. Usually when the marriage payment is received by the bride's parents her paternal and maternal relatives are invited to inspect it. It is here that all those present take their share of the drinks.

Naturally not every relative can attend such functions. A

---

[1] This is a round strong aluminium pan about eight inches deep and 30 inches in diameter.

portion is therefore reserved for those who call later. Many a time
some relatives call only to find that the bottles have already been
emptied. A person so treated may blame the bride's parents for
carelessness, but he also reserves the right to demand his own
share anytime from the groom, though it is not the latter's fault
that he is left out. In fact so unlimited is the number of relatives
entitled to share the marriage drink that a man may continue to
give marriage drinks throughout his whole life, depending on
when and where he meets affines who demand their drinks. At
many social gatherings such as funerals, dances, and market-places
it is not uncommon for affines to demand drink. Sometimes also
a man visits a neighbouring settlement and meets a person who
happens to be a distant affine. Tradition demands that he should
there and then give one *lobovi*, i.e. half a pint of locally brewed
gin, to his affine. It is not even considered to be against decorum
for the affine himself to demand the drink.

In some marriages certain relatives refuse the drink if they do
not favour the union. Since accepting the drink implies at least
tacit approval of the marriage, abstention is the surest way of
registering one's protest against the marriage while at the same
time saving oneself future embarrassment should it fail.

7. MARRIAGE AND FILIATION OF CHILDREN

The rights conferred on a man over his wife in Anlo marriage are
what Bohannan[1] calls rights *in uxorem*, or rights over her sexual
services. If after their wedding the woman is unfaithful, it is her
husband and not her father who initiates legal proceedings against
her seducer. Though the marriage payment and the *eto* powder
are both considered necessary elements in a properly conducted
marriage, the latter is the more important. It is claimed that the
eto powder establishes the husband's monopoly over the wife's
sexual services, and without it he cannot sue for adultery. It is
evident that this was the case in the past. Today however the payment, the handing over ceremony and the ring especially, are
considered sufficient.

The husband's sexual rights are personal and end with his death.
His widow is then free to remarry anyone of her choice if she
chooses to remarry. The levirate, as a rule enjoining a widow to

[1] 1949, p. 278.

be remarried to, or inherited by, her husband's brothers or lineage, does not exist in Anlo, though his agnates are equally eligible to remarry her with all others.

The children of a woman's second and subsequent marriages belong to the social group of their genitor. This is in line with the Anlo attitude to the relationship between biological fatherhood and paternity. In all cases the known genitor is the pater. An adulterine child belongs to its genitor and not to its mother's husband. It is inconceivable in Anlo for someone's biological child to be incorporated into the clan of another. When I told my informants that it could happen in some societies, the expression of disgust in their faces sufficiently showed how foreign such a possibility was to their social reality. 'That will be *dzidehlɔmi*', they said, literally meaning 'a false recruit into a clan', a pejorative term for Anlo of dubious paternity who are incorporated into the lineages of their mothers' husbands. If a person's alien paternity is an established fact he is regarded as Blu, a member of the foreigners' clan.

Since in the final analysis it is the known genitor who is pater, Anlo marriage in effect does not transfer rights *in genetricem* to the husband. But as the husband has a legal monopoly over his wife's sexual services, he is placed in a good position, if he is fruitful, to recruit children by the woman into his descent group. Therefore the Anlo husband does not acquire by mere marriage, paternal rights in the children of his wife. His own active participation in the procreational process is necessary, in addition to marriage, for a legal claim on the wife's issue as his children. In such a system, therefore, there is no point in an impotent man marrying a wife and asking another man to sleep with her for the purpose of raising seed to his name, as is the case in many patrilineal societies.

Our distinction between pater and genitor is here necessary largely for analytic purposes only. Normally there is no reason for disputing a man's paternity over his wife's children, and their recruitment into his lineage and clan is a matter of course. A woman may commit adultery that may bear fruit. If she is unwilling to leave her husband for her seducer, and her husband is ignorant of her adultery, only the two culprits will know that her husband is not the genitor of their child. This is illustrated by an Anlo saying which means 'only the mother knows the father of her child'. A few persons were pointed to me as not the children

of their paters. In all cases the husbands of the women concerned
were believed to be ignorant of the fact. However, since sterility
is very much loathed, a sterile man may condone his wife's
adultery with a fertile man if she intends to remain with her
husband.

A wife's infidelity is considered a great spite on a husband.
Should a husband know of his wife's adultery or the dubious
origin of any of her children, he may either divorce her or repudi-
ate the child. It occasionally happens, however, that a man refuses
to divorce an unfaithful wife even if she has had children by another man as shown in the following case.

Case No. 2

Kwadzo had three wives in 1958. When he went on a fishing
expedition to Abidjan he took two of them with him and left
the third with her mother. While he was away she had an adulterine child with a young carpenter. On his return in 1961 Kwadzo
was reconciled to her. Action for seduction was taken against the
carpenter, who was fined £5 and two bottles of local gin. His
(the carpenter's) mother took possession of the adulterine child.

Kwadzo's situation is not uncommon in these days, when
seasonal emigration to Abidjan and other West African fishing
centres takes place on a massive scale. But his reconciliation to the
adulteress was most unusual, though not unprecedented. Many
husbands do not divorce adulterous wives, but it is rare to take
them back after children have been born to other men.

A husband is not bound to take action against his wife's seducer,
though he is expected to and many do.

8. SECOND MARRIAGES, IRREGULAR UNIONS AND PATERNITY

Our discussion so far has been centred on normal matrimony.
There are, however, other forms of domestic union. One of the
spouses may die and the survivor enter into another union.
Divorce may occur and be followed by the remarriage of one or
both of the divorcees to another person. Moreover, in the first
unions not all couples pass through the normal marriage procedures before settling down to live together.

We have seen that the levirate, as a rule enjoining a widow to be inherited by her dead husband's lineage, does not exist.[1] On the death of their husbands Anlo women perform an elaborate and strict mourning ritual, *ahoxɔxɔ*,[2] which lasts for about sixteen months and is regarded as the transitional period necessary for the ritual separation of the dead husband from his wife. The ritual of separation involves a fair amount of expenditure, which must be borne by a male relative of the deceased, or failing him by any of her own male relatives. This man has become the guardian of the widow and her children, and any man wishing to marry her must first pay him the expenses of the ritual. If the guardian happens to be a relative of the deceased, then he himself would like to marry her if she agrees.

After the end of the mourning period the widow may either choose to remain in her husband's house or move away to live in her parental home. Her decision depends largely on the number and age of her children, the relative cordiality between her and her affines and her plans for the future.

Some indication of the extent to which widows remain with or are married to their dead husband's kin is given by data from Woe and Alakple. Altogether 171 in our sample had experienced widowhood. Of this number 15 were remarried to the dead husband's brother or some close relative. In 52 cases the widow took a new husband not related to the dead one. In the remaining 104 instances she had not remarried and was living independently.

A man may die at any stage of his marriage. If he has given the marriage payment and died before the consummation, the payment will have to be returned. Similarly if a betrothed girl dies before she is married, the betrothal will have to be nullified by the return of the marriage payment. Once the marriage has been consummated there is no question of return of the payment in the event of one spouse's death. If a girl dies soon after betrothal, however, her parents may give her sister to the groom, but this is not obligatory.

Young widows normally remarry. Only economic sufficiency

---

[1] Westermann (1935, p. 56) refers to the practice of widows being remarried by their husbands' brothers, but it is clear from Foli's (his informant's) statement that he only meant marriage with the widow's husband's brother was allowed. It was not a rule.

[2] Men also perform this ritual, but theirs is less elaborate and lasts a much shorter time, usually two weeks. See Appendix VI.

and old age prevent widows from remarriage. Anlo believe that a woman, like a man, cannot live for long without sexual intercourse, so that if a young widow remains single for a long time she lends herself to accusations and gossips of wanton behaviour. Almost all the widows in the sample who were living on their own became widows when they were over fifty years of age, though some above this age have remarried.

Widow marriage needs neither marriage payment nor ceremony apart from the *ahowɔho*, the expenses of the mourning ritual. The proposal is decided and agreed upon by the widow and her suitor. Drinks, about two bottles of *akpeteshie*, local gin, may be offered in prayers to the ancestors and the deceased.

Another form of second marriage is the remarriage of a divorced woman. This is usually more expensive than widow marriage, though here again neither marriage payment nor ceremony is involved. If her divorce is due to her adultery with the man she now marries, he will have to repay the marriage payment to the first husband in addition to all debts incurred by the latter on behalf of the woman. If, however, the first marriage has been legally dissolved before their marriage, the subsequent marriage will cost the second husband nothing more than a few bottles of drinks and some gifts.

The general atmosphere in which second marriages are conducted may throw some light on the need for the parents' active participation in the selection of partners in first marriages. In second marriages the parents of the spouses are less fastidious about what they expect of their affines by way of character and kinship affiliations. The reason given for this indifference is that in their first marriages the young couples are not experienced enough to know much about their partners and their parents. They are also charmed by qualities which are not necessarily good in married life. But their own experience in their first marriages enables them to judge better in their next choice.

The conduct of second marriages has been discussed only from the point of view of the condition of the women entering into them, because it is their marital conditions which are considered crucial. A widower marrying a maiden is expected to perform all the normal marriage rites for her. In the same way a divorced man who is marrying a maiden has to follow the same procedure.

Similarly all subsequent marriages of a married man to maidens must be conducted from the girls' point of view as if both were being married for the first time. But where a man who has not been married before is marrying a woman who has already been married, the normal procedures described for first marriages are not required.

In all the forms of union so far described the woman was legally married in the first instance. But not all women go through the proper ceremonies in their first unions. I now describe a type of union in which the woman has never been married.

The interference of parents and relatives in the choice of partners often results in disagreements between the girls and their parents. This gives rise in some cases to elopement and open revolt against parental authority. The parents, finding that they cannot control their daughter, let her do as she pleases. This may mean allowing her to live with a man of whom she is very fond, but who has not won the favour of her parents to make possible the performance of the ceremonies which bring about the marriage. Others in this category are those who have borne children before marriage and have not been married to their lovers, but have continued to live with them despite the objections of their parents.

A girl who finds herself in such a union must have considerable trust in the sincerity and ability of her lover, because she cannot expect the same support from her parents in family disputes as a wife can. This is the kind of union Evans-Pritchard[1] called 'simple concubinage' among the Nuer. Among both the Nuer and the Anlo this union, despite its name, is a permanent one, the primary aim of which, like that of any legal marriage, is the procreation of children and the establishment of a family. The couples call and refer to each other by terms appropriate to spouses. The difference between simple concubinage and legal marriage lies in their different origins and not in the relationship between the spouses. A man does not treat his concubinary 'wife' differently from a legal wife, and one cannot know, in a household containing both types, who is a legal wife and who is a concubine by mere observation of behaviour. A man may even treat a concubine with greater consideration than a legal wife, because the only control he has over her is what his personal influence gives him. Obviously he

[1] 1951, p. 117.

cannot claim compensation in case of her infidelity, neither can he restrain her should she wish to leave him for a new lover.

It is difficult to determine how frequent non-legalized unions were in the past. Both Spieth[1] and Westermann[2] mentioned them, but gave no indication of frequency. Spieth, for instance, differentiated between properly and improperly conducted marriages, while Westermann gave instances of girls having children and living with men to whom they were not married. My informants were unanimous in their opinion that this was quite rare, though not non-existent. This seems to be correlated with the greater authority of parents in the past. Of the 105 women (out of 474 married women) who fell into this category in Woe and Alakple in 1962, only two were over fifty-five years old. This may mean very little, since the number of older women in the population, and consequently in the sample, must of necessity be much smaller than that of the younger generation. However, case histories show that the frequency of non-legalized unions could not approach the high percentage we have today, about 18 per cent of all unions (105/579).

Certain conclusions follow from this account of Anlo marriage. Though a woman may be married more than once, only her first marriage must be accompanied by payment and ceremonies. Second and subsequent marriages, though lacking in ceremonial and payments, constitute proper marriages all the same, because not only are the purposes implicit in them found in legal marriage, but also because their creation and form are socially accepted. Of primary importance are the procreation and establishment of legitimate families, economic co-operation and companionship.

The difference between these second and subsequent marriages on the one hand and concubinage on the other is that the latter, though a first union, lacks ceremonial. The marriage ceremony is something more than a formality for transferring the bride's sexual services to her husband. It also goes beyond a mere occasion to test her virginity. To the bride it marks an important stage in her social development. We see in the consummation a solemn expression of sex as a prerogative of married life. This is illustrated by the Anlo attitude towards virginity. But it does not matter for the function of the ceremony whether the girl has had a previous affair. What matters is that, for the first time in her life,

[1] 1906, p. 183.   [2] 1935, p. 58.

society has given her ceremonial permission to indulge in sex for the purpose of procreation, and for this reason she must be associated with a man. Ceremonial then becomes the social qualification for married life. It is in this sense a rite of passage.[1] But the ceremony also has through its sanctions the effect of promoting premarital chastity.

If it is accepted that marriage in Anlo is a rite of passage *per se*, then the absence of ceremony in second marriages becomes understandable, because those involved have already passed through these rites. In fact, it is only on this explanation that legal marriage differs from concubinage, since they cannot be differentiated according to the legitimacy of the children resulting from them, because it is known biological fatherhood and not proper marriage which is the basis for establishing paternity.

The position in Anlo, then, is as follows. For women adulthood and the married state appear coterminous. To pass from the category of child to that of adult a girl must go through a full marriage ceremony with a youth. That the ceremony is associated primarily with girls is difficult to explain, but it is probably not unrelated to the polygynous nature of marriage and the greater moral stigma attached to premarital sex relations for women than for men.

9. DIVORCE

The stability of marriage, which the Anlo believe was absolute in the past, apparently was actually high. This statement holds, in view of what we have already said about paternity, whether we are speaking of the stability of the jural or the conjugal relationship.[2] This was the unanimous opinion of my informants, who maintained that Anlo regarded marriage as ideally a permanent union between the spouses and their kin groups, and divorce was allowed only for flagrant breach of the husband's obligations to his wife, her parents or any of his close affines, for childlessness and for the wife's adultery. The important thing, however, is that it did occur. But in the absence of statistical evidence it is impossible to assess correctly the actual frequency of these 'rare' cases. All earlier writers on the subject of marriage were almost silent on the subject, and Ward,[3] commenting on this fact, observed that 'this

[1] See Spieth, 1906, pp. 183–99, and Westermann, 1935, pp. 53 ff.
[2] See Schneider, 1953.   [3] 1949, p. 140.

is possibly partly to be explained by what appears to be the . . .
difficulty and infrequency of divorce in Eweland, attested by all
Ewe informants in London.' Case histories and genealogies of the
older members of the population also tend to give general support
to these views. We may also mention in this regard the fact that
infidelity and adultery, both important causes of divorce and
broken marriages, though not unknown in Anlo were severely
punished in the past.[1] Divorce was also considered immoral,
especially on the part of women. These legal and moral sanctions
must have greatly reduced the number of divorces. As Evans-
Pritchard observed long ago, marriage 'derives its stability from
the restraint imposed by law and morals'.[2]

Even if it is true that divorce was difficult and rare in the past,
there is reason to believe that since the turn of the century significant changes have taken place, due largely to the curtailment of
the power of the traditional government which used to enforce
the sexual morality of the citizens. Now divorce is comparatively
common, and it may be useful to have some quantitative estimate
of divorce frequency. In our measurements we have followed the
methods suggested by Barnes[3] in his articles on the subject. One
aspect of the occurrence of divorce is presented in Tables 1–5,
where the marital experiences of men and women of different
ages at Woe and Alakple are set out.

It will be seen that the mean number of divorces per head of the
married population is 0·18 for females in Alakple; 0·28 in Woe;
and 0·48 for males in Alakple and 0·66 in Woe. Combining the
figures for the two settlements we find that the mean number of
divorces per head of the married population is 0·59 for men and
0·23 for women (see Table 5). The difference in the figures for
men and women may be due largely to the greater reluctance on
the part of women than of men to admit to divorce. I have reason
to believe that many informants, especially women, were very
reluctant to tell their marital history in full because of the moral
stigma that divorce entails. And the difference in the figures for
the two villages may be due partly to the varying reliability of
their informants and partly to their different degrees of assimila-
tion of western influence. The higher figures for Woe may be

[1] See Westermann, in Adzomada, 1950, pp. 7–8; Wiegrabe, 1938, p. 45;
S. Obianim, 1957, p. 92; Fiawoo, F. K., 1943, pp. 3–5.
[2] Evans-Pritchard, 1934, p. 172.   [3] 1949, pp. 37–62, and 1951, p. 50.

explained by its greater exposure to social change, which results in greater fluidity in the social set-up, and the greater mobility of the population, which creates the environment for divorce.

To make the Anlo figures comparable with those of other societies we can express as a ratio the relationship between the number of marriages that ended in divorce and the number that did not or have not yet done so. This we have tried to do in Tables 6–8.

TABLE I. Marital Experience of Males by Age: Woe 1962

Age in Years	All Males with Marriage Experience No. of marriages experienced since birth						All Males with Marriage Experience No. of divorces since birth						
	1	2	3	4	5	total	0	1	2	3	4	5	total
18–25	6	2	0	0	0	8	8	0	0	0	0	0	8
26–35	19	3	4	1	1	28	15	6	5	2	0	0	28
36–45	14	8	3	2	0	27	19	7	1	0	0	0	27
46–55	12	7	7	2	1	29	19	4	5	1	0	0	26
56–65	6	8	4	1	3	22	11	5	1	1	1	3	22
66–75	7	4	2	1	4	18	13	4	1	1	0	0	19
76–85	2	0	2	0	0	4	1	2	1	0	0	0	4
86	0	0	0	0	0	0	0	0	0	0	0	0	0
Total	66	32	22	7	9	136	86	28	14	5	1	3	137

TABLE 2. Marital Experience of Males by Age: Alakple 1962

Age in Years	All Males with Marriage Experience No. of marriages since birth						No. of divorces since birth						
	1	2	3	4	5	total	0	1	2	3	4	5	total
18–25	2	0	0	0	0	2	2	0	0	0	0	0	2
26–35	7	3	0	0	0	10	8	2	0	0	0	0	10
36–45	13	9	3	0	0	25	15	6	2	2	0	0	25
46–55	5	3	3	0	0	11	7	3	1	0	0	0	11
56–65	7	8	3	0	0	18	12	5	1	0	0	0	18
66–75	6	6	1	1	0	14	8	3	1	2	0	0	14
76–85	4	1	0	0	0	5	4	1	0	0	0	0	5
86	1	0	0	0	0	1	1	0	0	0	0	0	1
Total	45	30	10	1	0	86	57	20	5		0	0	86

TABLE 3. Marital Experience of Females by Age: Woe 1962

Age in Years	All Females with Marital Experience									
	No. of marriages since birth					No. of divorces since birth				
	1	2	3	4	total	0	1	2	3	total
18–25	61	0	0	0	61	61	0	0	0	61
26–35	58	5	2	0	65	58	5	2	0	65
36–45	19	17	1	2	39	13	14	10	2	39
46–55	8	21	4	0	33	23	9	1	0	33
56–65	9	16	0	0	25	19	2	2	2	25
66–75	26	9	2	0	37	35	2	0	0	37
76–85	4	2	0	0	6	5	1	0	0	6
86	2	0	0	0	2	2	0	0	0	2
Total	187	70	9	2	268	216	33	15	4	268

TABLE 4. Marital Experience of Females by Age: Alakple 1962

Age in Years	All Females with Marital Experience										
	No. of marriages since birth					No. of divorces since birth					
	1	2	3	4	total	0	1	2	3	4	total
18–25	53	2	0	0	55	53	2	0	0	0	55
26–35	25	2	0	0	27	25	2	0	0	0	27
36–45	20	4	2	0	26	25	1	0	0	0	26
46–55	14	8	1	1	24	19	1	3	0	1	24
56–65	23	7	3	1	34	22	5	3	1	1	32
66–75	19	6	2	0	27	25	2	0	0	0	27
76–85	1	4	4	0	9	8	0	1	0	0	9
86	2	1	1	0	4	4	0	0	0	0	4
Total	157	34	13	2	206	181	13	7	1	2	204

TABLE 5. Mean Divorce per Head: Woe and Alakple 1962

Locality and Sex	Mean per Head
Alakple females	0·18 (38/206)
Alakple males	0·48 (42/86)
Woe females	0·28 (75/268)
Woe Males	0·66 (90/136)
Combined Figures: Woe and Alakple	Mean per Head
Females	0·23 (113/474)
Males	0·59 (132/222)

TABLE 6. Divorce Ratios: Woe

Ratio	Value	
Males only		
A	34·6%	(90/269)
B	40·7%	(90/221)
Females only		
A	20·7%	(75/362)
B	25·4%	(75/288)
Both sexes combined		
A	26·1%	(165/631)
B	32·3%	(165/509)

TABLE 7. Divorce Ratios: Alakple

Ratio	Value	
Males only		
A	30·2%	(42/139)
B	36·8%	(42/114)
Females only		
A	14·0%	(38/272)
B	18·0%	(38/210)
Both sexes combined		
A	19·4%	(80/411)
B	24·2%	(80/324)

TABLE 8. Divorce Ratios: Woe and Alakple Combined

Ratio	Value	
Males only		
A	30·34%	(132/435)
B	39·4%	(132/335)
Females only		
A	17·4%	(113/634)
B	22·7%	(113/498)
Both sexes combined		
A	22·9%	(245/1069)
B	29·4%	(245/833)

A. Divorce figures expressed as % of all marriages.
B. Divorce figures expressed as % of all marriages except those ended by death.

One general feature about divorce in Anlo is that it is initiated by women. The Ewe term for divorce is *atsugbegbe* that is, literally, 'refusing the husband'. It is said that a man may not refuse his wife but must be divorced by her, as it is believed that vengeance for his taking the action will be exacted of him by the spirits of his lineage ancestors, whose interest in large families he has violated. Related to this view is the belief that a boy accused by his lover of being responsible for her pregnancy, even though he is certain that the accusation is false, may not refuse, because if he did it would be held that he had refused a first child and hence would himself be punished, again by the dead, by never having other offspring.

There seems to be another reason why it is women and not men who must take the initiative in divorce. It will be seen later that one of the principal reasons for divorce is childlessness. This could be satified by further marriages. Marriages are potentially polygynous but not polyandrous, so that from the lineage point of view and that of the relatives it is unnecessary for a man to divorce his first wife before taking another. On the other hand a woman in the same predicament has no choice but to divorce before remarrying.

In the past it was possible to divorce without taking the matter to the courts. Kinsfolk of the spouses met together, discussed the marriage, and agreed among themselves on its dissolution. The party in the wrong was fined to *kpata* (pacify) the offended party. Today, however, while marriage is established without the knowledge of the Anlo Native Authorities, since there are neither marriage certificates nor registrations of any kind, divorce cases very often involve resort to the courts. The court hears the case, awards damages as appropriate, and, if it thinks fit, declares the couple divorced.

But even today it is possible and quite common to get divorce without going to the courts. The case may be referred to an elder of one of the spouses' lineages, and he dissolves the marriage.

A woman usually seeks divorce because of cruelty, desertion or childlessness. Cruelty often takes the form of beating. Anlo men are fond of beating their wives in quarrels. A wife may also be beaten for not cooking in time, for not coming back in time from a trading trip or for general disobedience. A woman's parents are always averse to the idea of a husband beating their daughter. The husband will naturally be warned, and even fined, several times, but if he remains obdurate the only thing is 'to take the wife from him', as it is put by the vulgar.

Desertion is another common ground, usually when a husband leaves his wife behind while going on a fishing expedition abroad without making adequate provision for her support. A variant of this ground is lack of support, which is different from the former only in the fact that here the husband refuses to or cannot, look after his wife though they are living together. Fifty-two per cent of divorced women alleged that lack of support and desertion were the principal causes of their divorce.

A husband's liability for the support of his wife is stated in specific terms. He is expected to *na asigbe* (i.e. give market-day money) to his wife. This is the money with which she provides food for the household. The actual amount given in any household depends on its size, the husband's financial position and the market conditions, and varies generally from 5s for a family of three to 10s for a family of eight in a 'market-week' of four days.

When I was there my calculations of family budgets showed that wives depending solely on this *asigbe* money needed a good deal of economy to make both ends meet. But many do not have to depend on that alone. Their husbands have fruit and vegetables in the garden and fish from periodic fishing trips. But these are not regular supplies. The only regular addition a wife makes to *asigbe* is from her own independent income.

One often hears wives complaining that their husbands give *asigbe* money at very long intervals, sometimes once in two months instead of once in four days. There were even more serious cases. In one instance a father of nine, who was being provided regularly with food by his wife, gave *asigbe* only twice in 1961.

Situations of this kind are likely to arise in polygynous families where a husband has attached himself to one wife to the neglect of the other or others. When it is found that the husband is not being fair to his wife, she may be taken away from him. Men do their best to support their wives, but in polygynous families, if a man finds himself unable to give *asigbe* regularly to all his wives he is guided in his choice by each wife's economic standing, the number of children she has and how regularly she provides him with food. But refusal, or rather inability, to give adequate *asigbe* is a social problem. At Woe the women's dancing group, *Nyayitoviawo*, even went to the length of composing a song about it, and what a popular song it proved to be! It runs:

Ne eɖe nyɔnua enue wòɖuna. . .
Ne eɖe nyɔnua avɔe wòtana. . .
Esi nedzoa fe nenie enye sia. . .?
'Matsɔ ɖonye daɖi. . .
'Wo abe ɖe metɔa. . .?
If you marry a woman she must eat. . .
If you marry a woman she must have clothes to wear. . .
How long is it since you deserted me. . .?
And if I remain your wife. . .
Don't you think others would think me worthless?

The implications of this song for marital stability are quite clear. If a husband fails to maintain his wife, she will be forced to seek divorce.

Another frequent cause of divorce is inherent in the institution of polygyny itself. The relationship between co-wives, as will be shown later, is always potentially explosive. A husband will have to be a big flatterer to maintain the balance of his affection between them. This is not always easy. Love is not amenable to mathematical calculations. Neither is the congeniality of the wives to the husband likely to be exactly equal. A man must needs love one wife more than the other, however much he may try to behave to the contrary. The result is friction. In the long run it is the fittest, naturally his favourite, who survives. Of the 113 women divorcees only 19, about 16·5 per cent had no co-wife when they were divorced

Childlessness is another important cause of divorce. A sterile husband does not find favour with his wife or with her relatives, who want her to have children to care for her and themselves in old age. A barren woman is in the same difficulty with her husband's relatives. Sterility and impotence are both shameful diseases, and men do not easily admit to them, especially the latter. Anlo clearly distinguish between sexual vigour or desire, *lili*, and the power of procreation, *vidzidzi*.[1] They know that a man who is sterile, *tsidzẽnyela*, i.e. 'producer of coloured semen', lacks the latter but is not necessarily deficient in the former. (It is said that the fertile sperm is white and the unproductive coloured.) A case in point is Wotɔga, who up to 1962 had married nine wives, all of whom left him without issue. The uncharitable believed that

[1] *Vidzidzi* here refers to 'the ability to produce a child'. This usage is to be distinguished from the more common usage of the term as 'childbirth'.

he was impotent, but others were prepared to give him the benefit of the doubt. No one except his wives knew the true position. He himself maintained, however, that he was not impotent. The *Ametutu*, impotent man, lacks sexual vigour and hence automatically the procreative power.

If medicines fail to cure a husband's sterility, and it is suspected that the trouble lies with him rather than his wife, she will be advised to leave him and try her luck elsewhere. But sometimes a woman remains barren while sleeping with a fertile man. Anlo explain this by *vumasɔmasɔ*, or 'disagreement of blood'. Credence is given to this theory because when a barren couple separate, their subsequent marriages sometimes bear fruit.

Barrenness is a great social handicap. When it is believed that a change of partners may remedy it, little time is wasted to bring about the change. The seriousness with which Anlo regard barrenness may be found in the words of this informant:

We regard childlessness as most unfortunate. The procreation of children is the principal function of life in this world. A dead tree is resuscitated by its own seed. So it is with us human beings. When we die, our children replace us. Our concern about the disease is demonstrated in no uncertain manner. When an adult dies childless special rites are performed on the dead body. A dead man has a stick thrust into his genital organ, and *nyakpe* leaves are tied on that of the woman, with the injunction, 'you must not come into the world in this manner again'.

The most important single reason for which a man can divorce his wife is adultery. But he will not divorce her if he has great affection for her, and especially if the fault is not her own. In adultery cases it is the adulterer, not the adulteress, who is fined by the courts. This is based on the reasoning that the adulterer has violated someone's rights in the woman, while the woman is more of a victim than an offender.

It is difficult to accuse a wife of adultery if she herself does not admit it, since coitus never has a direct witness, so that unless the culprits are caught *in flagrante delicto* the husband could not take action and hope to be successful. I never witnessed any case of a couple being caught in this state. Information on the occurrence of adultery in specific instances was based on village gossip and accusation in the courts, and not on admissions by those concerned, who are naturally very reticent. If, however, a woman is bent on leaving her husband, she may leave his house on any flimsy excuse and go to her parents' home, where she can make public her relationship with a lover, and thus provoke the husband into taking action.

Today divorce proceedings are not always initiated by women. Besides adultery, for which a man could initiate divorce even in the past, a man can now divorce his wife on a number of grounds, namely laziness, quarrelling, the interference of affines and anything considered to be contrary to accepted wifely behaviour. Usually it is a combination of these which make divorce necessary.

Case No. 3

Yaovi married Mesi as his second wife. Soon afterwards a great quarrel took place between his wives, in which he ignorantly took her side. Mesi by making unfounded allegations of misconduct against the first wife, forced her to leave Yaovi for another man. Mesi, whose main aim was to remain alone with Yaovi, became more and more impossible as soon as it was rumoured that Yaovi was about to marry another woman. Her behaviour towards her affines too became eccentric. Things came to a head when Yaovi's mother's paternal half-brother gave his daughter to him in marriage. Mesi was so infuriated at the idea that when she next met this girl at the village well she picked a quarrel with her and inflicted such a severe beating on her that the girl's face was badly swollen. Yaovi, until then unconvinced of Mesi's ill-temper and unpardonable misbehaviour, decided at last to take the most obvious course. He divorced her in the village chiefs' court.

Sometimes a man just gets tired of his wife without any fault of hers. Such a man does not need any specific reason for getting rid of her. Since he cannot take her into court without good reason, he may resort to all sorts of subterfuge to provoke her to take action. His principal weapon is a technique of making himself insupportable should a court case arise. A wife in such a position is given no presents and is provided with, if anything at all, only the barest necessities. He absents himself from home to go visiting when it is her turn to sleep with him, neither eating her food nor having much to do with her in other respects. Such treatment is the strongest disciplinary force that can be brought to bear on a woman. In a compound where many wives strive for the favour of their husband, the material for divorce is not difficult to find in these circumstances, because the wives who are in favour lose no chance to taunt those who live unnoticed by the husband. In most Anlo compounds a woman who in the opinion of the husband merits treatment of this kind is also beaten if she breaks any of the ordinary rules of wifely conduct. This being the harshest method of discipline, a man who takes a thorough dislike to a wife will most certainly employ it much more often than he would otherwise have done. He may even go further. At dances or funerals he may intentionally get drunk, and insult his parents-in-law and other affines when he meets them. In due course a family council is called by her parents to discuss his behaviour. He ignores the summons and by his action compels the council to pronounce a divorce.

A man who takes to this behaviour need not necessarily be cruel or foolish by nature. He only simulates this attitude to get ride of this wife.

It is left entirely to the wife and her people whether they take action against a husband who is thought to have offended her. Some women in spite of many harsh treatments do not take divorce action, either because of their great affection for their husbands or because social or economic considerations militate against the desirability of divorce. Others who are more sensitive to such treatment seize the least chance to bring their husbands to book.

Sometimes a couple separate without any formal divorce. The process most frequently begins with the woman leaving her husband's house with her children, if she has any, for that of her parents, complaining of maltreatment, lack of support or disagreements with co-wives. She disregards her husband's entreaties to return, and remains there unless her parents are willing or able to persuade her to do so. She starts informing potential suitors that she is not going back to her husband, while dismissing as false any arguments favourable to his point of view. She then attaches herself to a lover and as time goes on there comes a visible sign that they have been sleeping together. This is not divorce. There is only formal divorce when after leaving the husband an attempt is made, normally by her parents, to thrash out the disagreements

and only when it is agreed that divorce is the only solution. It
should be mentioned that though the initiative for divorce is
usually taken by women, some of them do not seek a legal dissolution before they attach themselves to new lovers. The effect
of this practice is to transfer the burden of the offence from the
woman to her new lover. This disregard of the family tribunals
and local courts is easy because of the supremacy of biological
paternity. The husband need not renounce any claims in her
before transferring paternity to children she might have by the
lover.

It is for the husband to choose whether he will claim damages
(*tɔ du*) from the new lover. If he does not like his wife to leave him,
he will prefer to claim damages, which in effect will mean formal
divorce. My interviews with men in this situation give the impression that many of them are not anxious to press their claims
unless they have incurred heavy debts on their wives' behalf. But
some who have the law on their side quickly seize their advantage.
A husband is most likely to take action against the seducer of his
wife if she has not been long married to him, and if he gave a
substantial marriage payment, but these considerations alone are
not decisive. Many factors work in combination, as the following
case will show.

Case No. 4

Gbato's marriage to Bensa, a proud middle-aged man, was her
first and his third, his two previous marriages having been ended
by death and divorce respectively. From the outset her mother
was against the marriage, because he is given to bullying his wives.
On Gbato's own insistence, however, the marriage was concluded
with a payment totalling nearly £40. But when she was expecting
her first baby, Gbato, who is not very presentable by Anlo standards, began to show some dirty habits, much to the dislike of her
husband. This was fuelled by a stealing case in which she was
involved after her first child was born. After this incident, Bensa
refused to visit her for nearly a year, and it was to his great relief
that she was impregnated by a schoolboy. Naturally he didn't
raise a finger at this.

It must be made clear that it is considered a great disgrace for a
man to have his wife taken away from him either by her parents

or by a seducer. A husband normally guards his rights in his wife, and only serious maladjustments result in, or create, the atmosphere for a break-up.

10. SOCIAL STRUCTURE, MARRIAGE PAYMENT AND DIVORCE

The break-down of any given marriage depends on a variety of causes, including the economic situation as well as maladjustment between the spouses. These factors, operating adventitiously together in different cases, produce an overall divorce rate which does not differ much within the same society from year to year unless something dramatic takes place. However, certain major determinants of divorce rates can be isolated in different societies to explain their trend, following the method used by Durkheim[1] in his study of suicide. Durkheim argues that a variety of factors affects the incidence of suicide, but the rate is determined in different countries by a few major social variables. Divorce may also be studied in this way. In assessing the causes of any one divorce case it will be necessary to take into account all possible relevant factors operating in the society. This we have tried to do in the last section, where we mentioned as the main causes of divorce adultery, childlessness, desertion, lack of economic support for women and cruelty. When, however, it comes to the understanding of the trend of divorce in general in Anlo, the influence of the major determinants, as recommended by Durkheim, becomes of paramount importance.

The first application of this Durkheimian methodology to the analysis of divorce rates was made by Gluckman in 1950.[2] His original argument was that kinship was the dominant feature in traditional African social life, and therefore the kinship structure must have a decisive effect on the divorce trend. This led him to put forward his famous hypothesis that divorce is rare and difficult in tribes with corporate patrilineages, such as the Zulu and Nuer, and common among those which are either matrilineal or bilateral, such as the Lozi. Although he recognized that other aspects of the social system, such as legal institutions and moral values, could have some influence on marital stability, he did not consider these factors decisive.

[1] 1952.   [2] Gluckman, 1950, pp. 167–206.

Since that time Schneider, Leach, and Fallers,[1] among others, have taken issue with Gluckman and offered modifications to his original hypothesis. Schneider drew attention to the need to distinguish between conjugal stability and the stability of jural relations which arise out of marriage because there is, for instance, 'a greater degree of probability that a Nuer man, once married, will remain undivorced, than there is that his wife will remain with him...'[2] This distinction is necessary because of the rule common to the Nuer and some other patrilineal societies, that a woman may remain her husband's legal wife while having children by copulating with lovers 'in the bush'.[3] Gluckman later admitted that he 'dealt only with the jural stability' of marriage but recognized the need for working with two rates, (1) a rate for jural divorce of spouses and (2) a rate for conjugal separation.[4] The distinction is, however, not crucial in our discussion, because in Anlo conjugal separation is usually followed by legal divorce.[5]

In this section an attempt will be made to relate the Anlo material to Gluckman's original hypothesis and its later modifications. We shall then consider certain other factors which, though not necessarily extraneous to the kinship structure, were not directly discussed in Gluckman's framework.

It has been seen that, although the Anlo have corporate agnatic lineages, they lack some of the institutions, such as the levirate, sororate, sororal polygyny, and the 'house-property complex' which, according to Gluckman, help to perpetuate the marriage tie in patrilineal societies, notably among the Zulu and the Nuer. Anlo marriage also does not transfer rights *in genetricem*. The absence of these institutions makes the Anlo kinship structure more akin to the Lozi than the Zulu type where marriage 'transfers a woman's fertility absolutely to her husband's agnatic kin group' and 'once a woman is betrothed her fiancé's kin have a

---

[1] Schneider, 1953; Leach, 1957, pp. 50–7; L. A. Fallers, 1957, pp. 106–23.
[2] Schneider, 1953, p. 55.   [3] Evans-Pritchard, 1951, p. 115.
[4] Gluckman, 1953, p. 142.
[5] Cases were however being encountered where conjugal separation was not followed by legal divorce. These cases have not been treated as divorce because the spouses gave conflicting reports of their relationships. In most of such cases it was the wives who maintained that they were separated while the husbands held that they were still living as husband and wife. Though these could not be categorized as either a divorce or married state it was found necessary to find the incidence of such cases (2·4 per cent of all marriages at Alakple and 3·5 per cent of all marriages at Woe).

right to claim her in ghost marriage'.[1] But the absence of these
institutions in Anlo and Lozi social structures does not have the
same effects on their divorce rates. In Anlo divorce was not frequent in the old days, but Lozi marriage has always been unstable.

Our main contention here is that the difference in the divorce
rates of Lozi and old Anlo is due partly to the different moral and
legal codes of the two societies and partly to the attitudes of the
traditional goverments to the problem. In traditional Anlo a
seducer was punished by death, while for a woman her adultery
constituted a grave public disgrace. Among the Lozi, however,
Gluckman[2] reports that even in the past 'should a man take a liking
to someone else's wife he will have an interview with her and
bring her home'. Lozi women were very loose.

It must be admitted at once that in Anlo the presence of the
agnatic lineages may have been responsible for the rigid attitude
of the traditional government towards sexual immorality. This,
however, remains to be proved. At the same time the difference
between this system and that of the Zulu is that in Anlo the
restraining factors on the breaking of the marital bond were not
inherent in the kinship structure or principles of filiation or
descent as such, but were introduced by the power of the government. This view supports Gluckman's explanation of the present
high divorce rates among the Azande, who were 'organized on
father-right but without the agnatic lineage'. The Azande had
rare divorce in the past, but it is rife at present, and he suggests
that the reason for this change in the rate may be that in the past
'the state power prevented women from leaving their husbands if
they wanted to .. when that authority was restricted by British
occupation divorce became rife'.[3]

If this view is accepted, the difference in the rates in old and
present Anlo will be accounted for partly by the influence of the
state power in the past and its curtailment after the establishment
of British rule. The acceptance of this view presupposes the presence in the Anlo traditional kinship structure of elements of
marital instability which remained dormant in the past only
because of the traditional government. It will therefore be necessary to have a further look at some of these 'elements of instability' in the kinship structure. This will require the analysis of the
whole kinship structure with the divorce question in mind.

[1] Gluckman, 1950, p. 189.   [2] *Ibid.*, p. 181.   [3] Gluckman, 1950, p. 203.

The first point which comes to mind is the strength of the sibling bond. As both Audrey Richards[1] and Leach[2] have observed, the marital bond is likely to be weak where the sibling bond is very strong. The relationship between siblings has already been discussed at length. It may be mentioned here in addition that the continued closeness of the sibling bond even after brother and sister have been married is reinforced by the fact that a woman remains under the protection of her paternal and maternal ancestors and the religious cults which she joined with her siblings before marriage. This provides not only the opportunity for frequent meetings between her and her brother but also a community of interests supported by supernatural sanctions. These sanctions are further strengthened by Anlo funeral customs. Though the husband has certain rituals to perform at his wife's funeral, the corpse belongs to her own lineage, and the management and organization of the mortuary ceremonies are entirely their responsibility. A married woman therefore has one foot in her parental home and another in her husband's, and the problem that faces every husband now and then is how to reconcile his affection for his sister with the love he owes through marriage to his wife. The wife is usually regarded by her husband's sister as the person most likely to poison his mind against her. Indeed many a quarrel between spouses results from what a wife considers to be interference by her husband's sister. Also the husband's sister, because of her inheritance rights in the property he uses to maintain his wife, looks on her in this regard as an outsider. Yet kinship obligations require that a man must never support his wife against his own sister. 'A bad sibling is like the palm leaf of the borassus tree, it may serve as a shelter during the rains.' In addition, after a quarrel with her husband a woman is sure to get from her brother any economic advantages she might forfeit as a result of the quarrel. This ready presence of the brother as an alternative support for the wife does nothing to strengthen the marital bond in any way, and indeed makes a close marital bond difficult, as will be shown in the next chapter. This view closely resembles that of Fallers. In his study of the Basoga he put forward the view that 'where a woman ... is socially absorbed into her husband's lineage, patriliny tends to stabilize marriage; where a wife is not so absorbed and thus remains a member of the lineage into which

[1] 1950, p. 250.   [2] Leach, 1957, p. 53.

she was born, patriliny tends to divide marriage by dividing the loyalties of spouses.'[1] But this single cause explanation of a complicated phenomenon such as marital instability is far from satisfactory. It is true that the non-incorporation of women into their husbands' lineages after marriage may strengthen the sibling bond at the expense of the marital bond. But this alone cannot be the decisive factor, as our several examples have shown.

The relation of co-wives also has an adverse effect on the marital bond in Anlo. The absence of tension-reducing mechanisms, such as sororal polygyny and the sororate in the co-wife relationship, is another threat to it. Though separate rooms are provided for each wife, joint activities with the husband, and quarrels resulting from troubles among their children, bring co-wives into frequent direct confrontation. The trouble between Yaovi and Mesi is a case in point (Case 3). Yaovi's first wife would not have left him but for Mesi's mischief-making and Mesi herself would not have been dismissed if the quarrel had not arisen over the next wife.

The filiation of children and the social position of adulterine children are other factors which may affect the stability of marriage. The separation of spouses is perpetuated and easily transformed into divorce when children are born out of wedlock, because of the supremacy of biological fatherhood as the basis of filiation. First, marriage loses its function as an important prerequisite for the establishment of legal families, since procreation of legitimate children does not necessarily have to be a product of legally constituted unions. Secondly, since the taking back by the husband of an adulteress who had had a child by a lover is frowned upon, an adultery which is fruitful must in most cases eventually lead to a new union. But in the past adultery, a common prelude to many a marital separation, was severely punished, sometimes by death. Without such drastic sanctions the atmosphere created by the principles of filiation might have led to more adultery and consequently a greater incidence of divorce. Our view is that it was only the attitude of the traditional authority that kept in check the unstable marital tendencies which filiation on the sole basis of biological fatherhood gives rise to.

Another cause of instability inherent in the marriage system is the initiative of parents in the choice of marriage partners. We

[1] Fallers, 1957, p. 121.

have seen that this is why most Anlo marriages are not love-matches. Parental interference imposes on girls and youths a choice which they have little power to oppose at the time of the marriage, when they are young and dependent. Such a marriage ends in divorce as soon as one of the spouses is in a position to precipitate it. Though a girl is expected to agree to a proposal before the marriage is arranged, respect for parental authority and the pressures often brought to bear on her make her independence only nominal.

II. CONCLUSION

With Gluckman's theory in mind we have tried to show that, though the Anlo have agnatic lineages like the Zulu, they lack some of the institutions which, in the latter, perpetuate the legal aspect of the marital bond. Moreover, certain aspects of Anlo social structure, as well as some of their values, make divorce basically easier than in many patrilineal societies. Despite these differences the Anlo have great regard for marriage stability. In the past, helped by strong paternal authority and the power of the traditional government, it was possible to enforce marriage stability through strong moral and legal codes. But since this was imposed by the political authority and was inherent neither in the principles of filiation nor in the rights conferred by marriage, the disappearance of the traditional state power under British occupation has given free scope to the inherent elements of instability.

In addition, certain changes in marriage ceremonial might be held responsible for the increased incidence of divorce. The elaborate ceremonies of the past included the *eto* powdering, the consummation and the bride's seclusion for several months during which she was subjected to advice on ideal wifely behaviour. This elaboration of ceremonial, as Gibbs has shown in a recent article on the Kpelle of Liberia,[1] emphasizes the importance of the marriage to the couple and their kinsfolk. It also served in the past to bring home to the married pair the seriousness and solemnity of their undertaking. But today the *eto* powdering and the seclusion no longer form part of the ceremony. The result is that it has lost its message to the couple and their kinsfolk and its function for society.

[1] Gibbs, 1963.

The influence of supernatural beliefs on the marriage must also be mentioned. The religious sanctions which made the powder the legalizing substance in the old marriage rites stemmed from the mystical powers associated with the *eto* tree, from which it is made. *Eto* is said to have been associated with one of the gods of the Anlo when they were at Hogbe, the Ewe name for their place of origin. Pieces of the bark of this tree were used there as the official seal for concluding agreements. On their departure from Hogbe they brought with them branches of the tree, some of which can be seen to this day. In view of its importance in legal and religious spheres it was used to give legality to marriage rites. That is why the *eto* powdering occupied such an important position in the old marriage ceremony. The ring, which is replacing the *eto* powder, has not the same religious backing.

Gluckman also suggests that marriage payments fall in value with decreasing dominance of patrilineal descent, but he regards the influence of property on marriage stability as secondary. He claims that 'it is rare divorce which allows high payment rather than high marriage payment which prevents divorce'.[1] To this view Leach[2] has added the fact that 'high' and 'low' marriage payments are relative terms and must be related to the economic resources of each society. This point is very important, because in view of the differing economic systems of African societies it is impossible to speak of high or low marriage payment in absolute terms. In Anlo, though the items making up the marriage payment have changed considerably since the turn of the century, considering the relative cost of living, little difference may be observed in value between the old and the new payments. To raise £25 for a major undertaking such as marriage is not beyond the means of an ordinary Anlo youth. A year's fishing operations may yield a net income of about £100, while onion farmers get rather more. With a little thrift many youths should therefore be in a position to raise this amount with ease. Moreover, the differences allowed in the value of the payments from case to case, especially in kinship marriages, make payment easier than if there had been a fixed amount. Another element of flexibility in the rules governing the marriage payment is that though the seduction fee must be paid in court on the same day, the refund of the

[1] Gluckman, 1950, p. 192.   [2] 1953, p. 180.

marriage payment by a man who has married an adulteress may be made in instalments, say within one farming season of about three months. On this score, therefore, the figures seem to support the Gluckman hypothesis. But the problem still remains complicated, since so many variables go to determine the rate.

4

The Family

I. THE HOUSEHOLD IN ITS PHYSICAL SETTING

Anlo young men become independent of their parents at marriage. This independence is emphasized by the Anlo ideal that a young man should have a house of his own before thinking of marriage. Invariably he does. In this chapter we shall try to describe the physical structure of the homestead, the kinship ties of its inmates and the interpersonal relations which obtain within it.

The traditional house forms in Anlo can be seen in old pictures and illustrations in missionary records.[1] Some description of them can also be found in the works of Spieth[2] and Westermann.[3] Usually a house consisted of mud and thatched rectangular huts, surrounded by rectangular walls of neatly woven coconut palm leaves (*kloba*). Each compound was clearly demarcated from the others, though sometimes compounds belonging to members of the same cluster of a lineage might have joint side-fences linking them.

A man built one hut for himself and his wife. If he was polygynous he would build one for himself and one for each of his wives. All huts were divided into two or more apartments by walls of mud, in such a way that each hut had a living room, *akpata*, and one or more *xɔdɔme*, bedrooms or *xɔga*, big rooms as bedrooms are sometimes called. The typical hut for a monogamous family comprised two bedrooms opening into a common living room (Figs. 12 and 13). The separate hut of a wife in a polygynous family was invariably a two-roomed hut comprising a living room opening into a bedroom. Every house had a kitchen, *dzodofe*, and a bathroom, *afekpɔe*. In polygynous houses each wife had a kitchen to herself. All huts opened into a yard and were surrounded by a rectangular fence about six feet high.

Developments have been continually bringing changes in

[1] E.g. Wiegrabe, 1938, pp. 15, 54.   [2] 1906, pp. 130–1.   [3] 1935, *passim*.

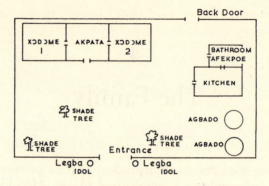

FIG. 12. The plan of a homestead: monogamous
family (1)

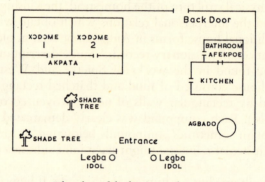

FIG. 13. The plan of the homestead: monogamous
family (2)

housing styles. In the latter half of the nineteenth century the
Bremen and Basle missionaries introduced a fashion for wooden
houses built on two storeys with wide eaves and balconies. More
recently concrete houses and storeyed houses have been erected by
private persons, commercial firms, Government and mission
authorities. The mud houses also now differ considerably in size
and complexity. In Keta I counted only three mud houses, all the
remainder having been replaced by concrete cement bungalows
and storeyed houses. But in the more remote villages, such as the
islands in the Keta Lagoon and settlements further inland, mud
huts similar to the old buildings are still common.

Whatever form the house takes, the kitchen occupies a special position. It is usually built on the leeward side of the main huts to prevent smoke from disturbing the latter and since winds are normally south-westerly it is built east of the huts. For the wife the kitchen is the centre of her life. It signifies her status as a wife. Foodstuffs, cooking utensils and other household materials are kept there. Besides using it for cooking and dining she receives her visitors there, and her neatness is judged by the way she keeps it.

But in a tropical climate, especially in dry weather, it is often more convenient to be out of doors, and it is the open space in front of the kitchen, especially if the roof projects over it, which provides shade for visitors. Shade trees are also planted inside and outside the compound to provide shelter. Open hospitality is an obligation of Anlo social life, and the living space is flexible enough to make visitors welcome.

A man entertains his visitors in his *akpata*, living room, and also under the shade provided by the eaves and trees. Children belong to the huts of their mother. Some sleep with her in her bedroom, others in her *akpata*. In a monogamous family the wife's apartment usually falls into the hands of her children, since she often spends her nights in her husband's. In a polygynous house a woman may spend her turn with the husband either in her own room or in his.

In many houses on the littoral one finds square or circular structures of mud about five feet in diameter and four feet high with roofs of thatch. These are *agbadowo* (sing. *agbado*) which are used by women to smoke fish in commercial quantities. They are also used as shelter for poultry in the night.

Another characteristic feature of Anlo homesteads is the *legba* mud idols erected in front of the houses of members and owners of *vodu* (cult) or *trɔwo* (deities).

In many settlements one can distinguish two different styles of housing. In the original village residential areas and the older sections of the settlements known as *afedome*, lineage homes, lack of space makes spatial expansion of compounds difficult. This is because the lineage founders acquired these residential areas for a much smaller number of members than exist today and all suitable land nearby has been taken by other lineages. The result is that for some time now many compounds in the *afedome* are already crowded to capacity and even beyond through the building of more and more huts. Compounds here are small and closely packed together.

As already noted, this overcrowding makes it necessary for some members of the lineage to move out of the *afedome* and found new residential areas on their lineage lands outside the original home. These new residential areas, called *kɔfewo* (sing. *kɔfe*), may be as far as one mile from the *afedome*, though many are much nearer. The distance of a man's *kɔfe* from his *afedome* is dependent on the distance of available and suitable lineage land from the *afedome*.[1] Because land is normally abundant in the *kɔfe* areas, compounds here are more spacious than in the *afedome*. Here every homestead has a large expanse of land round it planted with such crops as maize and cassava. Everywhere, both in the *afedome* and *kɔfe*, coconut trees abound. *Kɔfe* settlements are not regarded as independent villages, but as sections of the parent village or town.

Not all villages have enough land for use of their surplus population in this way. This applies especially to island settlements. Here overcrowding has no outlet to any available land nearby, and in case of acute shortage of land complete emigration from the village is the only solution. In these villages the compounds are much smaller and the population very dense.

Woe and Alakple are good examples of the two residential and housing patterns. Woe is on the littoral, and while its *afedome* occupies an area of just about thirty acres, its 3450 inhabitants are now spread over an area of over three square miles. Alakple on the other hand is an island in the Keta Lagoon. Its total area is a little less than one square mile, of which only half is suitable for human habitation. All Alakple's 1351 inhabitants are crowded into this space. The contrast between the spatial distribution of the houses in the two settlements can be further illustrated by comparison of the number of houses in them. In 1960 there were 541 houses spread over the three square miles at Woe, and no less than 242 squeezed into Alakple's small area.

In the following discussion every building, whether it is a single hut, fenced or unfenced, mud or concrete, which is looked upon

---

[1] In the old residential areas lineages are localized, in the sense that the houses of members occupy a continuous stretch of land and are visibly demarcated from those of other lineages. Outside the *afedome* the lineages have bush and farmland scattered here and there within the village boundary. It is these bush areas which are now being converted into *kɔfe* residences. One effect of this is to disturb the localized nature of lineages. Since some lineages have bush land in more than one place, and there is no rule as to where a man should build his *kɔfe*, it is possible to find many colonies of the same lineage in different sectors of the village.

by the inhabitants themselves as a unit, is termed a dwelling. The essential features of a dwelling are its separateness and independence. A dwelling is separate and independent if a person or group of persons can isolate themselves from others in the community for the purpose of sleeping, co-operating in its upkeep, preparing and taking their meals or protecting themselves from hazards of climate such as storms and floods. The inmates form the dwelling group, and it is this unit that we shall refer to as the household.

2. THE COMPOSITION OF THE HOUSEHOLD GROUP

In every society the kinship ties between members of a household are determined by the rules of post-marital residence. However, the uncertainties and complexities of social life make it impossible for the kinship composition of every dwelling in a community to be uniform. Thus in a patrilineal society with ideally virilocal residence, this ideal never attains 100 per cent. This is because in a society with limited welfare services to care for orphans, the disabled, the poor, the unemployed and the handicapped, the relationships that make possible the obligation to provide shelter and food extend beyond the ideal of a man, his wife and unmarried children. There is also the question of the degree of freedom of choice of postmarital residence. Nevertheless the actual residence pattern will approximate in varying degrees to the ideal. The extent to which this approximation has been attained can only be determined by quantitative analysis, which will be attempted in the following paragraphs.

The analysis is based on a random sample of 196 households in Woe and 168 in Alakple. These households may be divided into those with male and those with female heads. The latter numbered 84 (42·9 per cent) in Woe and 76 (45;3 per cent) in Alakple. The headship of households was determined in terms of age and authority structure. Where married couples formed the nucleus of the household unit, the husband was taken as the automatic head. Where the household was built around an adult man he was taken as the head. In households with no adult males, the oldest woman was regarded as the head. The figures show some significant differences in the composition of households headed by men and those headed by women. These differences will be considered presently.

In Woe all except 6 of the 112 households headed by men were built around nuclear families, while 48 (about 42 per cent) were composed of the head's simple family alone. In fact the household consisting of a man, his wife and unmarried children was regarded by the Anlo as the ideal, and this is still largely the case today, though it is not always realized in practice.

From the remaining 58 per cent of the male-headed households it is possible to discover the kind of relationships which in practice seem to carry with them the obligations for the provision of food and shelter.

There were only six households in which the dependents were not kin of the head or any member of his family; five were headed by teachers, and the other by a stranger in the town. The unrelated dependants were described as *gbɔvi*, or attendants, all young boys and girls between the ages of eight and fourteen, who helped with the housework and attended school in return. The keeping of distant relatives and unrelated children as *gbɔvi* of this kind is a common practice among middle class families throughout Ghana.

Kinsfolk in the household who were not members of the head's own simple family seemed to fall into four main groups: head's siblings and their children, head's parents, head's children's children, and affines. There were only three old mothers and two old fathers living as dependents of adult sons. The men were incapacitated and were being looked after by their sons. All the women were widows. Other old women living as dependants were eight affines, widows of the heads' brothers, but not remarried to the latter, however. They were living there because they had no adult sons or daughters to care for them. Their husbands died when they were too old to maintain households by themselves, and they decided to remain in their marital homes.

The dependants of ten heads included relatives of their wives, mostly school-children whose parents were away in Abidjan. It was stated that they would return to their parents' compounds when the latter returned. In fact, I was around when some of the parents came back, and they were immediately joined by these children. Other affines included relatives of the head's wives married from other settlements, who were living in Woe during term-time because of the educational facilities there. The boarding-out of children of school-going age with relatives of any kind is quite common in Ghana wherever there is a good school.

From these figures it is clear that the attachment of young affines to these households is the result of special conditions such as the absence of their parents and the quest for educational facilities. Their presence in these households is purely temporary.

Twenty-seven heads had younger brothers and sisters living with them, either because their parents were away on fishing expeditions or because their parents were divorced or their mothers widowed. Most of these dependants were unmarried. This was certainly true of all the youths. Three of the sisters had children but were unmarried, while six were married to men who went abroad. The latter were temporary cases, because they would go back to their husbands' houses as soon as they come back. All the women, both married and unmarried, who were living with brothers admitted that they were there only because their mothers were not alive or were not in town at that time. They would have preferred living with parents to living with their married brothers. This view underlines further the tensions which mark the relations between a woman and her brothers' wives especially if they happen to live together.

TABLE 9. Kinship Ties of Household Members with Male Heads
(Members of Nuclear Family Excluded)

Relationship	Woe		Alakple	
	No.	%	No.	%
Parents	5	2·9	3	3·2
Siblings and their Children	72	41·9	34	35·8
Affines	37	21·5	12	12·6
Children's Children	34	19·8	36	37·9
Other relatives	24	13·9	10	10·5
Totals	172	100·0	95	100·0

Siblings' children living with male heads were fairly equally divided between brothers' and sisters' children. Thirty-three households included such relatives.

The only households composed of members resembling an extended family were those in which married and unmarried children and their children were living with the head. There were only eleven households of this kind at Woe and twelve at Alakple, and in all but one the head's children were daughters. The only man in this category was a young man of 22 whose wife had died leaving a two-year old baby who was being cared for by his aged mother. He said he did not want to live alone and so had left his own house to live with his parents. Seven of the daughters did not want to live with their husband because he had his first wife with him.

It is now quite common for a young wife to remain in her parental home for some time after marriage, especially if her husband already has other wives living with him. Others prefer to have the first child in the parents' house before moving to the husband's, because it is thought that the first travail needs great attention, for which the young mother's own mother's presence at the time of the pains is considered necessary. Many such women leave their parental homes soon after the first birth, while others stay on if there is no pressure from the husbands. A wife is also likely to remain in her parents' house if she is the youngest daughter of parents who are old and need assistance in the home. Other women found with their children in their parents' homes were those whose husbands had left them behind when going abroad.

In the 48 households at Woe composed entirely of members of the nuclear family there were seven married daughters and four married young men. The four young men had just married and had built their own houses, but they wanted their wives to move in before they left their parents. The married women were in identical situations. They were newly-wed girls who were preparing to leave soon for their husbands' houses. There were also three young women living with their parents but spending the night and one or two days of the week with their husbands. Sleeping with the husband in this way is called *ahiaxɔdɔdɔ* (lit. sleeping in a lover's room). *Ahiaxɔdɔdɔ* has become common with the abandonment of the seclusion ceremony. It will be recalled that traditionally, immediately after the marriage, a wife had to live in seclusion in her husband's house for about six months. Nowadays the bride instead starts sleeping with her husband while still in her parents' house, before finally moving to his house.

Not all households were dependent on male heads, and it is now necessary to examine the composition of those dependent on females. There were 84 such households, 42·9 per cent of the total sample at Woe. The most striking feature about them was the difference in the type of kinsfolk composing their membership. Only 30 per cent of the 201 dependants were the heads' own children, as compared with 61·1 per cent in households with male heads. On the other hand, the heads' grandchildren formed 48·7 per cent, compared with 20 per cent in male-headed households.

These differences are to be explained partly by the ages of female household heads. Of the 84 such household heads only 15 were below forty years of age. As a result many of their children had been married and moved into their marital homes. The ages of the female heads affected their overall marital status too. Fifty-one of them were either widows or divorcees. Twenty had their husbands away in Abidjan, while four, though married, were living in their parents' houses, where they became heads because their parents had died and their brothers had established their own households. Six women were living with their husbands in houses built by themselves. In all six cases the husbands were not natives of Woe. Uxorilocal marriage is not only disapproved, it is considered very contemptible of a husband to move into his wife's house. In only one case did I find a native of Woe in uxorilocal marriage.

But a woman need not be widowed or divorced before finding herself at the head of a household. Many had remained in their parents' homes after marriage for one or other of the reasons mentioned above and became household heads after the death of their parents. As we have seen, this is likely to happen when a woman's husband has another wife living with him. Such women do not have to set up their own households. They emerge as heads when the death of their parents have left them in charge of the houses.

TABLE 10. Female-headed Households: Classification of Members' Ties with Head

Relationship	Woe		Alakple	
	No.	%	No.	%
Own children	60	30·0	103	41·2
Daughter's children	75	37·3	67	27·0
Son's Children	23	11·4	17	7·0
Siblings and their children	11	5·3	25	10·0
Affines	20	10·0	20	8·1
Husbands	6	3·0	11	4·4
Others	6	3·0	6	2·3
Totals	201	100·0	249	100·0

As with the male-headed households, all the adult children were either unmarried daughters with children or married daughters

and their children who were living with their mothers, either
because their husbands had left the village or because they were
second wives. The marital status of the female head also accounts
for some of the differences between the figures of their dependants
and those of male-headed houses. Only 10 per cent of the persons
dependent on female households were affines. This is less than half
the percentage of affines in male-headed households. The obvious
explanation is that a widow or divorcee in many cases brings her
children by previous marriages to her new husband's house. A
man also accepts relatives of his wife as dependants when they are
in difficulties. Some women extend the same hospitality to their
husbands' kinsmen, but the decisive factor in the difference between the figures seems to be the large proportion of female heads
who were divorcees and widows. A divorced woman living
independently, or who has returned to her parents' home, is most
unlikely to accept as dependants in her house any relatives of her
divorced husband other than her own children. Similarly, only
special circumstances would make it necessary for a widow to
have the relatives of her dead husband as her dependants. Consequently the few affines in these houses were found where the
heads had been managing the houses for their absent husbands.

Daughters' children in female-headed households exceeded
sons' children in a ratio of about three to one. This was probably
because most of these were children of the daughters of the head
who were themselves living with their mothers. An adult son as a
rule does not live in his parents' house, and his children live with
their grandmother only if he himself has gone abroad, has died
or has been asked by the mother to allow some of his children to
live with her.

TABLE 11. Age and Marital Status of Female Household Heads: Woe

Age Group	Unmarried	Married	Widow	Divorced	Total
20–24	0	0	0	0	0
25–30	0	0	0	0	0
31–40	2	11	2	0	15
41–50	1	14	0	5	20
51–60	0	1	7	9	17
61–	0	4	26	2	32
Total	3	30	35	16	84

TABLE 12. Age and Marital Status of Female Household Heads: Alakple

Age Group	Unmarried	Married	Widow	Divorced	Total
20–24	0	3	0	0	3
25–30	0	3	0	0	3
31–40	0	0	0	0	0
41–50	0	11	3	0	14
51–60	1	8	16	0	25
60–	1	16	14	0	31
Total	2	41	33	0	76

It would seem that dependants of female household heads were predominantly females. In Woe there were 151 females to 50 males and in Alakple the ratio was 190 to 59. In contrast there were in male-headed households in Woe 225 females to 200 males and in Alakple 188 females to 121 males. One reason for this difference is that Anlo believe a boy can only be properly trained by a man, otherwise he will grow up to be a *nyɔnugbɔme*, one unlearned in the skills that make the perfect man. Parents therefore do their best to see that, whatever the circumstances, their sons do not live long with women. Grandmothers especially have the reputation of being too soft to their grandchildren. This tenderness is considered detrimental to the development of a man. A girl does not face similar problems, since every household, whether or not it is headed by a woman, has a woman to look after her feminine interests.

The preceding paragraphs lead us to certain general conclusions about the composition of Anlo households. One fact that stands out clearly is the absence, as a unit, of the extended family of parents and their sons and the latters' children. Wherever the household existed as a three-generation unit members of the second generation were daughters of the head. This is in accord with the independence attained by men on marriage and the values associated with it. One of the important considerations that qualify a youth for marriage is the possession of his own house. On marriage, therefore, he automatically establishes his own household and becomes independent of his parents. Marriage is thus obviously virilocal rather than patrilocal, in the sense that a wife on marriage moves into her husband's and not his father's house.

Ward arrived at the same conclusion on the Ewe in general, though none of her figures were taken from Anlo. Commenting on the figures from Vane in northern Ewe, she wrote, 'it seems . . . that the building of extended families is not a regular feature of Vane domestic organization. . . The development of extended families elsewhere in Eweland will be unusual, occurring when it does either as a temporary measure or in order to meet a break-down in the more usual system of independent simple family groups.'[1]

In Anlo, a patrilineal society with ideally virilocal marriage, the usual form of extended family would have been a patriarchal one with married sons and their families under the authority of their father. This does not exist. The three-generation variant, in which married daughters and their children live with their parents, is largely a temporary phenomenon. It becomes permanent only in response to a special contingency, as when a last-born daughter is asked by the father to live with him in his old age. Though independence in men is cherished it is clear that a similar value is not put on women setting up their own households. All women heads of households found themselves in that position because they were widows, divorced, or past childbearing. All had at one time or another depended on a husband. The only exceptions were those who could not, or did not want to, move to their husbands' houses because they were second wives. The need for the dependence of young married women was also shown by the fact that whenever circumstances made it impossible for them to live in the households of their husbands, they attached themselves to their parents or brothers for moral support. Here it may perhaps be necessary to explain the case of the six young women household heads found in Alakple and the fifteen at Woe who were below 40 years (Table 13). The six young women at Alakple were all living alone with their children in their husbands' houses. At the time of the enquiry the husbands were away in central Ghana as seasonal labourers on cocoa farms. It is likely that the husbands would return to their wives before long. The case of the fifteen young women at Woe is more difficult to explain. They were all in their late thirties and most of them were married. Six, as already explained, had married strangers who were living with them, so that in actual fact the wives were rather owners of the homestead

[1] Ward, B. E., 1949, pp. 176–7.

than heads of the household. Three of the fifteen were widows living in their dead husbands' houses. One was a divorcee, and as a successful trader had built herself a house. The remainder were either unmarried or were keeping the house for their absent husbands.

TABLE 13. Age Distribution of Household Heads

	Male Household Heads				Female Household Heads			
Age Group	Woe		Alakple		Woe		Alakple	
	No.	%	No.	%	No.	%	No.	%
20–24	1	0·8	0	0·0	0	0·0	3	3·9
25–30	3	2·5	4	4·3	0	0·0	3	3·9
31–40	32	28·6	22	23·6	15	18·0	0	0·0
41–50	22	19·6	20	21·5	20	23·8	14	18·4
51–60	25	22·3	16	17·4	17	19·2	25	33·0
61–	31	27·2	30	33·2	32	39·0	31	40·8
Totals	112	100·0	92	100·0	84	100·0	76	100·0

The comparatively large number of female-headed households in a patrilineal society calls for further explanation. As far as numbers are concerned, and given that divorce and widowhood are important factors making necessary the establishment of independent households by women, this high proportion may be attributed to the reluctance of old widows to remarry and the relatively high frequency of divorce. But since an independent household presupposes economic self-support, it would seem that women cannot maintain their households unless they are economically self-sufficient.

The economic enterprise of women has been indicated, and will be discussed more fully later. Here it is sufficient to point out that the fact that a woman does not need to depend much on her husband in economic matters makes it easier for women who have nothing more to gain from marriage because they are old to decide to live on their own. Even then it would seem that economic self-sufficiency alone is not crucial here. A woman does not have to pass the menopause, be divorced or widowed before embarking on independent economic activity. Women of all ages and of all marital states do indulge in one economic activity or other. This being the case, the fact that setting up, and living in, independent households is largely limited to women of advanced

age, mostly those without husbands, can be explained by the ideal
of post-marital residence. Where women set up households or
manage existing ones this is not due to a desire for independence.
It is because their marriage ties have been broken and they have
no need to attach themselves to men. A wife should live with her
husband in the latter's house. Where this has not happened it is
because the husband has either left the village or died.

The composition of households with female heads suggests
that they will be more unstable than those headed by men. In
other words there is likely to be more frequent change of person-
nel as well as of the kinship ties linking the members. Actually
instability is inherent in all households. We have seen that children,
both sons and daughters, leave their parents on marriage; therefore a group composed of parents and offspring is not likely to be
a stable one. The instability in male-headed households is alleviated by the tradition of virilocal residence, partly because, when
divorced or widowed and when his older children have left, a man
can, if he so wishes, marry other young wives and produce more
children. There is no way out for a woman. The instability of a
woman's household is increased by the fact that this is a patrilineal
society, in which the children of a widow or a divorced woman
can expect less from the estate of their mother's lineage than their
father's. But a woman herself has no rights in her deceased or
divorced husband's lineage property. Therefore in most cases, if
a widow or divorced woman remains unmarried, she must as a
rule go back to live on her own lineage land, and her male children, having less to hope for there, leave on marriage to set up
their homes on their own lineage land, while the females leave
for their husbands' homes.

The discussion so far has shown that Anlo post-marital residence
is essentially virilocal. This usually gives rise to two-generation
households comprising parents and their unmarried children,
with or without other dependants living with them. But the household group is not a static one. It grows, decays and sometimes is
reborn. It is therefore a cyclical system. In its ideal form, its life
starts from the establishment of a household by a man on his first
marriage. It reaches the height of its development after the wife or
wives have finished their reproductive functions, and ends with
the death of the last surviving spouse or the marriage of the man's
last child, whichever is the later. But the ideal growth is not

attained by all households. In many cases, in the course of its life-span some external circumstance brings persons outside the nuclear family into the group. The most important factor is introduced by the failure of some married daughters to follow the normal pattern of post-marital residence, so that although they are married they remain with their children in their parents' homes instead of joining their husbands. Another complication is introduced when divorced women and widows return to join the households of their parents. Some of these daughters even grow up to become heads after their parents have died. But the important thing is that these households, which later include the heads' married daughters and their children, also start with only members of the nuclear family.

Viewed from this angle the nuclear family and the domestic group of which it forms the core are only the starting points in this growth cycle, and the other forms of domestic group, such as female-headed households and a man's household containing his married daughters and their children, may be regarded not as deviations but rather as phases in the cycle.

These findings are generally in line with the three phases of development of the domestic group formulated by Fortes.[1] He holds that the domestic group not only grows but that its growth is cyclical. He mentions three phases of development after which growth may be restarted. The first he calls 'the phase of expansion'. This lasts from the marriage of two persons and establishment of a household until the completion of their period of procreation. The second stage he calls 'the phase of dispersion and fission'. This begins with the marriage of the oldest child and continues until all children are married. The last phase is 'the phase of replacement', which is marked by the death of the parents and the replacement in the structure of the family by the father's heir amongst the children.

These phases of development have been borne out to a large extent by our figures and findings. What they amount to in effect is that the term 'virilocal marriage' when applied to the Anlo residence pattern must refer only to the first phase. In the second and third phases the life experiences of the inmates and former inmates begin to affect its structure. It ceases to be a unit comprising parents and their unmarried children only, for it is

[1] Introduction to Goody, ed., 1958, pp. 4–5. See also Fortes, 1949, pp. 54–84.

at this time that the head's daughters, if unsuccessful in their marriages, begin to make their way back into their parental home, while others who fail to move to their husbands' houses add to the number.

But it is difficult to fit into Fortes' schema the case of a divorced woman or a widow who sets up her own household. It seems we have to regard this as another birth of a household because it does not develop from any previously established one. If so, then it is only here that we may speak of a deviation from the ideal residence pattern.

At this stage of the discussion it will be useful to examine a few actual cases of households at different stages of development in order to see how the processes we have described work out in practice.

Case No. 5

Gomela, a carpenter of Woe, was 34 in 1962. In 1954, when he was 26, he built his house of concrete cement just outside the old village site because his lineage's residential area there was over-crowded. Living with him were his 29-year-old wife and their four children between one and eight years. His household represents the ideal simple monogamous family type described.

Case No. 6

The household of Kwaku Mensa, 59 in 1962, was the largest in our sample at Alakple. He and his seventeen dependants were living in a house comprising three two-bedroomed mud and thatch buildings. The whole group of buildings was surrounded by a wall of woven reeds. In this house was living Kwaku Mensa himself, his three wives, seven unmarried daughters, two un-married sons and two married daughters and their children. The house of his eldest son, 28, opened into his through a gate in the wall which separated the two compounds.

Kwaku Mensa's house represents a typical lineage house in the old sections of the settlement, for Kwaku Mensa is the head of the large Soɖokpo lineage of the Dzevi clan at Alakple. He himself built one of the three mud huts when he married his first wife some thirty years ago. The dividing fence between this house and that of his father was removed to merge the two into one when his father died ten years ago and he took control of the entire house. His mother and her co-wife were living there at first, but left for their parents' homes later. Kwaku Mensa's mother was still alive in 1962.

Ablewɔ, Kwaku Mensa's eldest daughter, 25, was married and had two children. She was living with her parents because a doctor at Abidjan had said the climate there was not suitable for her. She had to leave her husband and co-wife to return home. So she was living with her parents awaiting the return of her husband. Mansa, the third daughter (the second was not living in the house), was at this time spending leave at Alakple with her husband, a rubber plantation worker at Bunso, about 200 miles away. Kwaku Mensa's eleven children were all living with him.

Kwaku Mensa is a *bokɔnɔ*, a professional diviner belonging to the Afa divination cult.[1] Sick persons and those suffering from misfortunes of any kind, or believed to be threatened by witches, were brought to him for diagnosis, treatment or advice. There were also in his house, just before the census was taken, novices whom he was training for qualification in the Afa cult. Living in his house, as I did for two days on one of my expeditions, therefore put me right in the hub of Alakple social life. Despite his reputation as a diviner, Kwaku Mensa could not be described as rich by local standards. Divination was bringing him a fluctuating income of between 10s. and £3 a week. Occasionally he would get about £5 a week and sometimes nothing at all. He himself told me that but for the assistance he was getting from his wives he would find it very difficult to run his large household. His relative poverty was shown in the mud-thatched buildings found in his house. Houses are great status symbols in Anlo. Concrete buildings with roofs of corrugated aluminium sheets are the goal of every man. They are the mark of prosperity. It is most unlikely that Kwaku Mensa will ever build one. His first wife Nɔvisi, whom he married in 1934, was baking *abolo*, corn bread. Half the product was being bought at home by near neighbours, while the remainder was hawked around in the more distant neighbourhoods by her two young daughters. Every morning she would give a small loaf of bread, *asikloe*, to each of the children in the

[1] The Afa divination cult in Anlo is similar to the one described for the Dahomey. Herskovits, 1938, vol. 2, pp. 201–31.

house, including those of her co-wives, who were not really always happy about this gesture, which they regarded as simulated benevolence. Nɔvisi was self-supporting. Kwaku Mensa told me that he didn't have to give her *asigbe*, market money, because 'she is rich'. The second wife, Dasi, as her name suggests, worships Da, the Snake Cult. She was doing petty trading, dealing mainly in tinned foods such as pilchards, sardines and corned beef. She was also selling *akpeteshie* or *kele* (locally brewed gin), an occupation which is very rewarding in a diviner's house, where no trans-action could be undertaken without a bottle of *akpeteshie* being offered.

Twenty-six-year-old Dzatugbui, the third wife, had not yet engaged in any occupation. She was the only one of the wives who was then looking to her husband for financial support.

Case No. 7

Kɔsiwɔga, who was 64 in 1962, had a household consisting of her youngest daughter, the latter's children, and her eldest daughter's daughter and her baby. The present composition of the household came about as follows. Kɔsiwɔga's husband died in 1937, when her youngest child was only two. For nearly five years she lived in his house with the children. Later she decided to remarry, and as this move was opposed by his brother, who himself wanted to marry her in vain, she was turned out of the house by her brother-in-law. She moved to her father's house, where her widowed mother was also living alone. Soon afterwards her eldest daughter Yawo married a man from Monenu, some 45 miles north of Woe. In 1944, after Yawo had had only one child, Vicey, her younger sister, who had just reached puberty, visited her and was drowned in a river nearby. Because of this, diviners said the dead did not approve of Yawo's marriage. She was therefore divorced, and came back with her one daughter to live with her mother. Yawo had since left for Accra, where she was trading, but her daughter, though unmarried, had a baby in 1962 by a schoolboy, and was still living in her grandmother's house. Adzovi, Kɔsiwɔga's youngest daughter, was married to a driver and had three children by him. She was the driver's fifth wife, and he said he had no room in his house for her.

Case No. 8

Kokui was living in her father's house with her younger sister Abui. Also living in this house were Kokui's three married daughters, Gbeḍa, 25, Ami 23, and Mansa 21, and their children. Abui's three children between the ages of 2 and 9 were also there. This made a total of ten in the house. The household was formed in this way. When her mother died in the 1920s Kokui was the only female child old enough to look after her father and her younger siblings. She was soon to marry, but after the marriage her father asked her husband to allow her to remain with him. Her husband readily agreed, as he already had another wife living with him. Before her father died in 1938 all her brothers had married and established their own households. Kokui therefore decided to make her father's house her permanent home. The only one of her siblings still living there was Abui. She had a child in 1944 when still a maid. The relationship with her lover was legalized later, but she left him and was in 1962 the concubine of a wealthy fisherman who had no less than six wives before adding her to them. Kokui engaged in all sorts of occupations, as a fishmonger, *abolo* baker and *kaklo*[1] frier. She was also growing groundnuts and cassava. Kokui's daughters, all married, helped her in her various occupations. Abui traded many petty items – pans, cooking utensils and imported clothes.

These four cases show the composition of the household group at different stages of development. Case one shows a household composed entirely of members of the nuclear family. That this household did not include any relatives outside the nuclear family was due partly to the youth of its head and partly to the fact that both his parents were alive and his younger siblings were living with them. In fact, every household started with only members of the nuclear family has every potentiality of developing into a unit incorporating dependants outside it. This has been illustrated by all the other cases. In some cases the nuclear family ceased to exist as a unit. This happened usually in the third phase of the developmental cycle. In these instances the household was nothing more than a collection of relatives united with the head by various ties of kinship. On the other hand, the younger the household the greater the likelihood of the presence of the nuclear family.

[1] *Kaklo* is a popular Anlo food made by frying balls of cassava dough or corn flour.

The household in its development may assume several forms. Description of all these could fill volumes. In the examples given only key cases have been mentioned to indicate the general pattern to which the rest approximate.

The figures and examples given represent present-day conditions and refer only to Woe and Alakple settlements. But there is little doubt that conditions in Woe and Alakple are similar to those in most settlements in Anlo. In Alakple, where the lack of bush land makes impossible the development of *kɔfe* outside the old residential area, it might have been expected that the ideal of setting up a new household on marriage would be in many cases unrealizable. But in fact the figures on household composition in Woe and Alakple show no significant differences.

In Alakple the development of three-generation households with married sons under the authority of their fathers has been avoided by more intensive use of the lineage residential areas, the reclamation and use of less hospitable land for residence and also by emigration. The result is that in Alakple the area occupied by houses is much smaller and more congested than in Woe, where the least sign of congestion gives rise to moving out and the establishment of *kɔfe* houses by younger members of the lineage.

The present composition of households is not a departure from the traditional practice. The establishment by a man of his independent household after marriage has been emphasized by Spieth.[1] It is difficult to reconcile this view with the presence of extended families. My informants were unanimous in their view that what differentiated an adult from a child both in the past and the present was the former's establishment of an independent house and *ipso facto* his independence of his father.

Westermann's sole informant, Foli, however, mentioned the existence of extended families in Glidzi. Ward, whose findings, as we have mentioned, did not support Foli's claims, suggested that Foli, living in Berlin, 'was . . . speaking only of the large dwelling group in which he himself, as a member of the royal lineage of Glidzi, was brought up.'[2] This is most likely to be the case in view of another description by Foli of his grandfather's dwelling as a small hut. Moreover the actual composition of these 'extended families' has not been made clear. Possibly he was here referring to

[1] 1906, pp. 183 ff.   [2] Ward, B. E., 1949, p. 179.

a three-generation household of the Kwaku Mensa type (*Case* 6 above).

3. THE INDIVIDUAL'S STAGES OF DEVELOPMENT

In order to round off the description of the developmental cycle of the household group, we shall now consider the development and life experiences of the individuals who make up the group. This in a sense is introducing a new perspective into our analysis. We are now concerned with the individual rather than the group. However, in dealing with a society as a whole, it is necessary to remember that the social fabric is but a composition of the strands woven by the lives of the individuals who compose that society. Because of this, a study of the institutions found in any social system can be complemented by an investigation into the manner in which the individual takes his place among his fellows and how he responds to the patterns of behaviour that arise out of the traditions of his society. But we are here mainly concerned with the way in which individuals are brought up to fit into the social structure and not with their development as personalities in the psychological sense, though the latter aspect also cannot be totally ignored.

Birth and early childhood

Until recently childbirth has always been a village affair. This is partly due to the fact that up to about ten years ago the hospital at Keta was the only one in Anlo and was not within easy reach of many villages. Another reason is that Anlo still have great faith in their own traditional skill of midwifery. Even today, though almost every expectant mother at Woe receives medical advice, and two out of every five do so in Alakple, it is only in difficult cases that a woman in labour is taken to hospital, even though there are now hospitals within fifteen miles of every Anlo village.

Childbirth in the traditional manner is both tedious and painful, even considering that childbirth anywhere is never without pain. So great is the labour that on many occasions the cries of mothers in pain send alarm signals to neighbours, who come and flock around the bathroom, *afekpɔeme*, to await the outcome. While she is in pain the older women in the house pray for good delivery to

Mawu, The Supreme Being, and to the deified ancestors of the family. If before birth the child had been vowed to a deity, as often happens, this spirit too would be called upon for help.

Most of the difficulty lies in the traditional method of midwifery itself. As soon as the first signs of travail are sensed a midwife is sent for. Her main job is to assist the birth by manipulation and pressing the abdomen. An old woman stands behind her and supports her shoulders in her hand. Both the midwife and the women present from time to time call on the expectant mother to push out the baby. If necessary the midwife would put her hand inside to bring out the baby.

When at last the baby is born the first sign looked for is whether it gives the initial cry which shows that it is alive. If this is not heard the midwife asks that pepper be put on fire and brought to its nose. If it is alive it sneezes and there is rejoicing. The umbilical cord is cut and buried with the placenta in a bathroom. When on the fifth day the remaining cord is severed from the navel it is also buried there. No special significance is attached to this place apart from the coconut tree which may be planted there. As soon as the cord is cut, one of the women in attendance bathes the child in tepid water, while another bathes the mother in hot water.

The birth of a child is followed by another payment by the mother's husband, known as *vidzĩnu* (lit. baby's things). This consists of four gallons kerosine, several packets of matches, a mosquito net, clothing for the baby, a half piece of garment for carrying the baby and one *kente* cloth for the same purpose. All these items are necessary for use by the baby and its mother in the few weeks following the child's birth. *Vidzĩnu* must be given at every birth not only as an appreciation of the event but also as a sign of the father's recognition of the child. It is however only with the first birth that many men are particular.

Several customs are performed for children between birth and puberty. The first of these is naming. This takes place eight days after birth. This is also the day on which the child is entrusted to the care of the ancestors and the other gods who are believed to have made the birth possible. The occasion is marked by a simple ceremony, to which relatives and friends are invited.

Much attention is paid to naming. Different circumstances determine what name an Anlo child takes. The first important fact is the cult groups served by the parents. All cult groups have their own names for their members. Also, special circumstances surrounding a child's birth may determine its name. Thus we have such names as Zanu for a boy, and Zasi for a girl born in the night, Tsigbe for a girl or boy born on a rainy day, and Asinu for a girl born on a market day. Children who survive either after their older siblings have died young or after their parents have had a number of still births also have special names. They are given absurd names such as Ati (stick), Ekpe (stone), Elo (crocodile), or Modzaka (pastime). It is believed that death will spare them if they are not called by names appropriate to human beings. There are also names of allusion,[1] advice, exhortation and of thanksgiving to the Supreme Being, all relating to some experience of the parents. Some of these names are Goyimwole (they are only boasting, they can't do anything), Tɔnyɛwonya (they only know of my misdeeds), Hoenyega (money is supreme), Dzigbɔdi (patience), Mawuli (there is Mawu, Supreme Being). Also each of the fifteen clans has its own pair of names, one for males and the other for females. There are also a pair of names for each day of the week, but these and clan names are often superseded by the special names mentioned earlier. In all cases it is the names of the cult groups which take precedence over others if many circumstances surround a child's birth. For instance a girl born on a market day is called Asinu, but if she is the first daughter of a diviner she will be called Adugba.

From its birth until weaning the infant feeds on its mother's breast and on *akatsa*, a pap made from corn flour. Orange juice is also used by some mothers. The child is fed at least three times a day, that is, at ordinary meal times and also whenever it cries. A child is expected to eat whenever the time comes for it to do so, otherwise forcible feeding is resorted to. This is done as follows. As the child lies or sits in its mother's lap, she supports its chin on the palm of her left hand, while pressing together the nostrils with the index and the second fingers of the same hand thus forcing the child to open its mouth to breathe. As it does this she forces the pap into the open mouth with her right hand.

---

[1] These names of allusion are usually directed against the behaviours of neighbours and relatives of the parents, 'Tɔnyɛwonya' for instance means that neighbours who may be guilty of more serious offences have been gossiping about the parents on a trivial matter.

Weaning takes place when the child is able to walk properly by itself, because this is the time for its parents to resume cohabitation. From the time of its birth till it is weaned its parents are not expected to sleep together. It is believed that cohabitation at this stage affects the quality of the mother's milk and therefore has an adverse effect on the baby's health.

Weaning is achieved in several ways. It is normally started by encouraging the child to associate more and more with its elder siblings, and its subsequent introduction to more solid foods. Access to the breast is made difficult by fastening cloth around it. The nipples are also smeared with juice from the leaves of the *gbɔti* tree, which is very bitter. Many children try to get round this by quietly wiping the breast with a damp cloth, and the mother, marvelling at the ingenuity of the child, lets it have its own way for a time. Mild beating is finally resorted to if all these fail to sever the child from its mother.

Before weaning it is not difficult to see how close and intimate is the relationship between a mother and her child. During the day while the mother busies herself about the compound, the child lies in its bed in the bedroom or on a mat supported by cloth in a shady corner of the compound under the eaves, but always within sight of its mother. If it becomes restless she will produce the breast and then put it astride her back, inside a cloth which she ties in front. She then proceeds to go about her work regardless of whether the child is awake or asleep, pounding okro or palm kernel in a mortar, or cooking, washing or sweeping, while the child's head rolls this way and that as the mother moves. Even at dances it is a common sight to find women dancing with their children lying at their backs. The infant wears no clothes until it starts walking, but may have a string with a few beads about its middle as it grows older.

Weaning is followed by toilet training. Practices hitherto disregarded are now strictly regulated. The child is taught to call its mother at night whenever it feels like easing itself. Even before this time the child may have had some impressions about this. For it is put down from its mother's back when she feels that it is about to perform its excretory functions. Thus in time, usually after two years, the training process is almost completed. If a child does not respond to this training and manifests enuresis at the age of four or five, soiling every now and then the mat on which it sleeps, its contemporaries are informed. A date is arranged and if he soils the mat again he is wrapped in the wet mat and taken into the lagoon, pond or the market place where all the children clap their hands and run after him singing: *ɖuɖɔgo yayaya! ɖuɖɔgo yayaya!*, urine everywhere! urine everywhere![1] This is repeated until he corrects the habit.

As already noted in Chapter 2, Anlo believe in the reincarnation of the soul. It is thought that all dead persons return to the world of the living through their offspring, siblings or any relative. It is also believed that every person is a reincarnation of some dead relative, and sickness and suffering may be attributed to the latter's displeasure. When the child is about ten months old, sometimes earlier, it is taken to a diviner to find out which dead relative it represents. The diviner, it is believed, sends *Fiele*, the messenger of the gods, to *Tsiefe*, the abode of the dead, to enquire about the origin of the child. From *Tsiefe* the ancestor responsible is believed to come to the diviner in the form of a ghost, introduces himself, advises the parents as to the best way of making him comfortable, and reminds them of his likes and dislikes. A person is expected to follow in the footsteps of the dead man whose reincarnation he is, and if possible take to his profession. Sometimes the dead man advises that the child be named after him. In this case the name of the ancestor is given to the child as its second name, but in the case of members of certain cults, especially members of the Yeʋe, the cult name replaces the first. Although it is an ancestor who is known to return, the child is also known to be the result of the action of its human father and mother.

The belief in reincarnation serves as a reminder to the parents and kinsfolk of the ever watchful presence of the dead. It is one of the principal means by which the lives and practices of past generations are recreated in the present. In this way it is an important influence in linking the past and the present.

Circumcision is compulsory among all Ewe tribes. It takes place once a year during the dry season in December and January, when the wounds are supposed to heal well and quickly in the dry harmattan weather. Every village has at least one expert cutter. He announces and arranges the time for the operation. Boys are circumcised some time after they have been weaned, that is when they are about two years old. Those who have passed beyond this

[1] Cf. Herskovits, 1938, Vol. I, p. 273.

age without it are derided by their contemporaries. Boys who are circumcised together form a friendship group of age mates which later develops into a work party of youths called *Fidodo-habɔbɔ*. Girls are not circumcised.

Abnormal children receive special treatment. The most conspicuous is that of twins. First, their birth is heralded by a flute. They are regarded as sacred, and are treated as such lest they bring disaster on their parents and the community. The first-born of the twins is called the younger, Etse for a boy or Xetsa for a girl, and is regarded as the messenger of the second, Atsu or Xi. Attempts are made by the parents to placate the spirits of twins who die young by offering them worship. There is indeed a strong cult of twins. Dead twins are represented by wooden images decked in cowrie shells, which may be placed in a shrine or carried about by their mothers, and are honoured with gifts. A child that has lost its twin may be seen wearing the carved wooden doll image tied in front or back of his or her cloth. It is also said that a twin or a mother of twins does not receive a gift in singles, and for a child who has lost his twin partner, if he is given a gift the same gift must be given to the image of the dead twin he carries.[1]

Childhood to adolescence

Boys and girls enjoy much freedom until about ten years old. This is because they are not yet strong enough to cope with the work which helping their parents demands. This is more true of boys than girls, because the latter have to help their mothers from an earlier age than boys. Up to the age of ten, boys spend most of their time in little gangs in the bush or in the water – hunting. They catch ground birds, shoot others with stone and catapults, dig for rats in the termite hills or holes, and chase as valuable booty any animal that happens to cross their path. The transition from play to work is almost imperceptible. It is made easy because most games and early childhood activities are imitations of adult activities, so that work seems to the boys to be more like an amusing game than a hard task. Those who are lazy, or slow in mastering the techniques of the various occupations, are simply laughed at by their contemporaries. Skills considered necessary for a boy are swimming, hoeing, rowing, onion sowing, and

[1] See Appendix 5.

weaving of fish traps. All these he learns from his elder brothers and contemporaries.

From about ten years children begin serious economic activities by helping their parents, especially in the farm. In fishing communities too, though the hazards of sea-fishing make it difficult for youths under fifteen to participate fully in the main activities, such as rowing, swimming long distances, and net-dragging, there are many minor roles usefully filled by boys. They help in mending the net, carrying ropes and nets, and running errands.

The fact that major fishing and farming in Anlo are seasonal occupations gives boys much time during the off-seasons to pursue their own occupations, occupations which fall outside the domain of adults and are not seasonally demarcated. Anlo have great sense of property. Even small boys at this age are taught to pursue economic activities which give them substantial incomes which greatly alleviate much of their dependence on their parents. Boys acquire income by gathering and selling firewood, rowing women to the marketplace, rearing fowls or goats, climbing coconut trees to harvest the nuts, and doing small services to relatives and neighbours.

Sometimes a father may allot a small plot of land to his young son. The harvest from this belongs to the boy, who may give some of it to his mother for the household, but she will buy the greater part from him, keeping the money for him and buying with it whatever he decides upon, or he may go to the next market himself and there trade on his own behalf. Each year the size of these little plots increases and so does the pleasure the boy gets from the sale of the crops, or the proceeds of his firewood gathering or his fishing, and he soon begins to think of his marriage payment and of the wedding expenses to which he must contribute at least a part.

Girls have little or no time to acquire independent capital at this stage, because women's occupations, unlike those of men, are not seasonal, and girls are always helping their mothers. The commonest female occupations are petty trading, baking, and fish curing and selling. As soon as a girl has learned how to talk she is taught elementary addition and subtraction. From that time she takes charge of selling the mother's products. The bread, or whatever it is, is packed in an *akpaku* or calabash which she carries on her head and sells throughout the whole village and sometimes outside it. She returns very late in the afternoon only to start work on the following day's produce. Girls are praised for their *zaza*, i.e. 'brilliance', the ability to speak clearly, to give the correct balance or change and prevent cheating by buyers. One of the familiar noises one often hears in the morning in Anlo villages and towns is that of girl hawkers announcing their wares at the top of their voices.

> *Abolo dzodzoe lae (nye esi)!*[1]
> (Come and buy the hot *abolo!*)
> *Yakayakɛ kple akla tɔe (nye esi)!*
> (I am selling *yakayakɛ* and *akla!*)

Even after they have started to work both boys and girls have much time for play. On moonlit evenings they gather to tell stories and riddles. The meeting place is usually the market place, or any open space in the neighbourhood. At these sessions stories are told about animals or about *Ayiyi*, the spider trickster, who is the hero of many Ewe stories. Most of these stories carry morals and are held by elders to be an important means of learning the precepts of the good way of life.

Until puberty boys and girls play together freely, and clandestine affairs are sometimes reported. There are about three games played by combined teams of boys and girls which often serve indirectly as instruments of first adventures into seduction. One such game is *bebi*, a kind of hide-and-seek played in singles and in couples. When played in couples, one couple close their eyes while the rest disappear in couples to find hiding places. When the signal for the search is given the couple who have closed their eyes go about looking for those in hiding, and the pair discovered first must conduct the next search. It is said that in this particular game the interest of boys is not in the game itself. When hidden in the various convenient places precocious boys may start to make love. A game of similar nature, *avɔɖɔli*, 'exchanging of clothes', as the name suggests involves changing of clothes by the participating pairs, while someone who has hitherto been in hiding comes out to identify one of those who have exchanged clothes, the latter completely covering themselves and lying down close to

---

[1] *Abolo*, corn bread, is a common food for breakfast, it is very appetizing when taken hot with stew or soup. *Yakayakɛ* is another bread taken at breakfast. It is made with a mixture of cassava dough and corn flour and cooked by steam. It is usually taken with *akla*, fried balls of ground beans.

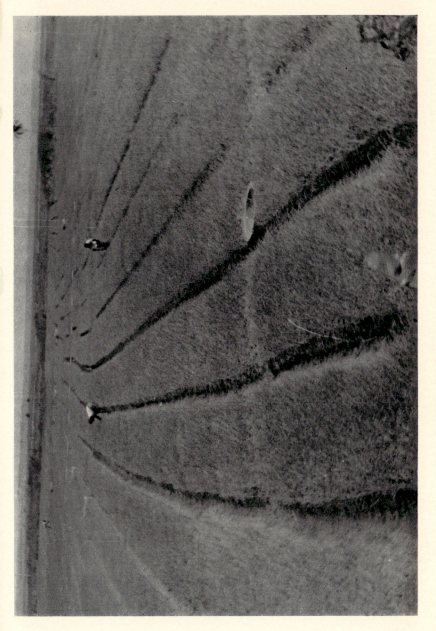

1. A layout of shallot beds at Avume, near Anloga

2*a*. A canoe-load of women from the hinterland arriving at Keta on a market day

2*b*. A lineage head of Woe prepares to pour libation to his ancestors

each other. Some informants claimed that coitus may take place during these games, a claim disputed by my women informants.

Children are taught early to distinguish relatives from other people, to use the correct terms in addressing their seniors, to be willing to help others, not to take anything without permission and not to enter a house where there are no relatives. They are also discouraged from eating in the houses of neighbours. If they do this it will appear to neighbours that they are not well looked after in their own homes. They may not take anything from other villagers without express permission, least of all from 'foreign' traders in the market. They are also told that if they take cassava, corn or mangoes when they are on their way to fish or to fetch firewood, that is stealing. From these instructions children acquire the kernel of customary education. This forms the essence of *amebubu*, 'respect for persons'. This in effect means respect for elders and all their seniors. The sharpest reproof of all is '*ɖevi sia mebuna ame o*', 'this child is disrespectful – to elders'.

Certain offences are regarded as especially bad in children. These include the use of abusive terms like *lã*, beast; *avu*, dog; *dawò*, your mother; or *fofowò*, your father, especially against a senior. Among adults these are insults which could be taken to court. Calling a senior by his name is also strongly resented. An older person must be addressed by the term appropriate to his or her kinship tie with the child.

But on the whole there is not much punishment. In Ewe the term for 'to punish' is *he to*, that is 'to pull the ear'. This ancient method of punishment is still used on children today, as well as beating with a stick and curtailment of food, tying the child's hands or cutting its fingers and rubbing them with pepper. These latter punishments are applied only for especially heinous offences, such as habitual stealing or using swear-words against their parents.

In general, however, children are allowed to go their own way, especially by their mothers. If a child is afraid of punishment he will run to his father's father's house nearby or to his mother's brother and stay there until the father's wrath is past. If a task given by his mother seems distasteful, the child may say '*megbe*', 'I refuse. I won't do it', and the mother may laugh and acquiesce. The child could not speak so to the father without serious consequences. As already mentioned, when a father is beating a child its mother often complains, 'How can you beat him? He is only a child'. Punishment is often checked in this way by the mothers. Parental love, especially from the mother, is the general need of all children – hence it is said of children that it is better to lose a father than to lose a mother.

We earlier discussed what may be called 'adolescent culture'. We described in some detail how youths and girls on reaching puberty leave behind their childhood behaviour and begin to mould their general deportment on lines that would make them acceptable to members of the opposite sex. For both sexes this adolescent culture is the link between childhood and adulthood, though the processes of transformation differ.

For the girl, the onset of menstruation and her gradual incorporation into domestic tasks form a focus for her maturity. The well-marked changes are the growth of the breast and her more meticulous use of clothes to cover her genitals and breast, which have hitherto been bereft of shelter. These developments are immediately followed by the puberty rites already described.

It is thought that girls should reach a certain age, about fourteen at least, before their breasts develop. If they appear before this time they are broken down. This prevention of premature protrusion of the breast is significant as an expression of the importance attached to age rather than physical development as the essential index of social maturity. The fear, it seems, is that since physical development, puberty rites and marriage in girls follow each other almost automatically, premature development of the body may undermine the age limit for marriage and sexual intercourse.

For a boy the transition from childhood to adulthood is almost imperceptible. It is not marked by any rites. There are also no such well-marked changes to punctuate the progress of his development. The outward changes that take place in him, his deportment and carefulness about clothes, are his own social reactions to the inward physiological developments taking place in him. This reaction is itself greatly influenced by the adolescent culture in which he participates, which is mainly concerned with courting and preparation for marriage.

For both youths and girls, the final stage in reaching adulthood is marriage. Marriage, which is automatically accompanied by the establishment of an independent household, gives a man his adult status. The same is the case for a woman. After her first child is born, whatever her age, the young mother becomes 'mother of so-and-so'. It is now more customary to address her in this way than to call her by name. The same applies to the young father.

Old age

Old age automatically confers honour and elicits respect. Increase in years brings an increase in responsibility, in the number of offices held and the exercise of leadership. Old men and women continue as managers of their households. They also continue to run their farms and to pursue their other economic activities. Unless a man is sick or infirm he continues to work no matter how old he is, and one often sees men of seventy and over going off to their farms and fish traps every day.

Despite this there is great respect for age. The saying, Ðevi mekpɔa amegãxoxo fe ŋku me o, 'a child does not look at an old man's face', is a sufficient indication of this. A man reaches the height of his prestige when he becomes the lineage head. As lineages are over eight degrees of genealogical depth this position extends his authority beyond his household and the segment he heads. Since the lineage head is the oldest surviving member of the group, by the time a man reaches this position he is really old, but the physical weakness is compensated for by the new authority he acquires as the head of his lineage, a position which carries with it, among others, the arbitration of disputes and the administration of ancestral shrines.

Even without the status of lineage head old age *per se* carries great respect. An old man is regarded as a storehouse of traditional knowledge and secrets of success in life. And because of his age he is generally identified with the dead and the fear and awe associated with them. For these reasons, old men enjoy a good deal of respect not only within the lineage but also in the community at large.

For women old age is the time when most of them return to the parental home. They then find themselves really valuable in lineage affairs, both in the settlement of disputes and in ancestral rites. Both old men and women sit on the lineage tribunal which settles disputes among the members. The advice of old women is sought in all matters. In the ancestral rites too, though women do not officiate, those who have passed the menopause can approach the ancestral stool and the shrines and participate fully in all activities with men, for in Anlo, as in many other societies, the segregation of men and women, as we shall soon discover, and the latter's prohibition from many sacred functions, result from their association with blood, regarded as unclean, which starts with puberty and ends with the menopause. At ancestral rituals old women are very useful as repositories of knowledge on genealogies and ancient rituals. They are always ready to remind the lineage head of the names of the important ancestors he forgets, and are consulted whenever doubt arises on details of the ceremony.

4. INTERPERSONAL RELATIONS WITHIN THE FAMILY

The relations within the domestic group comprising a man and his wife or wives and their children, the core unit of Anlo households, are standards to which all households approximate in their interpersonal relations and co-operative activities. In every compound men and women have their special roles to play in the upkeep of the house. So do children. There are also specific behaviour patterns between spouses on the one hand and between children and their parents on the other. The latter we have already discussed, the former is the subject of this section.

Anlo homesteads are built, so to speak, in relation to the number of persons found in them. In the monogamous family there is the main building and the kitchen. In this main building there are apartments for the spouses and their children. If there is only one kitchen one knows that there is only one woman-wife in the house.

The polygynous family, on the other hand, is a unit of a number of wives (each with her kitchen) and their children, linked together only by the common father. By virtue of their relationship to the husband-father, children and their mothers belong to one family unit. But the children of each wife also belong exclusively to her apartment and kitchen. They eat with her and sleep in her apartment and kitchen. In effect each wife and her children in a polygynous family together with her husband form a nuclear family. Viewed from this angle the polygynous family is but a compound of a number of nuclear families.

Though the home is run by the combined efforts of all its members, between men and women there is a clear and complementary division of labour. Certain tasks are performed by one sex while others fall exclusively within the domain of the other. The man generally does the work which demands great physical strength, such as clearing the bush, constructing the woodwork in the building of a house, making fences, and cutting roads from the home to the farm.

The work of the woman is no less difficult. She has to provide the daily food for the family. Food preparation involves more than cooking. There is the grinding of corn, pounding of okro, mashing of pepper, and fetching of firewood. Fetching water from the well or river is also a woman's work. Assisted by her daughters, she must every day fetch water, often from a long distance. She must also sweep the compound and the rooms. Before the evening meal, she must heat water and take it to the bath for the husband. She must also bathe the children. In fact, all the day to day maintenance of the household falls on the women, while most of the men's tasks are periodic operations from which only their physical weakness excuses the women. It should be remembered that the marketing of fish and all farm produce is also the responsibility of women, as is the transportation of these goods. No man, not even a bachelor, will do any of these things. To all intents and purposes, therefore, the man is the master of the house.

Though the division of labour between husband and wife does not by itself express different evaluations of the sexes, the man in many respects feels himself the superior. He is the woman's protector, and in this he is supported by the position allotted to women in the society at large. The defence of the state and its administration are in the hands of men. Women as a group, if they have grievances, only present petitions to the elders and the chief for remedies. They have no direct say in the affairs of the community.

The marital relationship is marked by the complete obedience of the wife. Every wife is expected to obey her husband. He may beat her for disobedience, disorderliness and any suspicion of unfaithfulness. A wife addresses her husband as *efo*, which means 'elder brother'. She may also call him the father of one of their children, e.g. Kwasi-*fofo*, i.e. Kwasi's father, or simply, *wofofo*, i.e. the children's father. But on no occasion should a wife

call her husband by name. The superiority of men over women
is seen in all aspects of Anlo social life. One conspicuous example
is the manner of greeting. A woman must go down on her knees
when greeting a man.

This relationship is held responsible for the segregation of the
spouses, both at home and in public gatherings. At home men sit
and relax with friends. Women do the same. It is considered
unseemly for a wife to enter a conversation with her husband and
his male colleagues unless invited to clarify a point. Spouses may
not eat together. Men eat with the older boys in the *akpata*, living
room, women with the girls and smaller boys in the kitchen.

The separation of the sexes is no less rigid in public gatherings.
It is remarkable to find at public ceremonies and meetings men
sitting separately on one side and women on the other. Again,
though dances are organized by both sexes, men sit on one side
and women on the other. The dancing is open to both sexes, but
here again they are usually segregated in the actual performance. Men dance in groups of two, three or four and women the
same.

In the home the strict division of labour is seen also in the economic aspect of household management. The family is an
economic unit in so far as its members jointly provide for their
daily needs. But they cannot be said to co-operate in a joint economic venture. Men farm and fish. These are by far the commonest
occupations, employing over 90 per cent of the total population.
Wives of farmers help to sell the farm produce on market days, for
which service they are rewarded with a commission in cash. In
fishing, however, the catch is sold to the women, both wives and
women unrelated to the fishermen, who cure it before taking it to
the market. Besides these every woman follows her own occupation as baker, trader, basket weaver or fishmonger. It is also
common to find a woman carrying on a regular farmer's business
independently of her husband, engaging men to cultivate for her.
From these occupations many women derive considerable independent incomes.

Spouses only contribute part of their incomes to the expenses of
the household, the remainder is their own. Thus a woman can
acquire a fortune to which the husband has no claim. It is therefore
not surprising to find a family in which the wife is very rich while
the husband is poor. I found several women who were the credi-

tors of their husbands, and even children the creditors of their parents.

The far-reaching economic independence of the spouses makes close marital union difficult. This is especially the case in polygynous families, where each wife in turn cooks for four days, corresponding to the market week, for the husband and shares his sexual services, and is comparatively free at all other times. It is true that husband and wife live in a common house and share in the education of the children. But in the main the interest of the husband is with his male equals in age, his economic undertakings and matters of public life. A man who is too fond of his wife is called a kitchen man, a man whose interest lies in women's activities.

For the woman her interest, apart from her children, is with her friends, neighbours and own relatives. Her welfare is as much the concern of her parents and brothers as it is of her husband. The former always make sure that no injustice is done to her. The wife feels herself more closely linked to them than her husband and his family, knowing that she will always find refuge with them. Even after marriage she retains her affiliation with her own lineage. On her death it is her brothers who are responsible for her funeral. In the religious sphere too the separation and independence of the spouses are marked. Each may serve different gods and belong to different cult groups. Perhaps the most important significant factor here is the influence of filiation and the ancestors on membership of cult groups. A person must join the cult group of his or her antecedent. This injunction is voluntary in some cults, compulsory in others, and is automatic in that of Yeʋe, the god of thunder, which is by far the most widespread of the traditional religious groups. This has the effect of further concentrating kinsfolk in the religious groups of which their ancestors were members.

One important aspect of the Anlo family which has not yet received any full treatment is polygyny. The incidence of polygyny is comparatively high in Woe and Alakple. Although only 42·4 per cent, representing 94 out of the 222 men, had more than one wife at the time of our census, 64·4 per cent had experienced polygyny at least once in their lives.

Polygyny earns prestige and respect. According to the Anlo themselves, if you have only one wife she will not respect you because she knows she is the only one living with you. If you have two, both will be vying for your love. But the economic implications of polygyny prevent many aspirants from realizing it. More wives mean more marital responsibility. First, each marriage involves a new payment and new expenses towards the ceremony. Moreover, as the women's song says, 'If you marry a woman she must eat'. For her own maintenance and her contribution toward the family budget she needs capital, part of which at least the husband should contribute. Polygyny from the husband's point of view means a larger family and more children to look after. In its initial stages, therefore, it is an expensive venture. It is not surprising, then, that only the rich indulge in it.

TABLE 14. Incidence of Polygyny and Monogamy among Males, Woe and Alakple combined

Age Group	18–25	26–35	36–45	46–55	56–65	66–75	76–	Total	%
Monogamy	6	28	30	22	21	14	7	128	57·6
Polygyny	4	10	22	18	19	18	1	94	42·4
Totals	10	38	52	40	40	32	8	222	100·0

TABLE 15. No. of Wives per Married Man in Woe and Alakple

Location	1	2	3	4	5	Total Polygyny
Woe	74	40	9	4	3	56
Alakple	54	27	11	0	0	38
Totals	128	67	20	4	3	94

The economic gains from polygyny are not so clear. In Anlo, owing to the nature of the economic activities of men and women, the common argument that many wives are an economic asset is not really applicable. This is especially true of fishing, which is an exclusively male occupation. Women only buy the catch, cure it and finally sell it. The catch is not so big as to demand many hands to cure one fisherman's share. Moreover, there are many fish traders other than the wives of fishermen, so that a fisherman's wife is not necessarily a fishwife and fishmongers are not always fishermen's wives. It is not uncommon for wives to take occupations totally unrelated to their husbands'.

Onion farming may be a little different in this respect. Here, though sowing is done by men only, weeding, harvesting, and the preparation of the seeds for market, though predominantly male affairs, are sometimes done by women because many hands are required for them. A polygynous farmer may therefore have assistance from his wives if they are free. Indeed, although normally farmers have to employ professional weeders and farm labourers each season, those with large families are able to depend on them. But, as has been emphasized, women cherish their independent economic activities. Only a few help their husbands in this way.

Also, comparison between families of fishermen and onion farmers show that fishing-net owners, who are on the whole richer than farmers, tend to have more wives than they do. Not a single fishing-net owner in Woe in 1962 had fewer than two wives. Among ordinary fishermen the average number of wives is just about the same as that of farmers. Even among the farmers the tendency is for the richer ones to have more wives. It is therefore quite legitimate to conclude that polygyny and the desire for large families are not motivated by economic considerations. On the contrary, it is prosperity which makes it possible and even increases the desire for it.

In a society where extra-marital affairs are frowned upon, the strongest case for polygyny is sexual satisfaction. The case for this view is strengthened by the taboo on sex during the period between birth and weaning, which is about two years. Husbands who cannot wait so long may find polygyny necessary if they have the means. This will mean regulating the births in such a way that while one wife is breast-feeding her child the other will be in a position to provide sexual services for the husband. Observation shows that this calculation is never in the minds of polygynous husbands. One often finds co-wives having children within a few months of each other, and accordingly spending the weaning taboo period together. It is also common knowledge that monogamists as well as polygynists often violate the weaning taboo.

In a polygynous family the relations between spouses are complicated by the husband's relations with his other wives. Many actions by the husband which, in a monogamous union, would have been regarded as mere peccadilloes are here given more serious twists. The position is usually aggravated by the presence of favourites among the wives. As is usually the case, and as is inevitable where many wives fight for the love of one man, one gains special favour, perhaps through her beauty or her character. The most important consideration is, however, closeness of kinship. This may be both an asset and a liability, for it often places the husband in a dilemma. If he gives special treatment to his cross-cousin wife he is accused of preferring her to the others because she is a close relative. At the same time his uncles or aunts, her parents, expect him to grant her special favours. Many husbands do their best to be impartial in these circumstances, even if without success. No specific instances can truly give a representative picture of the various situations. It is a dilemma which runs through all polygynous families where some wives have closer kin ties with the husband than others.

The co-wife relationship itself is an explosive one. *Atsusi*, or *atsunyesi*, my husband's wife, in common usage means co-wife, but it also connotes, rather ominously, 'to be jealous'. In this latter sense it is often used outside the family circle to anyone who tries to pick quarrels out of jealousy. '*Atsuwòsie menyea?*' 'Am I your co-wife?' is a common question in this context. One understands why in local English *atsusi* is usually rendered by 'rival'.

It is often believed that wherever co-wives live together there is bound to be trouble. This is borne out by the fact that in many polygynous households the co-wives are never on speaking terms. This sad fact is responsible for the practice now in vogue of not allowing second and subsequent wives to live in their husband's homestead with the first wife even though they might have separate apartments or huts to themselves. Whenever possible a man builds a new house for his second and subsequent wives near his own house or in a different *kɔfe* where he has land. It is also considered more desirable for such wives to remain in their parental homes than to allow them to live under the same roof with their co-wives.

But real friendship among co-wives is not unknown. In some polygynous households one finds co-wives having joint economic activities and even cooking and eating together. But these are rare cases, and that such households are the object of favourable comment shows they are exceptional. It is said that for a husband to achieve co-operation among his wives he must sleep with them all together and copulate with each one in the presence and full view of the others. But it appears many husbands do not believe this.

The co-wife relation is the first source of fission in the polygynous family. The attitudes of co-wives to each other inevitably affect their children's behaviour. Each wife has her own cooking place, cooks for herself and her young children and advises them against eating from the other kitchens. When trouble breaks out it is to be expected that children from the same kitchen will side together against those from the others. Only the father maintains an uneasy truce amongst them. As each wife in turn cooks four days for her husband and thus at the same time for all his sons who share his meals, a wife must sometimes cook for the children of her co-wives. Westermann,[1] commenting on this fact, that is, half-siblings eating at the same table, said that, as a result 'it comes about that a close bond is formed between the sons of the same father by different wives'. My own view is that eating together, taken alone, is too formal an activity to achieve such a thing as 'a close bond' between them when it is remembered as Westermann himself noted that even 'conversation at meals is also bad manners for young people'.[2] It is also not uncommon for mothers when they cook special dishes, to call their own children and feed them on some of the choicest food after they had eaten at the common table with their half-brothers.

The other source of fission in the polygynous family which may be considered here is the pull of the children towards their mothers' relatives. Frequently the children go while still young to stay for longer or shorter periods with their mother's brothers, sisters, or parents. They know their visits will be welcome and they much enjoy going. They are made much of, given presents and food, made the centre of attention, so that they are always at home whilst there. It is the grandparents who most often have their daughters' children as visitors. Next in importance are the mothers' brothers.

Since there is no sororal polygyny, half-siblings always have different matrilateral relatives. From very early childhood, therefore, the relations of half-siblings move towards different directions. This will be accentuated in adulthood when some will have to utilize their rights in their mothers' lineages. Children visit their paternal relations also, but this fact does not affect the role of matrilateral kinship as a unifying influence on the full sibling bond.

[1] 1935, p. 29.   [2] *Ibid.*

5

The Effects of Social Changes on Kinship, Marriage and the Family

In the previous chapters, attention was focused primarily on the traditional features of the social structure. This somewhat detailed discussion of the traditional social structure, besides its ethnographic value, should enable us to grasp fully the nature of the changes brought about by contact between the Anlo and the Western World, for it is the traditional elements of the social structure which determine this.

In this chapter an attempt will be made to trace some of the changes produced in Anlo kinship and family life by the establishment of British administration and the introduction of Christianity. Before tackling these problems we must give a brief account of the introduction of these alien forces.

The earliest contact of any importance between the Anlo and Europeans was in 1853, when missionaries of the Norddeutsche (Bremen) mission established a centre at Keta, which has since developed into the largest town in the area. At first progress was slow, and by 1890 only three other centres were opened, namely Anyako (1857), a town on the northern shores of the Keta Lagoon, Woe (1887), and Dzelukofe (1888), two miles west of Keta. Missionary work in those days, as at present, consisted, in the main, of preaching the scriptures, conversion to the faith and the establishment of schools. In all these activities, the missionaries met with such insurmountable opposition from the traditional rulers that at first only freed slaves gave them any reasonable attendance at their schools and churches. It was due to the immense perseverance of the missionaries that by the end of the century they were able to ordain several Anlo scholars into the ministry.

Throughout most of this period the missionaries were operating with no backing of force from any European power. This made their work the more difficult. It was not until the passing in the Gold Coast of the Native Jurisdiction Ordinance in 1883 that a measure of indirect rule was introduced.[1] After this the Roman Catholic Church established a centre in Keta in 1890, to be followed later by the A.M.E. Zion Church, the Anglican Church and the Salvation Army. British influence was further strengthened by the establishment of Anlo as an administrative unit with a District Commissioner at Keta, following the Crowther recommendations.[2] From this time onwards the history of Anlo social institutions has been influenced by forces similar to those operating among all African peoples who have come under Western influence of this nature; the establishment of Government courts in addition to the traditional judicial procedures; the expansion of money economy; the establishment of schools and the creation of a more favourable atmosphere for missionary work. Today every settlement of a few hundred inhabitants has at least a school and a church belonging to one of the denominations mentioned. But the Roman Catholic Church and the Evangelical Presbyterian Church have by far the largest numbers of adherents.

Our subject here is not the total effect of this sequence of events on the Anlo, but only the results they have had on the institutions which form the subject of our discussion, namely kinship, marriage and the family.

We can distinguish a number of fields in which practices external to the indigenous system began to impinge on it and to become part of it. The establishment of white control brought to an end once and for all the inter-tribal wars in which the Anlo had been incessantly involved since their settlement in their present country.[3] This, besides lessening the hostilities between neighbouring tribes, increased communication between them and, along with the circulation of money, made exchange of goods over long distances easier. The Anlo were able to sell their salt and fish to the Akwamu, Krobo, Ga and Ashanti, and bought in return gold and farm products. The development of motor transport,

---

[1] *Native Jurisdiction Ordinance, 1883*, Government of the Gold Coast Colony.
[2] *The Gold Coast Review,* vol. I. III, No. 1. January–June 1927, pp. 11–55.
[3] See Ward, W. E., 1946, pp. 104–7, and 1958, pp. 134–6, 223–8, and 313–15; also Amenumey, 1964, *passim.*

in the shape of the 'Mammy Wagon', is an important factor in this respect, for it greatly increased both local and inter-tribal mobility. The establishment of British courts of law and administrative offices introduced new alternatives into the choices open to individuals and groups in the judicial field, while school education opened new avenues and tastes as well as new ways of satisfying them. Increased trade and new occupations made people less dependent on their kinsfolk for support. Moreover, as farm products started to be produced in large and commercial quantities the value of land increased, resulting in sale of surplus land by lineages who had it. Christianity began to affect traditional attitudes towards the ancestral cults and the mystical bases of kinship obligations.

All these changes in one way or the other affected the Anlo value system in general and undermined the traditional social structure to some extent. We shall try to analyze this process.

I. KIN GROUPS AND SOCIAL CHANGE

We described Anlo society as composed of clans, lineages and wards living in fairly large settlements. It is more than a mere aggregate of units. In it we observed a structure consisting of the relations between people who hold statuses and perform roles in these units. These relations are those of authority, in that the rules governing members place every individual in specific relationships to others who make up the total system. In the working of a system any significant change in one part of its structure is bound to affect the others.[1] Thus where the structure of the lineage is affected, as for instance when the sanctions which support the authority of the lineage head have become ineffective, this change is accordingly translated into the relations between its various segments. In view of the importance of the lineage as the basis of the traditional kinship structure the changes brought about by European activities in Anlo will be primarily related to it.

Of all the changes which came in the wake of British occupation, the money economy has been the most conspicuous and perhaps the most far-reaching. In the traditional system the lineage was largely responsible for the economic welfare of its members.

[1] This view of a 'system' is based on the analysis of it by Parsons in 1951, pp. 3–22.

The economic life of the individual was enclosed in the framework of the lineage system. A person's membership of the lineage entitled him to some land or creek which was the only capital good of any importance. The common interest in land resulted in a special type of relationship between lineage members. An important aspect of this relationship was the attitude of the lineage members to those who were believed to be the owners of the land. The belief that the ancestors expected them to live in peace and unity and to respect their leaders, coupled with the importance of the land to the individual members, greatly buttressed the authority of the lineage head and the other elders, who were to the living, because of their age, the representatives of the dead.

We have described the common interest in land and other properties as one of the important sources of lineage unity. From the economic point of view, the unity of the group and the authority of its head were sustained when heritable property was for many Anlo all they could depend on and when land and creeks were the only forms of capital. A person owed much to his kinsfolk on whom he depended. Now many occupations are open to the individual outside his lineage. Moreover he can now buy a house site or rent building land.[1]

Land ceased to be inalienable soon after the introduction of onions as a cash crop. Southern Anlo is still the only area in Ghana where onions are cultivated on a commercial scale. The 1948 census report describes the industry in the area as 'more systematic ... than is normally to be found among cultivators in the Gold Coast'. The crop was first introduced into Anlo round about the middle of the last century. But it was not until the beginning of the present century that cultivation started on any large scale. The boom which soon followed led many to convert their farms to onion beds. Even then only certain lineages had land of suitable quality, because the crop thrives only in the lower lands on the shores of the lagoons and on the banks of streams. Those who had surplus plots mortgaged some to raise cash to buy more expensive seeds from the Agu mountains in central Togo. At the same time congestion in the wards and land shortage in certain lineages had

---

[1] Today only building plots are sold outright. Onion farms are usually mortgaged for a certain period. Since the farming areas are normally not suitable for residence, it may be necessary to keep this distinction in mind. Some buy building plots and convert them to farms, but not *vice versa*.

led those who could afford it to buy building plots outside their own lineages.

About half the adult male population of Woe are onion farmers. They make on an average about £100 net during the three sowing seasons in the year, which is not bad at all for a rural community with a comparatively low cost of living.

An idea of the extent to which people have become independent of hereditary property for their living has been obtained by a case study of 120 onion farmers at Woe. Seventy-two (60 per cent) were farming land they inherited from their lineage or matrilateral kin. But 52 of these had other plots of farmland mortgaged to them by non-relatives. The remaining 48 were farming only plots mortgaged to them, although some of the latter had inherited land which they consider unsuitable for use at the time of the enquiry. [Compare these figures with the sample of farms in Chapter 2, (IV).]

Since farms are scattered in different parts of the settlement and many people have farms in more than one part of it, the above figures have little bearing on the residence pattern. But the fact that an Anlo can now build his house on land he has bought for himself has affected the degree of localization of lineages. As we have seen the local agnatic incidence, which is said to have been 'very high' in the past, was just 75 per cent in 1952.

Another economic fact which brought some measure of independence to the individual Anlo was the introduction of seine fishing into the area by European traders towards the end of the last century. A number of men, especially those without much land, turned suddenly from farming to fishing, which became particularly lucrative because of the large market for fish in the hinterland. That was the start of an industry on which now depend about half of the 50,000 people living on the Anlo coast. The nets are owned by individuals and groups who employ a number of of men, about thirty adults, for their operation. The group which works together on one net is called a 'company'[1] and is named after the owner, e.g. the Company of Kofiga (Kofigahawo). There are now nearly 300 companies in the area. Each is built around a group the core of which comprises the immediate kins-

---

[1] 'Company' is the term used by the fishermen themselves for the group working on the net, and has been retained by Polly Hill in her article already mentioned.

3*a*. A bokɔnɔ, or diviner at work

3*b*. Fishermen dragging their net ashore while children and a woman wait to help carry the fish

4. Two traders bargain with a shallot seller in Keta market

men of the owner or owners assisted by more distant kin and some unrelated men.

As Polly Hill[1] has observed, the Anlo coast is now one of the busiest fishing areas in West Africa. Actually the coast has been overfished, and the catch is no longer sufficient to support all those who depend on the industry. The result, as has been mentioned earlier, is that for nearly 50 years the fishermen have been inclined to migrate in search of richer waters and markets, sometimes for up to three years at a time. In this way the introduction of seine fishing has helped to increase many Anlo's contact with the outside world. But from the point of view of kinship authority the important thing has been the opening up of new opportunities for people whose lineages have insufficient land, or who have fallen out with their lineages, to turn to net owners, who may not necessarily be relatives, for employment.

In the inland areas, where fishing is still carried on only on a very small scale in lagoons and creeks, European influence made possible improvements in many other economic activities. Of these the making of cloths, baskets, mats and mattresses as mentioned in the introductory chapter is by far the most important. Other occupations introduced by these changes are handicrafts of all kinds, including tailoring, carpentry, gold and silver smithing and masonry.

But by far the most effective means to independence has come 3 through the opportunities offered by school education. This offers chances of employment which guarantees a steady and regular income. Through education the Anlo becomes to some extent wedded to European ideals which are foreign to his native training. One factor which accelerates the estrangement of the educated Anlo from his indigenous culture, and which at the same time reduces his influence on the traditional society, is the inevitable tendency to find his future not in his natal community but in a commercial or industrial centre. In the absence of great commercial and industrial centres in the Anlo district he realizes his ambition in most cases in the large towns outside Anlo country, such as Accra, Kumasi and Takoradi. A sizeable number too find work at Keta. Such educated migrants return home occasionally, and for brief periods, only when they are 'on leave' from their employers. This at least was the position before the Gold Coast

[1] 1963, p. 1455.

became indepedent, when almost 90 per cent of the school leavers had to go outside Anlo to find work.

The emigration of school leavers expresses the ordinary Anlo literate's attitude to farming, fishing or weaving. These occupations are considered unsuitable for educated men. This attitude has persisted because of the tendency among literates to live differently from the illiterates in their own community. One is made to think that the educated man is forced to adopt this attitude because the illiterate locals, among them his own relatives, do not expect him, after his education, to come back and 'be one of them'. They expect him to be a 'clerk', that is, to work with a European commercial firm or a Government Department. Any educated man who indulges in farming or fishing is bound to subject himself to derision of all sorts and even abuse. For instance two school leavers who were in a fishing company at Woe in 1962 complained that people had been saying they had failed their school-leaving examinations (which was untrue), otherwise they would have gone to Accra. The same applied to the handful of school-leavers who were helping their parents in farming. These complaints are not merely attempts to find excuses for leaving for the city. It is the unfortunate impression any observer is bound to have in this area. I myself heard derision of this kind several times. The term *klaki ɖigbɔ*, which in effect means 'a disappointed literate', is often used of these educated men.

One reason for this state of affairs is the fact that agriculture and fishing have not been modernised in a way which would make them more profitable and so more attractive to educated men. Until the last two years the tractor was a very rare spectacle, and motor fishing trawlers are only just beginning to appear.

The result is that many lineages are losing their sturdiest members. Also, since traditional values and customs are not learned so much by theoretical education as through participant observation, there is the added result of the gradual but steady disappearance, among the educated, of knowledge regarding traditional usages. For instance, it was found that nearly half the students at the two secondary schools at Keta did not know the totems and taboos of their clans. Yet of the illiterates of the same age group not a single one was ignorant of these facts.

This is also the case, but to a much lesser extent, with the illiterate fishermen who seasonally migrate to such places as Lagos,

Freetown or Abidjan. The influence of this type of migration on the traditional values is less disruptive than that of the literates, partly because the environment in which the emigrant companies live, almost to themselves, is not very different from what they have at home, and partly because they are less attracted to the European way of life wherever they may be. Thus when in 1962 some companies returned home from Abidjan, it was possible to find a marked difference between their behaviour and that of the literate Anlo on leave. Soon after their arrival the various lineages arranged special thanksgiving ceremonies to their ancestors and other deities. Gifts were offered in abundance and protection sought for future expeditions. In contrast it is only occasionally that the educated Anlo finds the time and need to take active part in such traditional activities.

The emigration of school leavers is now under some control. Since the country became independent in 1957, the establishment of the Workers' Brigade[1] and the state farms, and the Government's 'back to the land' campaign, and the formation throughout the country of young farmers' associations have modified the picture. First the state farms (there are several branches now in the area) and the Workers' Brigade are helping to change people's attitude to farming. The use of tractors and the fact that the majority of the employees are literate are the important contributory factors. Now nearly a quarter of elementary school leavers remain in the locality, not necessarily in their own settlements, but within easy reach.

Also, with the introduction of free and compulsory education there has been a great demand for school-leavers as 'pupil teachers', which has made it possible for many literates to remain in their areas. Many junior clerks are also required for the increasing number of District Commissioners' Offices now being opened,[2] as well as for the various Government agencies, such as the Food and Nutrition Board, women's organizations and the Department of Social Welfare and Community Development. Several settlements in Anlo now have these facilities, which were formerly to

[1] The Workers' Brigade (formerly Builders' Brigade) was established in 1957 by the Government to employ ex-servicemen and unemployed youths in the fields of agriculture, building and construction. School leavers form the bulk of the members.

[2] The Keta district, formerly administered as one unit, is now subdivided into six units each with its own District Commissioner.

be found only in Keta. The employment of school-leavers in these jobs enables them to work with their own people and to decrease the dishonour usually associated with school-leavers working in their own villages.

These new establishments open new vistas to the educated Anlo both in his own village and outside it. His employment offers him a new circle of acquaintances, or that continued from school, based both on occupational or professional interests and congeniality of personalities. In such environments mutual aid societies are the rule. These societies, which cut across kinship lines, are now more important in his life than the lineage or other kin groups. Many such associations have rules which govern the behaviour of members. Disputes are referred to their executives. To give financial and moral help to members in time of need is one of their important aims. Certainly in such a crisis as bereavement, the chief mourners will be lineage members and other kinsmen, but his comrades will offer him financial and moral support. He is therefore able to look outside his kin groups when the need arises. Indeed when he is far away from home it is his associates who play the major part in these cases.

Co-operation of this nature is not limited to the educated Anlo. Fishing companies also have their own rules, such as that disputes between members must be referred to the company's owner or business executive for settlement. Onion farmers too have formed themselves into associations which give their leaders wide powers, enabling them for instance to determine when farmers in each locality should start sowing or harvesting.

One result of the increased occupational differentiation is that junior members of a lineage may gain economic power which places them above the others. And since leadership in the associations is based on ability and professional qualification rather than age or birth, able men can easily rise to positions of leadership. School education *per se* may also give influence. In many lineage matters the advice of the educated members is sought, and family disputes are sometimes brought to them instead of the lineage head for settlement. This may have far-reaching repercussions on the structure of the lineage. The fact is that at the present time neither personal eminence nor the constitution of co-operating local groups is significantly determined, as it was in the past, by membership of or attachment to any kind of genealogically defined unit.

One or two examples may serve to illustrate this. Akakpoga, a renowned diviner and owner of several prosperous fishing companies, at 42 was a junior but most respected member of the Aʋako lineage at Woe. He was undoubtedly its richest member. In 1962 two brothers, sons of Akakpoga's second ortho-cousin, were drowned in the Woe area of the Keta Lagoon at the height of the floods. One of the bodies was found three days later and buried. It was not until the late evening of the fourth day that the second was found. Tradition decrees that no burial should take place at night, except for people who die from special diseases.[1] However the boy's father, finding that the body was not in a condition to be preserved till the following morning, suggested that burial should take place that night. He was immediately shouted down. Soon afterwards Akakpoga, who was noted for his revolutionary views, also spoke in favour of the night burial, and everyone murmured approval.

I also know of a group of siblings whose disputes are never settled until their educated brother comes home on leave, although he is not the lineage head. Several similar instances could be cited. The *de jure* structure of the lineage may persist; the oldest surviving male member may remain the lineage head; he may still be regarded as the only one who prays to the ancestors. But decision-making becomes more and more a function of the *de facto* power structure. Moreover, many other functions previously performed by the lineage are now outside its domain, and it is in these new functioning associations that men like Akakpoga are making their mark.

Missionary activities have also had a great influence on the social structure. In Ghana, as in many other parts of Africa, Christianity was a necessary concomitant of school education, because most of the early schools were run by missionaries, who almost always made baptism a condition for attendance. Those converted were soon to lose touch with most of their traditional values and beliefs, for the missionaries were not content with teaching the scriptures.

---

[1] All 'unnatural' deaths are regarded as 'bad deaths', *kuvɔwo* (sing. *kuvɔ*). They belong to two broad categories. One is that of executed criminals, mad persons and victims of death preceded by the swelling of the body. These are buried in the night with only summary ceremonies. The second are victims of accidents and childbirth. Their corpses are prepared for burial in a special 'house' of palm branches outside the family house. (For further detail see Gaba, 1965, especially pp. 251-2).

They considered many native practices unsuitable for Christians and were determined to crush them. As Professor Mair puts it, 'the Christian missionaries have set their faces against all the patently "uncivilized" aspects of native culture, whether or not they were directly forbidden by the scriptures: they have opposed polygamy, slavery, the payment of bride-price, initiation ceremonies, dancing . . . as all being equally repugnant to a civilization in which mechanical warfare is a recognized institution.'[1]

This attitude greatly alienated educated Anlo from their traditional beliefs and institutions, especially their faith in the efficacy of the power of the ancestors, which was the most important sanction on lineage unity and its leaders' authority. In the individual sphere too one finds as a result the disregard of clan taboos and injunctions which may now be regarded as superstitions. The extent of Christian influence can be appreciated if it is realized that Christianity has been fairly successful in Anlo. Once the initial difficulties were overcome rapid progress was made. At first the converts were mostly those who went to school. But in the last two decades especially, illiterates have been converted in increasing numbers. Girls form the greater proportion of these because as a result of their baptism and the lessons they take before confirmation they imbibe some of the qualities expected by educated men of their wives. This has been necessitated by the small number of girls who go to school as compared with that of boys, with the result that there is not a corresponding number of educated women to marry the educated men.

In Woe and Alakple about 40 per cent of the population are at least nominal Christians. Most of these accordingly stay away from ancestral rites and other indigenous practices which run counter to conditions laid down by the missionaries.

In the field of law and public order the direct outcome of European occupation has been the establishment of government courts with powers over and above the traditional procedures. The effects of this were mainly political, but it also affected the relations of the Anlo with their lineage leaders. In the traditional system, where the lineage head lacked the backing of force, the ultimate sanctions governing behaviour in everyday matters were religious. The adjudication of lineage matters rested solely with the head and the elders. Though cases were sometimes taken

[1] Mair, 1934, p. 3.

to the King's or the village chief's courts, matters concerning the lineage were settled within it. This meant that it was not necessary to sue a fellow lineage member at the Chief's court. Backed by the sanctions of the dead, the elders' decisions were considered final.

There is no pretending that these decisions were always just, or that the disputants were always satisfied with them. In the main the elders concerned themselves with reconciliation and the maintenance of harmony between kinsmen, rather than giving judgement on the juridical merits of a case. In other words, the punishments and compensations did not always measure up to the offence. This position was radically altered by the establishment of British courts. Disputes between lineage members, as well as inter-lineage ones, are still sometimes settled by the elders, but many litigants have taken advantage of the presence of the lay magistrate's court near by where they expect more impersonal treatment. In this respect the present trend has been helped by the cracks already appearing in lineage solidarity and the authority of the elders as a result of the increasing economic independence of the individual and doubts of the efficacy of the ancestral sanctions.

One of the greatest blows to lineage unity in this field has been quarrels concerning land. The quarrels are caused partly by improper distribution of rights, but mainly by sales without proper authority. As we have seen, land is no longer considered inalienable. People now sell their share of lineage land, and this is considered perfectly permissible. But there have also been instances when a head sells a portion of the lineage land without authority from the members and is taken to court by his juniors. Several disputes have resulted from such irresponsibility.

The alienation of land affects lineage unity in two ways. First, the lineage ceases to be a unit with a common interest in property. Secondly, the litigation which follows some irregular sales gives rise to situations with which the lineage heads are not fully equipped to deal. Consequently their authority is disregarded and cases are transferred from them to the magistrate's court, the decisions of which are considered more authoritative and more effective. The elders themselves sometimes indirectly contribute to this by mismanagement of lineage property. The overall result has been the disintegration of lineages and the consequent weakening of the elders' authority. And in this the new economic opportunities open to the ordinary Anlo have been the dominant factor.

One other index of the disintegration of lineages must be mentioned here. This is the dispersion of members. When lineages were localized in the ward, *afedome*, co-operation was much easier, and so was the regular expression of their corporate unity. Now, in addition to the seasonal movements of fishing companies and the migration of educated members, overcrowding has led to the dispersal of lineages even in the same settlement. Today at the ancestral rites, when the lineage used to meet in a body, only a fraction of its total membership is present. At impromptu meetings for *ad hoc* purposes people who live far away from the lineage home may find it difficult to attend. As Barnes[1] has recently observed, 'co-residence implies the possibility but not necessity of continual day-to-day face-to-face interaction, and in non-literate society, however clearly their rights are recognized, absent members cannot play as full a part in the activities of the group as do those who are present.'

This part of the discussion would be incomplete without a look at one aspect of kinship which has persisted in a different form despite all the changes. This is mutual help. When discussing the changes which have been taking place in kinship relations, the Anlo themselves think more of this than anything else.

It is obvious that in the past, in addition to the lineage's collective responsibility for the economic welfare of its members, kinsmen co-operated among themselves. Older informants maintain that 'in the past relatives used to eat from each other. Anyone who had a bad harvest had ready assistance from more fortunate relatives.' It was not even considered necessary for anyone to ask his brother or cousin, real or classificatory, before plucking a few ears of corn or a couple of sugar canes from his farm. Indeed it is maintained that a person could not steal a relative's property. He could only take it. And co-operation among kinsfolk was considered one of the most important obligations.

This aspect of kinship obligations is still taken very seriously by those who are in a position to help. But it seems that the range of kinsfolk now considered important is narrower and more specific. In what follows I try to give a rather detailed account so as to

[1] 1962, p. 7.

bring out clearly how the ordinary Anlo now feels about it. One way in which this spirit is expressed is the regular sums given by well-to-do members of the society for support of kinsfolk and the *ad hoc* financial assistance given to those in need.

Salaried workers and artisans, as well as farmers and fishermen, are known to be the principal benefactors in this respect, but the educated and the salaried men are by far the most important. In an area where there are frequent economic fluctuations on account of floods, drought and poor fishing seasons, the educated elements in the various kin groups have become the insurance institutions on which their relatives fall back.

The salaried workers interviewed were working at Keta, Anloga and Woe. In all they numbered seventy-two. Eighty-three per cent gave some regular help to at least one relative outside their household, apart from wives and dependent children, and over 50 per cent said they gave an average of over £1 a month. Since most of them were earning just about £15 a month, this contribution was a substantial part of their income. About 25 per cent spent over £5 on relatives and about 10 per cent over £6. These sums, it was claimed, did not include occasional gifts or the expenses of lineage rituals, which some of them are expected to bear.

Most of the help went to old people such as parents and grandparents, uncles and aunts and elderly cousins and related widows without children of their own. Apart from old people their main responsibility was the education of younger siblings, nephews, nieces and married sisters. Some were helping relatives of their own generation and others of their children's age groups. But of all relatives by far the most generally accepted responsibility was for the mother. '*Ame dada mefena na ame o*', 'one does not play with one's mother'. The mother must be helped. 'Anyone who doesn't help his mother must be a fool.' Ninety-one per cent of those interviewed whose mothers were alive regularly supported them. Where this did not happen it was because the mother was herself a wealthy woman in a position to help herself and her dependants. After their mothers, they most often gave help to siblings, maternal aunts, fathers, or paternal aunts in that order. Both men and women support their relatives, and a wife will try to set aside something for her family from trade or selling poultry, but the amounts are smaller than what men usually give.

The heaviest responsibility tends to fall on the eldest son, even while his father is still working. Akpelashie, a £25 a month school teacher in Keta, told me, 'I have two younger brothers and two sisters. They are all attending school. It is my intention to give them the best possible education. My father did a lot for me even when the going was bad for him. Now that he is getting old I must relieve him of some of his responsibilities. Next year Cudjoe, the second brother, is going to Mawuli Secondary School at Ho. The first brother is also a brilliant chap, but I have advised him to take up a teaching appointment so as to help me educate the younger ones. Both girls will go to the Keta Secondary Day School.' This teacher also was sending about £1 regularly to his mother, and another £1 to 'my small mother, who sometimes even asks for more when the need arises.' As soon as the father dies, responsibility for his mother and siblings falls squarely on the eldest son. It may be assumed by a younger brother if the eldest is not so well off, as in the case of Nani, the youngest of four brothers and the only one of his family to have gone to school. He was a bank official receiving about £40 a month. 'I have two wives and five children. But when my father died last year my responsibilities for my mother increased. My brothers were formerly fairly prosperous farmers, but we lost our onion beds in a lawsuit. Now they have no plots of their own. Two of them got some mortgaged farms with my assistance. But they have not yet found their feet. The third one has left for Abidjan. We don't even hear from him. So every month I send £2 10s or £3 to my mother. Other relatives are also asking for help'.

Where possible the responsibilities are adjusted to fall fairly on all earning members of the sibling group. A carpenter told me, 'My two elder brothers and I are fairly rich, so we have devised a method by which each one of us assumes a certain share of the responsibilities to our younger brothers' and sisters' education. We also built a new house for our mother after the death of our father. Our only married sister is now living with our mother. My own daughter is staying there to help them.'

In addition to these regular sums, there are also occasional calls for help. A mother's brother whose crop is destroyed by floods calls suddenly for help, and his sister's son will have to do something. A brother's wife falls sick, and help is readily sought from an elder brother.

Certain segments of lineages have quite rich and self-supporting members, and the regular exchanges described are no longer considered an important feature of inter-family relations. In other prosperous lineages, where every family is financially independent, the reciprocal exchange of gifts tends to balance up and no hardship is entailed. In a poor family, on the other hand, it is not uncommon to find a regular income earner who has to deprive himself of even the smallest luxuries for the sake of his kinsfolk.

The important thing about these gifts is not so much the amount or frequency as the spirit in which they are given. As informants always claimed, '*Mi Aŋlɔwo ɖe míewɔa fome*', 'We Anlo, we like to do kinship – honour our kinship obligations.' The best way to do this is to help relatives in need. Now that social and economic conditions have introduced differences in income, not all are able to reciprocate the favours they receive from their relatives. But in a sense the gifts given by the educated Anlo to their relations may be equated with the help given them by their parents and other kinsfolk when they were attending school. Thus, though kinship makes it necessary for them to help elders and parents who are in need, many educated Anlo, when giving help, recall what their parents, aunts, and uncles did for them, in the hope that their own children's generation will support them in their turn.

Not all regular income earners find it necessary to give help to relatives beyond parents and young siblings. Others do not even include siblings in their responsibility. They do not understand why they should be expected to look after others when they have families of their own to care for. One such man was Asigbi. He told me that 'the best way to deal with this mass of relatives is to be tough. If they know you are miserly they will stop troubling you. Once you start parting with money freely they take advantage. Boy, let me tell you. This *fome* (kinship) thing is a thing of the past and the illiterate folk should realize that. Yesterday I was just going to bed when a relative of mine, my father's sister's son, dropped in. He wanted to stay the night. He also wanted some money for their net. I managed to despatch him immediately. No money. The way I treated him he would never try again.'

There are some other people like Asigbi. Their attitude is usually a result of the treatment they received from their relatives during their school days. They are in the main those who went through school the hard way by looking after themselves. But they form a negligible proportion of the educated Anlo, though Asigbi's view of kinship as a thing of the past is increasing in popularity. It is necessary to add, however, that all the educated men interviewed, including those in the last category, agreed that close relations who are really in need must be helped.

This analysis of mutual help as an expression of kinship obligation shows that the modern conditions which alienate educated men from their traditional values provide also the means by which these very people help their kinsmen, whose economic weakness is a result of the same changes. But these benevolent gestures are not limited to the educated few. All fairly prosperous farmers, fishermen and young men of all descriptions who are in a position to help do so. It is also important to add that the help does not always go in the same direction, that is from the educated man to needy relatives. On occasion a clerk who loses his job tells his parents and uncles, and they all contribute a few pounds to secure him as a storekeeper in a commercial firm.

In general, therefore, relatives, especially those with regular earnings, still assume responsibility for the welfare of the less fortunate. As yet there are few welfare services in Ghana to relieve them of any of these duties. In the absence of these services this sense of mutual obligation will continue for a long time to sustain kinship ties as the dominant concern of everyday life. Every member of the kin group has rights, obligations and privileges, and enjoys the sense of security which they provide. Everyone is protected against the financial difficulties of unemployment, old age and sickness, and can look to close kinsmen for support in difficulty.

It is difficult to ascertain the degree of relationships which in the past carried with them the obligations of mutual help and support. Records are not specific. It appears from the life histories of some informants that the range was extensive. If this is so, then the economic individualism which resulted in the weakening of the lineage as a property-holding group may be held responsible for the present narrowing, for the important consideration which made help obligatory was not only the kinship tie itself but also the fact that the source of income was a common property.

2. MARRIAGE AND THE FAMILY IN THE CHANGING CONDITIONS

It has been indicated already that marriage no longer always takes the traditional form. Anlo marriage today is completely devoid of ceremonial and much of its ritual. The last *dedexɔ* (seclusion ceremony) I recorded took place nearly ten years ago. The consummation also has lost its significance, and virginity in a bride is now rare. In this section an attempt will be made to view modern marriage in the light of the changes now taking place.

Traditionally marriages were between two kin groups and were frequently arranged by the elders. Today young people are more and more claiming the right to choose their own spouses, though some stress is still laid upon parental approval.

Today, when a young man has chosen a girl, he requests his father, with the girl's consent, to approach her parents to discuss the union. The girl's parents then make inquiries regarding the character and position of the young man and his family: hereditary diseases, witchcraft, criminality and physical defects are still considered. If the results are satisfactory the young man's parents are informed that the proposal is acceptable and the two kin groups meet for the wedding. Nevertheless parental opposition is still common, as was shown by the case of Danu and Aku.

A typical modern wedding ceremony I witnessed at Woe in 1962 was remarkable for its paucity of glamour, ritual and ceremonial. Three days after the marriage payment was accepted, the two families met in the bride's father's house, where the bride was handed over with brief speeches of exhortation and a prayer to the ancestors. There was neither a consummation ceremony nor seclusion of any kind.

The Christian Churches allow marriages to be performed by the families before the couple come for Church blessing. Even if there is to be a Church wedding it is preceded by the customary one.

The fact that marriages are now generally discussed by the young people before they approach their parents introduces new elements into the relationship of the spouses-to-be. Nowadays the lovers are able to study each other well before making their final decision. One adverse consequence is that virginity at marriage is becoming rarer, since marriage is only the final stage in a relationship which the lovers themselves had already decided on. This in turn leads to the danger of premarital pregnancy. This danger is really grave in view of the young people's ignorance of contraceptives. 87 per cent of married men knew nothing about contraceptives, and of those who knew only about half considered their use worth while. Premarital pregnancy is now a social problem, and the free association of the sexes, helped by the schools and the Churches, is blamed for it. Even in the mission schools established by the Presbyterian and Roman Catholic Churches, inquiries showed that sexual experience among adolescent boys and girls is very widespread.

In the absence of contraceptives it is not surprising that many of these liaisons end in pregnancy. In one mixed senior elementary school containing 131 boys and 47 girls, about eight girls become pregnant every year. Among the town girls too premarital pregnancy is high, especially among the semi-literate.

Premarital pregnancy is not always the result of ignorance or accident. The Anlo stress on marriage as primarily for the procreation of children presupposes that a girl becomes a wife in order to become a mother, but the usual procedure of first becoming a wife has now tended to be reversed and some girls aim at first becoming pregnant and then considering how to make the men marry and maintain them. Equally, due to the present dubious sexual morality of girls, many young men wish to make sure that their girl friends are capable of bearing children before embarking on marriage.[1] Paradoxically enough, this tendency is more prevalent among those Christian literates who intend to make monogamous civil or religious marriages, because if the woman proves barren remarriage cannot take place without dissolving the first marriage on Christian grounds; and the Catholic Church does not approve of divorce on any grounds. Surrounding this practice is the popular superstition, mentioned to me by several informants, that a bride who is not pregnant before a church or civil marriage remains barren for life. They mentioned some cases in support of this.

The girl may wish to become pregnant because she is afraid her lover does not mean to marry her. She makes herself available to him because she knows their parents will bring pressure on him

---

[1] The popular belief is that many girls now cause abortion a number of times before getting married, and this is believed to affect fertility.

to marry her. In such matches love, which is supposed to be the primary factor, tends to be secondary to distrust and economic considerations; consequently tensions arise at the outset from the element of constraint imposed on the man.

It often happens that an unmarried girl finds after her pregnancy that her seducer is not in a position to maintain her, as is usually the case when the lover is in school. This may be risky for the girl, because it may be a sufficient cause for abandoning her unless his parents are willing to look after her.

Because of these dangers, the sensible girl from a good home still finds it necessary to rely on parental advice, knowing that if she marries without her parents' full consent, she will not be able to fall back upon them should the marriage prove unsuccessful.

The problems created by modern conditions go beyond the choice of partners and premarital pregnancy. We must recall that the establishment of British Courts curtailed the powers of the traditional authorities, so that they no longer have the power to execute hardened adulterers. Adultery is now punished by a fine of £5, which is not beyond the means of the ordinary Anlo. The attitude of Christians too, which derides the mystical retribution believed to be visited on sexual offences, has not helped. 'Since coitus has no referee', as an informant put it, the most important sanctions against illegal liaisons were the mystical beliefs associated with them. These beliefs were dispelled without the Christian Churches taking the trouble to bring strong sanctions to back the Seventh Commandment. If it is true, as is popularly believed, that many Christians do not take confessions seriously, then it is only after a person has been found guilty of adultery by a court or caught *in flagrante delicto* that any disciplinary action could be taken against him. In most cases this takes the form of suspension from certain Church activities. The difficulty of detecting adulterers is so grave that, although rumour and village gossip have it that adultery is relatively rife among Christians, there was not a single trial for the offence during our ten-month stay in the two villages.

Even if there are adulterers among the Christians, it is doubtful whether disciplinary action can have any effect on most of them, because only a few are practising Christians. At Woe, out of a total membership of nearly five hundred adults, only seventy women and seven men are said to be regular communicants.[1]

In discussing Anlo attitude towards sex offences it is important to distinguish Christians from pagans. If there is one aspect of Anlo social life in which the pagans have not yet been greatly influenced by Christianity, it is this. Curiously enough, adultery occurs much less frequently among the pagans. This may be explained in several ways.

In all the cult groups and pagan religious organizations, the faithfulness of spouses is one of the first injunctions. There is also the belief in the efficacy of the pagan deities, and in their power eventually to detect and punish every sin committed. It is also believed that failure to confess in the face of punishment, which always takes the form of serious sickness, will result in death or madness. There are many instances to remind the Anlo pagan of this. Every now and then a woman dies suddenly, and divination reveals that adultery is the cause. Mention was made in an earlier chapter of women who were believed to have died because of failure to confess their infidelity, and others who went mad for the same reason. I also saw a woman at Alakple who, after she was found out by her cult through divination, confessed to committing adultery with several men. The public horror provoked by such discoveries is in itself a strong sanction against cult members. In the case of *dema*, already described, confession may not always save the adulteress. Moreover, many pagan women believe that their husbands take magical precautions against their infidelity.

It is these beliefs which account for the differences in moral behaviour between Christians and pagans, though the two images presented are to some extent stereotyped. On the one hand, many Christian wives are very faithful to their husbands. On the other, quite a number of pagans could be found to be unfaithful, as evidenced by those who have confessed after divination has revealed their sins. Moreover, about 10 per cent of the pagans do not belong to any of the retributive organizations mentioned, and others have been disenchanted by Christian influence from the mystical beliefs associated with illicit sexual behaviour. But still,

---

[1] This does not mean that the non-communicants are practising pagans in Christian uniforms. Outwardly they behave like Christians on many social occasions, and they even look down on pagan practices, but they find it difficult to adhere to Christian principles.

Christianity and the indigenous religions have had great influence on Anlo sexual behaviour and, given the division into Christians and pagans, the above conclusions should hold.

Another important structural change that can be attributed to external influences is the decreased incidence of polygyny. In the old days a man acquired dependants by begetting, buying or capturing in war. Wealth consisted largely of dependants who could help him in his economic activities. The well-remembered names of the past are those of men who had several wives and slaves, whose offspring now form the core of some villages. As Westermann[1] puts it, 'The rule is that he who has sufficient means marries more. . . Those who do not are rare exceptions.' Nowadays, in addition to the fact that the Churches oppose polygyny, wealth and leadership can be obtained by other means. Moreover, polygyny demands greater expenses now than before. People who have many wives must be able to feed them in the first place. In the early days of colonialism the few people who were able to make money had limited uses for it. Giving marriage payments and buying slaves were the chief uses to which it was put. Now there are not only many other uses for money but it can be obtained in several other ways.

Nevertheless polygyny is still an important feature of Anlo family life. When the Christian Churches opposed polygyny, they were fighting an institution practised by the traditional leaders themselves, which was an essential aspect of the traditional social structure. This was one of the reasons for the relative failure of the missionaries in converting the Anlo to monogamy. Many Anlo still consider that marriage to a plurality of wives is a man's right, and most men cannot reconcile this belief with Christianity's preference for monogamy. The Presbyterian catechist at Woe told me that polygyny is the reason why the ratio of regular communicants is about ten to one against men. The Presbyterian Church's rule is that a man who marries a second wife ceases to be a communicant, and the same applies to the woman. This implies that only first marriages are given church blessing. He went on, 'But the truth is that practically all illiterate Christians are polygamous, and it is therefore not surprising that only a few men turn up for the Holy Communion.'

The low proportion of male Christians who receive Communion

[1] 1949, p. 50.

may also be explained by the apparent indifference of men in religious matters compared with the enthusiasm of the women. At service the pews for women are always full, while the men's are completely empty, or filled only by children.

But the ratio of monogamy to polygyny shows no significant difference between Christians and pagans, except for teachers, whose profession makes it necessary for them to be monogamous. Apart from teachers only a very small number of men, who are strongly influenced by Christian belief set a positive value on the strict observance of monogamy even when their economic standing might make polygyny desirable.

Thus Christianity has not very much affected the Anlo attitude towards polygyny, and if there is any difference between its incidence today and in the past the explanation must be sought in other directions. It is not easy to assess whether the incidence of polygyny as a whole has decreased over the years. Since our information on the past is based on genealogies, it is possible that it is incomplete on barren wives and the wives of men whose descendants are no longer in the localities studied. It is also not clear on the proportion of polygynists who made successive monogamous marriages, or 'diachronic polygyny' in Southall's[1] terminology. Making allowance for these limitations, there is evidence to indicate a decrease in polygyny, for in the past two out of three were polygynists, whereas today's figures show roughly two out of five.

Today many economic factors militate against polygyny. The financial implications in the initial stages have been mentioned. House-building is much more costly and difficult now, and a man must be very rich to provide adequate homes for many wives. This difficulty is somewhat offset by the increasing number of second and successive wives who prefer to remain in their parental homes. At the same time, as many wives now prefer to live apart from their senior co-wives, provision of houses for those who cannot or are not willing to live with their parents or other relatives means the establishment of a new homestead for each wife.

By preaching monogamy the Christian Churches were indirectly curbing the sexual rights of men over their wives and increasing those of the women. Monogamy puts the rights of

[1] 1959, p. 52.

husband and wife on the same level by limiting the husband's sexual activities to his wife as hers are to him. These are in complete contradiction with the male attitude mentioned above. The large number of polygynous marriages at Woe and Alakple (42·4 per cent) shows that quite a large number of Anlo women still accept the jural superiority of men. Others, such as the few literates and rich market women who have somehow emerged from tribal life, tend to interpret equality to mean permanent monogamy for both men and women. Those who are first wives try to prevail on their husbands not to take additional wives. Others who have co-wives have been able to persuade their husbands to get rid of them or make life impossible for them so that they leave.

On the whole, traditional male values on sexual rights have only been slightly modified. Female criticism and the Churches' pressure have had little result. On the other hand male criticism of laxity in women, being less revolutionary and backed by traditional values and Christian teaching, carries considerable weight. At the moment the conflict still remains unresolved, and looks like continuing in intensity with the increase in the number of educated women.

Compared with the above, the interpersonal and authority relations between spouses in the home have moved a long way towards equality. This has been greatly helped by the traditional economic independence of women, which now provides them with a strong basis for adjustment to the demands of modern conditions for an emancipated status. Conversations with many couples, especially those in monogamous unions, indicate that today as much weight is given to the wife's as the husband's view. It is true that matters concerning the upkeep of the home have always been under the direction of the wife, but the segregation of the sexes is no longer as rigid as in the past. Many decisions about the children are now taken by both parents together.

These new features of domestic life were clearly brought out during our interviews. On many occasions, especially in Keta and Woe, husband and wife sat together and answered our questions either independently or in consultation. On other occasions wives would insist on being present when the husband wanted to confide in us. The atmosphere in these homes always savoured of equality.

In an answer to questions on authority structure within the household, among 222 men 37·1 per cent maintained that the relationship between a man and his wife should be based on absolute equality. They said they didn't expect their wives to be subservient to them in any way, and always treated, and were treated by, them as equal partners. However, of all the husbands only 15 per cent were addressed by name by their wives, and all these were among the 37·1 per cent. The remainder were divided on the best form of address. Some did not find the use of the term *efo*, elder brother, the traditional term of obedience, for a husband, inconsistent with equality, since husbands are usually older than their wives. Others would have liked to be addressed by name, but as one informant explained, 'Owing to the natural respect for a husband a wife will prefer to address you in terms other than the personal name.' I never met an illiterate or pagan couple on first-name relationship, though there were quite a number whose relationship can really measure up to the equality described. Perhaps one might agree with the informant quoted that the right to call a husband by name is not an index of equality.

On the other hand, 62·9 per cent of the married men thought that the wife should be subservient to the husband. Despite this, there has been a great change from the attitude of total submission of the wife described by Westermann.[1]

In our earlier discussion we saw that the Anlo family, like any other group, normally functions as a unit in many respects. It is a domestic unit, either by itself or as part of a larger one. Among its main functions are co-operation in the upkeep of the household and the education of its younger members in preparation for their adult life. This last function has been undergoing some changes since the introduction of schools, and it will be necessary to consider it in some detail.

The introduction of schools means that a great number of children (now nearly all) between the ages of six and seventeen spend a significant part of their lives under the direction, and in the company of, people who are not their parents or siblings. There is therefore a sudden break in the natural development of the parent-child relationship. We have seen that in the traditional system a child between six and eight years old spends most of its time playing with its siblings and cousins, until at about ten it begins to follow the occupation of its parents and help in the domestic work. In this way the child is prepared for its future.

[1] 1935, p. 49.

Schools now have taken over the preparation of the child. The effects of this change are manifold. The child enters a group whose membership cuts across kinship lines. Through partial co-residence and co-activity it develops a permanent relationship with its teachers and colleagues approximating roughly to the parent-child and sibling relationships. These new relationships, especially the latter, can play a very important part in the child's development. After school hours, at week-ends and in vacation periods, many activities are organized on the basis of these special relationships. At these times, when they are not assisting their parents, school children can often be seen together in small work gangs collecting firewood for sale, fishing, or hunting for small game. They also visit one another and help their friends in household duties, such as grinding pepper for girls and mending fences for boys. The extent to which these relationships develop largely depends on the spatial proximity of their homes and the relations between their parents. In the present kinship composition of the villages, where the lineages are less localized, the correlation between kinship and membership of these children's groups is becoming more and more slight, while that between residence and membership increases.

Sometimes quarrels between parents may end or prevent close friendships between their children, although the latter may be very fond of one another. This was the case with Mose and Kɔwuvi, whose friendship suddenly changed to enmity after Mose's father was found by divination to have been responsible for the death of Kɔwuvi's sister. Earlier Mose's father's proposal to marry Kɔwuvi's sister had been opposed by her father. Here indeed is the difference between kinship and friendship which is always emphasized by informants. Kinship is a permanent relationship, unsevered even by the greatest animosity between those concerned. Friendship is based on consent and is therefore conditional. But where the atmosphere is healthy, friendship plays an important part in a person's life.

Close association between comrades and age mates through the medium of schools may increase the ties of friendship at the expense of sibling solidarity, especially where there are great differences in the ages of siblings. It should be possible to find some correlation between comradeship in fishing companies and childhood associations of this kind. The matter is however one of degree. Even in the past, though the Anlo attached a high value to agnation and kinship in general, also important in the organization of everyday activities were relationships of friendship and co-operation between neighbours without regard to kinship affilia-tion. Now, it seems, friendship is playing a greater part than in the past.

The two spheres of authority represented by parents and teachers introduce an element of uncertainty in the behaviour of children. Though they are not pampered, Anlo children enjoy a good deal of freedom in the home, and it is only serious offences like habitual stealing and disrespect to elders that are severely punished. At the same time the respect due to elders is epitomized by the saying that a child does not look into its senior's face. But in the informal setting of domestic life, respect for elders does not involve any separation of children from members of the older generations. What is meant by the saying is that a child, or anyone else for that matter, should give due respect to an older person, obey his orders, not be involved in argument or altercation with him, and not call him by name.

With this background children find it somewhat difficult to reconcile the formality of the classroom life, especially their relation with the teachers, with their parents' attitude to them. The teacher as a disciplinarian, with a stick in hand most of the time, is much less approachable, and is better able than parents to strike terror and inspire respect. While a child can refuse to go on an errand for its mother and get away with it, it could not behave in like manner towards its teacher without incurring the severest punishment. Hence there is a tendency among many children to take liberties at home, where they enjoy greater freedom than they can at school. An important index of this development has been the attitude of some parents, almost equal to resignation, of transferring their disciplinary functions to teachers. Many teachers told me that some children have become so uncontrollable that when they do something wrong at home the parents ask teachers to beat them at school, instead of themselves giving the punish-ment. I often heard the threat from many parents, 'Meyina ta wò trɔ ge na miafe tsitsa', 'I am going to report you to your teacher'.

Some parents also think that by sending their children to school they have transferred their socialization functions to the teachers; hence the remark one often hears today that teachers are no longer strict with children. It is true, however, that frequent association with contemporaries, prior to adolescence, when much of their time is spent away from the watchful eyes of their parents, develops in children behaviour patterns which traditional parent-child relationship might have avoided. The use of swear-words by children and their sexual precocity are some of the evils parents commonly attribute to the influence of schools.

What this discussion shows is that schools have taken from parents an important aspect of the tasks of socialization, the child's preparation for the life that lies ahead. But we should not argue from this that the family has lost its function as a unit for socialization. In the first phase of a child's development, when it depends entirely on its mother for everything, no agency has yet been able to relieve the mother. In its earliest stage of development the greatest needs of the child are food and shelter. Breast-feeding too means that the child not only depends on the parents for its food supply, but also that the mother's own health at this stage is very crucial. The period of entire dependence on the mother, assisted by father and older siblings, lasts until about three to four years when it can eat by itself. Even then its independence is only partial, for it still depends for food and shelter on its elders. Thus, up to the time it goes to school, all the care it needs is provided by the parents. Indeed the parents are still responsible during the period of training which was formerly done under parental direction, though now outside the home. Though tuition may be free, all other expenses are paid by them. Though a child's schooling may take him into a boarding institution, the payment of the bill is still the responsibility of the parents.

The function lost by parents to schools is therefore that of actual participation in the training process, not responsibility for provision of that training. Even here only part of this is taken over by the schools. It is now necessary in Anlo to distinguish between two forms of knowledge, namely *sukununya*, school education or book knowledge, and *afemenunya*, i.e. general knowledge, intelligence and etiquette. The former falls within the domain of teachers, while the latter is still the responsibility of parents. This is concerned with teaching customary etiquette and decorum. It is because parents have forgotten this dichotomy that they blame the children's reported disobedience on their teachers. After all, the child eventually spends the greater part of its life with the parents.

3. CONCLUSION

The aim of this book has been to give an account of Anlo traditional social structure with particular reference to kinship, marriage and the family, and to examine how the changes brought about by European activities have influenced it. Having attempted that, it is convenient at this point to take a general retrospective view of the ground so far covered.

Our study has involved a description of the structure and functions of clans, lineages and wards, the various events leading to marriage, and the domestic groups and relationships which result from it, and finally a discussion of the social structure in the present situation of change. The picture which has emerged from the study is that Anlo society, like all other African societies subjected to similar external influences, is transitional, in that the traditional social set-up has undergone some modifications.

In the traditional system the lineage as a localized property-owning group with the sanctions of its ancestors was the most important unit of the social structure. A person's membership or attachment to the lineage entitled him to a share of its property; there was little to compete for in private wealth; land and creeks were freely available for use, and everyone was either farmer, fisherman or small craftsman, enjoying a very uniform standard of living. Men could compete only for authority, but opportunities for this were narrowly circumscribed. Within the lineage, authority and status depended on age. Within the village it lay with chiefs, who derived their positions from their membership of lineages in which a hereditary right to fill the chieftaincy rested. In such a system respect for age was great, and parental authority reigned supreme. Group solidarity was strong, as was co-operation among kinsfolk. Any major undertaking in the life of an individual, such as his marriage, was the concern of all.

With the introduction of a money economy and the development of new material wants and needs, a new value system has been created. The money economy has introduced individualization and alienation of lineage property. It has become possible for people to earn their living without help from their lineage by joining fishing companies or entering the employment of the white man. It has led to migrant labour, the periodic exodus of people from their lineages. This has a disruptive effect on lineage solidarity. Money in the hands of individuals carries with it a certain freedom of action which gradually undermines the authority and solidarity of the lineage. A status formerly achieved entirely by age or genealogical seniority may now be attained by wealth or professional ability.

Like money, other agents of change, namely formal education and Christianity, generate tendencies which have led to the relative disorganization of the traditional structure. Associations such as the Church, fishing companies and the school have brought the individual Anlo into much closer contact with people outside his kin group. Finally there is the new political system, in which the old judicial procedures, elaborately buttressed by religious beliefs, are being superseded by new legal institutions.

As the authority of the lineage group is challenged, so is its claim to overriding loyalty. In the traditional society marriage was designed above all to ensure that the lineage would continue to flourish. To many of the new generation it offers, instead, a relationship of mutual affection which makes them less dependent for emotional security on the solidarity of the kin group. Now people begin to search for ways of satisfying their need for love which can be more easily reconciled with the new structure of authority. And in conformity with this trend most of the traditional sanctions which stabilize the marital bond have disappeared, the result being an increase in divorce and marital instability.

Perhaps in my attempt to show the changes that have overtaken the Anlo I have been led to overemphasize the disintegration of the traditional social structure. To a large extent, however, the predominant pattern of Anlo traditional kinship and family relationships remains. Although the individual's world view has extended far beyond kinship, contemporary Anlo ideas and values still derive from the traditional kinship system. This is because rural Anlo has not undergone any radical industrial revolution. No new major industries have been introduced since the establishment of national government. All the changes have been incorporated into a peasant and largely subsistence economy, so that lineages, though increasingly disintegrating, are still largely localized. So long as the great majority of the educated members of the society have to leave their homes for large commercial centres in other parts of the country, their influence on the traditional social structure must be limited. Those who have attained positions of power because of their wealth and professional skills are fishing net owners, traders and craftsmen, who need no formal education. They have not been able to imbibe many of the new ideas through which they might influence the system.

Moreover, the moral and emotional pressures on the individual to subordinate his personal interests to those of his kinsfolk are still powerful. But with the rise of economic individualism, the range of kinsfolk covered by mutual help is becoming restricted. Yet the lineage as a whole remains under the guardianship of one ancestral shrine. During ancestral rites all members in the locality renew their kinship ties in a religious context. This religious expression of kinship ties has been sustained despite the break in economic unity of the group, and shows the great deference the ancestors still command. It is this religious aspect which is still the most powerful sanction for lineage solidarity. At present its force is threatened on two fronts, first by the seasonal labour migrations and secondly by the attitude of Christians to traditional ritual. As we have seen, the effects of the first are not as great as those of the second. As more and more Anlo become Christians they are disenchanted with traditional religious beliefs. The strength of this threat is the more serious in view of the present education drive of the Ghana Government, by which at least elementary school education is regarded as compulsory. If this scheme materializes it will mean that all future farmers, fishermen, and craftsmen will have at least some taste of formal education and perhaps be converted to Christianity. It is important to emphasize that ancestor worship, and indeed the worship of traditional deities, is still an illiterates' affair. Though Christian converts may not necessarily be practising Christians, they none the less consider it improper to revert to traditional religious practices. The future of ancestor-worship as a unifying factor in lineage affairs therefore depends largely on the extent to which formal education and Christianity influence the next generation.

The degree of disintegration suffered by the various Anlo settlements is a function of the amount of western influence to which they are exposed. This study was primarily concerned with rural communities. Only Keta is, strictly speaking, outside this description. It is therefore to be expected that the fluidity of established social norms has reached a more advanced stage there than what has been recorded. It is not possible to be more precise than this at present.

Some details of Anlo Clans, including Totems, Taboos and Cults

1. LAFE

Totems: Monitor lizard (*eve*), Antelope (*se*) and sparrow (*atsutsrɔe*).

Taboos: Members of this clan are forbidden to kill or eat totem animals. If any totem animal is found dead its body must be covered with leaves or if possible given a burial. Violation of the taboo will result in death.

Clan cults: Aʋadoʋaklo, Kodzikli, Aʋadatsi, Tsiamitsi. The Lafe clan is regarded as the oldest of all the Anlo clans. Their legendary apical ancestor, Atsu Ʋenya, was reputed to have led the Anlo on their migration to their present country.

2. AMLADE

Totems: Same as Lafe.
Taboos: Same as Lafe.
Clan cults: Tɔgbi Gbe, Sui, Nyaga, Adebe. The founder of this clan was Etse, twin brother of Atsu, founder of the Lafe clan. The two clans have identical observances except for the cults.

3. ADZƆVIA

Totem: *Adzɔvia*, a small, brown perch-like fish related to *Tilapia melanopleura* (*Akpa*).

Taboos: Members of this clan are forbidden to eat totem fish. They are also forbidden to use unprocessed sponge (*Kutsamadogbeɖi*). They must not use the following local trees as firewood: *Aviatsi, Xe* and *Xetolia*.

Violation of these taboos will result in rashes.

Clan cults: Mama Tɔmi, Asimatsɔnu, Ʋanyevi, Afɔmagbetɔme. This is the senior of the two royal clans. The other is Bate.

4. BATE

Totems: Leopard, Hippo, Dog, Crab, Raffia.

Taboos: Members of this clan must not kill, touch or handle any part of a leopard, or sit on its skin. They are not expected to look at any part of raffia in the morning. If they inadvertently do so, they must lick the raffia. And they do not use raffia as firewood.

They do not eat *galadzeŋi* – that is a crab which turns upside down (legs up) when being cooked.

They are not to be licked by dogs. If a member is licked by a dog, he must kick it to ward off supernatural retribution.

When the wife of a Bate man is pregnant she is forbidden to receive anything from anybody across a fence. Violation of this taboo may result in the birth of *vɔ* (lit. python), an abnormal baby having the features of this snake.

Violations of all other taboos of this clan result in rashes or loose tongue.

Their taboos are believed to be among the most powerful. When they die members of this clan have their faces covered with leaves of raffia specially woven.

Clan cults: Bate, Fiazikpui.

The Bate are the junior of the two royal clans. The other is Adzɔvia.

5. LIKE

Totem: Saw-fish (*nyanyake*).

Taboo: Totem animal not to be eaten. Violation of the taboo will result in madness or death.

Clan cults: Ziɔ, Atsikpui, Dzomadoɖetɔŋgɔ.

6. BAMEE

Totems: Leopard, Monitor lizard.

Taboos: Not to kill, touch or handle the leopard, or sit on its skin. Not to eat any *layɔŋɔe*, i.e. spotted animal, or any animal resembling the leopard. Not to kill the monitor lizard. To bury or cover its dead body with leaves. Bamee babies must not be anointed with shea butter exposed to naked fire. Rashes will result from violation of taboos.

Clan cults: Gbaku, Gbekukuia.

7. KLEVI

Totem: Antelope.
Taboos: Antelope not to be killed or handled. *Klevɔ*, a small local bird, not to be eaten.
Violation will result in death.
Clan cults: Gbɔtonya, Kɔvi.

8. TOVI

Totem: Buffalo.
Taboo: Never to kill nor eat the flesh of buffalo.
Violation will result in death.
Clan cults: Mala, Kotsi.
This is the only clan whose members are occasionally spoken of as actual descendants of the totem animal.

9. TSIAME

Totems: Land-crab, cashew tree.
Taboos: Totem objects not to be eaten. Cashew tree not used for firewood, and its nut not eaten.
Violation of taboo will result in death.
Clan cults: Tsali, Dɔkutonyi.

10. AGAVE

Totem: Same as Tsiame.
Taboos: Same as Tsiame.
Clan cults: Kaklaku, Gbe, Tsixi, Dzemu.

11. AMɛ

Totem: Dog.
Taboos: Not to breed, handle or kill dogs.
Members are not to be licked by dogs. If a member is licked by a dog, he must kick it to ward off supernatural retribution. Members must not be held by the ear. If held by one ear by mistake the other ear must also be held.
They must not set foot on the creeping branches of the sweet potato plant (*ti-ka*).
They must not eat *etsɔ kple*, i.e. *akple* prepared the previous day (for *akple* see Chapter 3, Section 5, p. 82, fn.).

Violation of taboo will result in death.

Clan cult: Mama Blolui.

Members of this clan have the prerogative of settling any dispute between kinsfolk which has resulted in sickness for one or both parties (*nugbidodo*).

12. DZEVI

Totem: Leopard.

Taboos: Totem animal not to be killed, eaten or handled. Not to use unprocessed salt for cooking. Not to use salt from a bulrush-basket – *kevimedze*.

Violation of taboo will result in death.

Clan cult: Nyigbla. (This is a national god, but the Dzevi are its custodians.)

13. ƲIFEME

Totems: Antelope, Tortoise.

Taboos: Totem animals not killed, eaten or handled.

Violation of taboo will result in rashes.

Clan cult: Mama Asife.

This is the only clan whose members claim descent from a woman. Descent is however traced patrilineally from the male children of the ancestress, Ʋi. Ʋi is also believed to be of foreign origin.

14. X̲ETSOFE

Totem: Sheep.

Taboo: Totem animal not eaten or handled.

Penalty for violation is death.

Clan cult: Aʋadatsi.

15. BLU

Totems: Antelope, Tortoise.

Taboos: Totem animals not killed, eaten or handled.

Not to use *ɖɔka* – any piece of fishing net – as a sponge.

Not to eat a piece of egg – *azikakɛ*.

Not to eat dough prepared in *afianu* – a wooden tray.

Penalty for violation is rashes.

Clan cult: Nil.

Since members of this clan trace descent from ancestors in different foreign countries their observances differ from place to place. In any case the above taboos and totems are fairly widespread. And as they lack much of the solidarity characteristic of the other clans, they do not have a shrine where members could be 'inducted' into full membership. Instead every adult is expected to perform a special ritual known as *etretsyɔtsyɔ*. Evidence of this ritual is the calabash hung in the sitting rooms of Blu clan memers. It is said that this *tretsyɔtsyɔ* is equivalent to an induction into the Blu clan and after this has been done the totemic observances become imperative.

APPENDIX II

Anlo Clan- and Day-Names

1. CLAN NAMES

Group 1 Lafe, Amlade, Adzɔvia, Bate, Likɛ, Bamee, Tovi, Klevi, Xetsofe.		*Group 2* Agave, Tsiame.		*Group 3* Amɛ.		*Group 4* Dzevi, Ʋifeme, Blu.	
Male	*Female*	*Male*	*Female*	*Male*	*Female*	*Male*	*Female*
1. Fui	Kokui	Fui	Ʋi	Amɛ	Kui	Tete	Dede
2. Tsatsu	Abui	Tsatsu	Gbo	Adzɛ	Akoe	Tete	Kɔkɔ
3. Tsiɖi	Dzoe	Tsiɖi	Tolo	Tsiɖi	Tolo	Tɛ	Mable
4. Akɔli	Sa	Akɔli	Sa	Akɔli	Sa	Ɖa	Maɖui
5. Dɛ	Kuya	Dɛ	Kuya	Dɛ	Kuya	Ɖate	Aladze
6. Lotsu	Aʋayɛ	Lotsu	Aʋayɛ	Lotsu	Aʋayɛ		
7. Letsa	Aʋala	Letsa	Aʋala	Letsa	Aʋala		
8. Dra	Ʋala	Dra	Ʋala	Dra	Ʋala		
9. Akɔlɔ	Ʋalaʋala	Akɔlɔ	Ʋalaʋala	Akɔlɔ	Ʋalaʋala		
10. Akɔlɔtsɛ	Ʋalawui	Akɔlɔtsɛ	Ʋalawui	Akɔlɔtse	Ʋalawui		
11. Tui	Gbato	Tui	Gbato	Tui	Gbato		

(Culled from Kpodo, 1945. Part 1. p. 5.)

The clans are grouped in their naming according to the order in which they are believed to have travelled when migrating to Anlo country. Clans in Group 1 were the first and those in Group 4 the last. That the Dzevi and Ʋifeme are grouped with the strangers' clan of Blu is due to the fact that the ancestors of the former are believed to have settled in Krobo and Adangbe countries for a long time before joining the main body at Anloga. Their names are therefore the same as those of the Blu, who are mainly of Adangbe stock. It is also significant that the clan names of this last group (4) are similar to those of the Ga, Adangbe and Krobo peoples.

2. DAY NAMES

Day of birth	Male	Female
Sunday	Kɔsi	Kɔsiwɔ
Monday	Kɔdzo	Adzo, Adzowɔ
Tuesday	Kɔbla	Abla, Ablewɔ
Wednesday	Kɔku	Aku, Akuwɔ
Thursday	Yao	Yawo, Yawɔ
Friday	Kofi	Afi, Afiwɔ
Saturday	Kɔmi	Ami, Ama, Amɛyo

Grouping of Clans according to Mortuary Rites

Normally funeral rites in Anlo involve two 'vigils'. The first takes place on the eve of the burial and the second on the eve of *yɔfogbe*. On *yɔfogbe* day, two rituals of sacrifice are performed, the first at the graveside and the second in the ancestral home of the deceased. Two old women, one a clanswoman of the deceased and the other from his mother's clan, visit the grave-side to bring the spirit of the deceased to join the ancestors in the ancestral home. The *luvɔ*, or 'soul' of the deceased, comprising his finger nails and hair, is then buried in the ancestral home. This ceremony is known as *yɔfofo*. It may take place on the 5th, 7th or 8th day after the day of burial, depending on the clan of the deceased. The Anlo themselves group their clans according to the number of days which elapse between the day of burial and *yɔfogbe*. According to this classification, there are two broad groups of clans, namely *ŋkeke-kpui-tɔwo* (the short-period clans) and *ŋkeke-legbe-tɔwo* (the long-period clans). The *ŋkeke-kpui-tɔwo* are Lafe, Amlade, Adzɔvia, Bate, Bamee, Likɛ, Tovie, Klevi and Amɛ. They keep vigil on the fourth night and *yɔfofo* on the fifth day. The *ŋkeke-legbe-tɔwo* are in turn divided into two sub-groups. Tsiame, Agaʋe, Dzevie and Xetsofe keep the vigil on the 6th night and *yɔfofo* on the 7th day. Ʋifeme and Blu do theirs on the 7th night and the 8th day respectively.

APPENDIX IV

Fair and Market Days

One of the ways by which life among the Anlo is regulated is the fair, *asi*. It is held on every fourth day in all large towns in the area. The economic and cultural lives of the people are governed not by the seven-day week but by the four-day fair cycle. Many religious and social functions are prohibited on the fair day, *asigbe*, and are usually fixed for the day preceding or following it.

The fair is a great social occasion: it is the meeting place for relatives and friends from different localities; people go there to hear news from distant places; outstanding disputes are settled; and girls and youths may go there to find spouses.

The fairs are organized in a cycle, the main towns in the sub-districts of Anlo having theirs on different days. Keta has the chief fair and it is from this that the others take their names. The day-names based on the fair cycle are: *Asigbe*, fair or market day; *Asigbɔgbe*, returning day or day after the fair; *Domegbe*, minor fair; and *Asimbegbe*, last fair. The main towns and their market days are shown in the following table:

Keta-sigbe	Asigbɔgbe	Domegbe	Asimbegbe
Keta	Akatsi (Mɔnenu)	Afao	Dzita
Anloga	Denu	Dzodze	Tadzevu
Xevi			Agbozume

Thus *asigbe* at Keta is also *asigbe* at Anloga and Xevi. But *asigbɔgbe* at Keta is *asigbe* at Akatsi (Mɔnenu) and Denu, and so on.

APPENDIX V

Evewɔwɔ or Customs with the Birth of Twins

Twins, *venɔviwo*, are regarded as supernatural beings and their birth requires the performance of rites aimed at placating their spirits. Failure to perform these rites is believed to bring disaster to their parents and relatives. If propitiated, however, they are believed to bring abundant prosperity to their parents. The rites, which are many and complicated, may be spread over several months or even years, but it is desirable to perform them as early as possible. The ritual specialists are old women who are parents of twins, *venawo*, and have themselves passed through the rites. Only the important ceremonies will be described. Of these *alɔtɔtrɔ*, or changing of hands, is one of the first. It is performed a few days after the twins are born. A special climbing plant or raffia is tied around the neck, waist, wrists, ankles and knees of each of the twins and around the left wrists of the parents. This is followed by recitals and incantations by the ritual specialist. According to Gaba (op. cit., p. 231) *alɔtɔtrɔ* is directed towards making the twins identify themselves fully with the human life they have themselves chosen. Through this rite they are separated from the supernatural beings whom they have left behind in the spirit world and who make furious attempts to take them away. The non-performance of the rite might even lead to the deaths of the twins themselves.

Another important ceremony at this early stage involves the fixing of two pots at the main entrance of the building housing the twins. These are known as *Venɔvizewo* (sing. *Venɔvize*) or Twin Pots. Each pot contains water and herbs including seven palm nuts, *sede ku*. The safety of the twins is identified with the safety of the pots, and the latter must be kept in a very good state. The water they contain serves as a balm for the twins. When they are sick they are bathed with it. Gifts of money for them are put into the pots. The coins in the pots may be used only by them or their parents, or with their express permission. Any other person who takes any coin from the pots will be struck with kleptomania till confession is made and his body purified.

The final and perhaps the major ceremony concerns the parents and goes by the name *evewɔwɔ*. Here again only the important stages will be mentioned. The ceremony usually occupies a whole day. As with all major ritual performances in Anlo, those initiating the ritual, in this case the parents of the twins, send *edza*, an invitation with ritual payment (of only token monetary value) to the *venagãwo*, the ritual specialists and other parents of twins, *venawo*, and twins. Relatives who are not twins or parents of twins may also be invited. This invitation makes it incumbent on each of the twins and parents of twins to bring four cowries and a small quantity of corn to be used in the ceremony. The important opening events are fetching water from a nearby well by the twins' mother; collection of firewood from the bush and a visit to the market to buy *nukpotuikpotuiwo*, sundries. Then comes *Asaɖameyiyi*, the voyage to Asaɖame. Asaɖame is a small island town of 811 inhabitants on the northern shores of the Keta Lagoon. Its association with the ceremony is only symbolic. There is no actual visit there. The twin's mother and father enter a canoe which the latter rows a few yards on the lagoon, creek or pond and then rows it back. They then come ashore at 'Asaɖame' and enter the 'Asaɖame' market, where they buy corn and paw-paw. On their return from 'Asaɖame', they are welcomed home by the ritual specialists and all those assembled: '*Venawo miawoe zɔ*', 'Parents of the twins, you are welcome home', they say, and the couple reply: 'Yoo!' When they have put down their load the greetings are repeated. After this they are offered water to drink, as is the custom when someone returns from a long journey.

Next an improvised entrance is made in the fence enclosing the house. The chief ritual specialist leads the couple through this forwards and backwards four times. Then follows the eating of the ceremonial meal of several courses: chicken soup, ordinary okro soup, special okro soup (*fetri-ma*) with fish, rice and yams. This is eaten by all the participants in the ceremony, including those who are neither twins nor parents of twins. But before they begin eating, yams, rice and fish should be given as offerings to the Twin Pots. This concludes the activities of the morning.

The afternoon activities begin with the pouring of libation.

Special herbs are given to all the participants. A new bed bought for the occasion is picked up by the chief ritual specialist, who counts seven and then lays it down. She then holds the couple by the wrist and after counting seven seats them on the bed. She then gives them pieces of the herb which has been distributed to the others.

Then comes *adzɔxexle*, the incantation believed to restore normalcy to the lives of the couple. As the ritual specialist recites the words, all the twins and parents of twins come forward one by one and put the cowries and corn they have brought into three bags made of bulrush, *keviwo* (sing. *kevi*). Then the couple are led away from the bed, again by the ritual specialist into a room where they are made to sip *aɖima*, a form of okro soup, seven times. After this they are led outside amidst drumming and dancing, in which they join. They have to lead the singing for a while, asking their own favourite songs to be sung for them, before they themselves retire. This concludes the ceremony of *evewɔwɔ*. It only remains for the couple to visit and thank all the *venagãwo* and *venawo* and the twins who attended the ceremony.

By the performance of this ceremony the parents of the twins not only avert mystical danger but automatically acquire the power of osteopathy, which in Anlo is the prerogative of parents of twins who have gone through these rites.

It is difficult to understand the import of most of these intricate rituals. But they do indicate that the birth of twins is regarded with great concern.

Ahowɔwɔ or Rituals and other Customs concerned with Widowhood

Marriage commands great respect among the Anlo. Though the marital bond is generally subordinated to kinship ties, its importance is demonstrated in certain social situations, notably in mourning customs. The management of funerals as a rule is the responsibility of the kin of the deceased. The same applies to the funeral expenses. Yet the most formal and institutionalized aspects of the mourning are performed not by the kin of the deceased but by the spouse. This ceremonial mourning is known as *ahowɔwɔ*. This may take place some time after the death of the spouse, but the surviving spouse has certain taboos and ritual practices to observe before the period of *ahowɔwɔ* starts. As in the case of *evewɔwɔ* a woman has more to do in these practices than a man. As soon as a wife learns of the death of her husband, unless she is pregnant, she must start wearing her red cloth, *godui-dzi*, more securely around her private parts. This is a precaution against attempts by the husband's spirit to copulate with her. Should the spirit succeed the wife will become permanently pregnant. And on the day of *yɔfofo* she must go through the ritual of *yɔdzogbɔnono*, drinking the special 'funeral pap' to prove her innocence of her husband's death. She must also observe the practice of putting a piece of charcoal into her food, otherwise the spirit will partake of the food and harm her. This practice is also observed by men.

Ahowɔwɔ itself falls into two parts. First there is the period of confinement of sixteen days for both husband and wife. After this a wife observes a further mourning period of sixteen months.

The period of confinement is preceded by a special ceremony.

For this the bereaved spouse requires the following: sponge, cooking utensils, plates, calabash, pot (to contain water for bathing) and towel, all new. The ceremony begins in the evening of the day after the local market day, *asigbɔgbe*, one of the two *asinyuigbewo*, propitious days for religious ceremonies in the traditional four-day fair week (see Appendix 4). The ritual specialists are a man and woman who have been widowed and have themselves gone through the ceremony. The bereaved spouse is shaved of all hair and has the tips of the nails cleaned, and is then taken to the side of a lagoon, river, creek or pond, where a ditch one or two feet deep has been dug. The ritual specialist of the same sex as the bereaved spouse prepares *aɖitsi*, water mixed with herbs, and with it washes the head of the bereaved.

For purpose of description it will be assumed that the bereaved spouse is a woman. The ritual specialist washes the widow's head with clean water, and gives her the sponge to wash herself with the lagoon water. Then the ritual specialist pours *eflatsi*, another mixture of water and herbs, on the widow, who then washes herself all over again with clean fresh water. She is then taken out of the hole, and after wiping her body is brought home, hands across the shoulders, with only a piece of cloth around her waist. Back at home the bereaved is led seven times in and out of the 'widow room' which she will now occupy. On the seventh she is left inside to remain in confinement for the next sixteen days. Several rites and taboos are associated with the confinement. A widow must cook her own food inside her room, but a relative who has gone through the ceremony before will cook for a widower, and sometimes also for a widow. A person in confinement does not answer a call from outside. A visitor must knock four times, and be answered by knocking the bed or chair the same number of times, before entering. Again, to greet the widow the visitor must clap four times, also to be reciprocated. These measures, according to some authorities, are to prevent the deceased spouse from surreptitiously re-uniting with the survivor. The belief is that during this delay he would be recognized and would then disappear.

For a widower the ceremonial mourning ends with the completion of the confinement period. For a widow the confinement is concluded by another visit to the lagoon-side, where she is dressed in the black mourning attire she is to wear for the next sixteen months. On the following day, which is a market day, the widow, or *ahosi* as she is now called, is sent to the market to buy, among other things, corn to make *abolo*, bread. She must sell this first to *ahosiwo*, widows who have already gone through this ceremony. From this time until the end of the sixteen months she is at liberty to pursue whatever trading or economic activities she has normally followed before the death of the husband. She is indeed expected to work harder to save money for the clothes she will use when the mourning period ends. But she is still subject to some restrictions. She should not announce her wares as she sells around. Her usual response when called is no longer 'yee!', the usual response of women and girls, but rather 'agoo!', that of men. She may not greet anyone in English (using such salutations as good morning, as many do in these days) but only in the traditional way in Ewe. Finally she may neither sing nor dance. Reticence and detachment are the prescribed qualities of behaviour during the sixteen months.

At the end of this period, there is *ahotsilele*, the ceremonial washing of the widow. In the evening the *ahosi* is taken to the shores of the lagoon or creek or to the beach to see whether she has been seduced since the death of her husband. This is known as *zãmeyiyi*. As they reach the beach she steps into the water. It is said that she will be drowned if she has slept with any man, unless she confesses. The next day is an occasion of great joy and activity. All widows in the locality who have gone through *ahowɔwɔ* are invited. Two fowls, a cock and a hen, are killed and cooked for the *ahosi* to eat in the company of all her guests. Some of the food is placed at the road side for the spirit of the dead husband. Finally there is drumming and dancing in which the *ahosi* is expected to participate fully, leading the singing at one stage.

A widow must go through *ahowɔwɔ* before re-marrying. As the ceremony of *zãmeyiyi* has shown, she is regarded as the wife of the dead husband even during the mourning period. Any sexual activity at this time is still regarded as infidelity. It is only after she has been ceremonially washed at all the stages of *ahowɔwɔ* that she is free to enter into another marriage. There is no *zãmeyiyi* for a widower because access to other women is not offence against a wife, polygyny being a recognized institution. This is also responsible for the differences in the ceremonial mourning periods for widows and widowers. For a man a long period of ceremonial mourning with all its associated taboos would mean that for over sixteen months he will not be in a position to render his sexual services to his other wives. But a woman has no such reason to be exempted.

LIST OF WORKS CITED

BOOKS AND ARTICLES

ADZOMADA, REV. P. J. K., 1950. *Ewe dukɔ kple Kristotɔnyenye*. Augustin.

AMENUMEY, D. E. K., 1964. *The Ewe people and the coming of European Rule 1850–1914*, Unpublished M.A. Thesis, London.

BARNES, J. A., 1949. 'Measures of divorce frequency in simple societies', in *Journal of the Royal Anthropological Institute*, pp. 37–62.

——, 1951. *Marriage in a changing society*, Rhodes-Livingstone Paper No. 20.

——, 1962. 'African models in the New Guinea Highlands', in *Man*, pp. 5–8.

BOHANNAN, L., 1949. 'Dahomean marriage: a revaluation', in *Africa*, pp. 273–87.

BUSIA, K. A., 1951. *The Position of the Chief in the Modern Political System of Ashanti*, Oxford University Press.

CHAPMAN, D. A., 1943. *Our Homeland Bk. 1*, Achimota Press.

CROWTHER, F. G., 1927. 'The Ewe-speaking people', in *Gold Coast Review*, pp. 11–53.

DURKHEIM, E., 1952. *Suicide: a study in sociology* (translated by G. Simpson), London.

ELLIS, A. B., 1890. *The Ewe-speaking peoples of the slave coast*, London.

EVANS-PRITCHARD, E. E., 1934. 'The Social Character of Bridewealth, with special reference to the Azande', in *Man*, pp. 172–5.

——, 1940. *The Nuer*, Oxford University Press.

——, 1952. *Kinship and marriage among the Nuer*, Oxford University Press.

FALLERS, L. A., 1957. 'Some determinants of marital stability in Busoga. A reformulation of Gluckman's hypothesis', in *Africa*, 1957, pp. 106–21.

FIAWOO, D. K., 1958. *The influence of contemporary social changes on the magico-religious concepts and organization of the Southern Ewe-speaking peoples of Ghana*, Unpublished Ph.D. Thesis, Edinburgh.

FIAWOO, F. K., 1943. *The Fifth Landing Stage*, London.

FIRTH, R. W., 1957. *We, The Tikopia: a sociological study of kinship in primitive Polynesia*, 2nd edn., London.

——, 1959. *Social Change in Tikopia*, Allen and Unwin, London.

FORDE, D., 1950. 'Ward Organization among the Yako', *Africa*, pp. 267–89.

——, 1950. 'Double descent among the Yako', in A. R. Radcliffe-Brown and D. Forde, eds., *African Systems of Kinship and marriage*, Oxford University Press.

FORTES, M., 1949. 'Time and Social Structure: an Ashanti Case Study', in M. Fortes, ed., *Social Structure: studies presented to A. R. Radcliffe-Brown*, Oxford University Press.

FORTES, M., and EVANS-PRITCHARD, E. E., eds., 1940. *African Political Systems*, Oxford University Press.

GABA, C. R., 1965. *Aŋlɔ Traditional Religion*, Unpublished Ph.D. Thesis, London.

GENNEP, A. VAN, 1960. *The Rites of Passage*, translated by Vizedom and Caffee, London.

GIBBS, J. L., Jr., 1963. 'Marital instability among the Kpelle: Towards a theory of Epainogamy', in *American Anthropologist*, pp. 552–73.

GLUCKMAN, M., 1950. 'Kinship and marriage among the Lozi of Northern Rhodesia and the Zulu of Natal', in A. R. Radcliffe-Brown and D. Forde, eds., *African systems of kinship and marriage*, Oxford University Press.

——, 1953. 'Bridewealth and Stability of marriage', in *Man*, pp. 141–3.

GOODY, J., 1959. 'The Mother's Brother and the Sister's Son in West Africa', in *Journal of the Royal Anthropological Institute*, pp. 61–88.

GOODY, J., ed., 1958. *The developmental Cycle in Domestic Groups*, Cambridge Papers in Social Anthropology, No. 1.

HERSKOVITS, M., 1939. *Dahomey*, 2 vols., Chicago.

HILL, POLLY, 1963–64. 'Pan-African Fishermen', in *West Africa*, 28 December 1963 and 4 January 1964.

KODZO-VORDOAGU, J. G., 1959. *The Impact of Western Education on the Clan System of the Anlos*, unpublished thesis, St Francis Teacher Training College, Hohoe.

KPODO, G. C. K., 1945. *Anlo Names I and II*. Ewe Studies Nos. 3 and 4, Achimota Press.

——, 1954. *Srɔɖeɖe le Aŋlɔ me*, Unpublished manuscript.

LEACH, E. R., 1953. 'A note on bridewealth and marriage stability', in *Man*, pp. 179–80.

——, 1957. 'Aspects of Bridewealth and marriage instability among the Kachin and Lakher', in *Man*, pp. 50–5.

MAIR, L. P., 1934. *An African People in the Twentieth Century*, London.

MANOUKIAN, M., 1952. *The Ewe-speaking People of Togoland and the Gold Coast*, Ethnographic Survey of Africa, Oxford University Press.

MIDDLETON, J. F. M., 1960. *Lugbara Religion*, Oxford University Press.

OBIANIM, S., 1957. *Eve Kɔnuwo*.

PARSONS, T., 1951. *The Social System*, Glencoe, Ill., Free Press.

RADCLIFFE-BROWN, A. R., 1952. 'The Mother's brother in South Africa', in *Structure and Function in Primitive society*, London.

RADCLIFFE-BROWN, A. R. and FORDE, D., eds., 1950. *African Systems of Kinship and marriage*, Oxford University Press.

RICHARDS, A. I., 1950. 'Some types of family structure Amongst the Central Bantu', in Radcliffe-Brown and Forde, eds., *African Systems of kinship and marriage*, Oxford.

RIVERS, W. H. R., 1914. *Kinship and Social Organization*, London. New edition ed. Firth and Schneider, 1967.

SCHNEIDER, D. M., 1953. 'A note on Bridewealth and the Stability of marriage', *Man*, pp. 55–7.

SCHWAB, W. B., 1955. 'Kinship and Lineage among the Yoruba', in *Africa*, pp. 352–74.

SOUTHALL, A., ed., 1959. *Social Change in modern Africa*, Oxford University Press.

SPIETH, J., 1906. *Die Ewe Stämme*, Berlin.

——, 1911. *Die Religion der Eweer in Süd-Togo*, Berlin.

WARD, B. E., 1949. *The social organization of the Ewe-speaking People*, Unpublished M.A. Thesis, University of London.
——, 1955. 'An example of a "mixed" system of descent and inheritance', in *Man*, pp. 3–5.
WARD, W. E., 1958. *A Short History of Ghana*, London.
——, 1946. *A Short History of the Gold Coast*, 3rd edn., Longmans.
WESTERMANN, D., 1928. *Ewefiala: Ewe-English Dictionary*, Berlin.
——, 1930. *A study of the Ewe language*, translated by Bickford-Smith, Oxford University Press.
——, 1930. *Gbesela Yeye or English-Ewe Dictionary*, Berlin.
——, 1935. *Die Glidyi-Ewe in Togo, Züge aus ihrem Gesellschaftsleben*, Berlin.
——, 1949. *The African Today and Tomorrow*, Oxford University Press.
WIEGRABE, P., 1938. *Eve gbalexexle Akpa Enelia*, Berlin.

GOVERNMENT PUBLICATIONS AND OFFICIAL REPORTS

Native Jurisdiction Ordinance, Gold Coast Government, 1883.
Population Census of the Gold Coast Colony, 1891.
Annual reports to the League of Nations, 1919–39.
Gold Coast Census Report, 1948.
1960 Population Census of Ghana, vol. 1.

INDEX

Abidjan, 98, 128, 131, 139, 169, 176
Abor, 5, 8
Accra, 7, 167–8
Adangbe tribes, 21 n., 198
Adeladzea, 10
Adolescence, 80, 148 ff.
Adolescent culture, 152
Adultery, 70–71, 97, 111, 119; incidence of, 181–2
Adulterine children, 119
Adzomada, 84 n., 104 n.
Adzovia clan, 9–10, 22–23, 193, 198
Affines, and marriage prohibitions, 64–67
Afiadenyigba, 5
Afife, 8
Aflao, 5–6, 8, 201
Agave, 8
Agave clan, 22, 195, 198
Agbametsi, 23
Agbozume, market day at, 201
Agnates, basic behaviour patterns among, 38–42
Agnatic incidence, Local, 47
Agu Mountains, 165
Ahiadzidzi, 80; *see also* Courting
Ahiakɛ, 83
Ahiaxɔdɔdɔ 130
Ahoxɔxɔ (*Ahowɔwɔ*) 99, 205–8
Akan, 11 n., 13 n., 21 n.
Akatsi, market day at, 201
Akwamu, 11 n., 163
Alakple, 29, 47, 60, 71, 116 n., 127, 129, 133–4, 138–9, 142–3, 172
frequency of divorce in, 104–7
incidence of *fomesrɔ* in, 72
intra-clan marriages in, 74
number of polygynous marriages in, 185
number of wards in, 14

reasons for selection as fieldwork centre, 18
residential and housing patterns in, 126
royal stool of, 24
Alɔkpli, 69–70
Amɛ clan, 22, 24, 52 n., 74, 195, 198
Amelor lineage, 33–7
Amenumey, D. E. K., 9 n., 163 n.
A.M.E. Zion Church, 163
Amlade clan, 22, 24 n., 193, 198; priestly functions of, 23
Amutinu, 5
Ancestral home, 28
Ancestral shrine, 28–29
Ancestors, 25–26, 29, 48, 144, 192
Ancestor worship, 27–28
Anglican Church, 163
Anlo Migration Festival, 22
Anlo proper, boundaries of, 8
Anloga, 3, 9–10, 12, 22, 29, 80, 175, 198; market day in, 201
Anyako, 5, 162
Anyanui, 8
Asafohenegāwo (Military leaders), 11
Ashanti, 11 n., 13 n., 21 n., 25, 163
Atiavi, 5, 7
Ave, 3
Avenor, 8
Avadada, 12
Awoamefia (King), 9–13
Azande, 117

Badagri, 6
Bamee clan, 22, 194, 198
Barnes, J. A., 37, 104, 174
Basel missionaries, 124
Basoga, 118
Bate clan, 9–10, 22–3, 194, 198
Be, 3

LONDON SCHOOL OF ECONOMICS
MONOGRAPHS ON SOCIAL ANTHROPOLOGY

Titles marked with an asterisk are now out of print. Those marked with a dagger have been reprinted in paperback editions and are only available in this form. A double dagger indicates availability in both hard cover and paperback editions.

1, 2. RAYMOND FIRTH
   The Work of the Gods in Tikopia, 2 vols., 1940. (2nd Edition in 1 vol., 1967.)

3. E. R. LEACH
   Social and Economic Organization of the Rowanduz Kurds, 1940. (Available from University Microfilms Ltd.)

*4. E. E. EVANS-PRITCHARD
   The Political System of the Anuak of the Anglo-Egyptian Sudan, 1940. (New edition in preparation.)

5. DARYLL FORDE
   Marriage and the Family among the Yakö in South-Eastern Nigeria, 1941. (Available from University Microfilms Ltd.)

*6. M. M. GREEN
   Land Tenure of an Ibo Village in South-Eastern Nigeria, 1941.

7. ROSEMARY FIRTH
   Housekeeping among Malay Peasants, 1943. Second edition, 1966.

*8. A. M. AMMAR
   A Demographic Study of an Egyptian Province (Sharquiya), 1943.

*9. I. SCHAPERA
   Tribal Legislation among the Tswana of the Bechuanaland Protectorate, 1943. (Replaced by new volume, No. 43.)

*10. W. H. BECKETT
   Akokoaso: A Survey of a Gold Coast Village, 1944.

11. I. SCHAPERA
   The Ethnic Composition of Twsana Tribes, 1952.

*12. JU-K'ANG T'IEN
   The Chinese of Sarawak: A Study of Social Structure, 1953. (New edition revised and with an Introduction by Barbara Ward in preparation.)

*13. GUTORM GJESSING
   Changing Lapps, 1954.

14. ALAN J. A. ELLIOTT
   Chinese Spirit-Medium Cults in Singapore, 1955.

*15. RAYMOND FIRTH
   Two Studies of Kinship in London, 1956.

*16. LUCY MAIR
   Studies in Applied Anthropology, 1957. (Replaced by new volume, No. 38.)

†17. J. M. GULLICK
   Indigenous Political Systems of Western Malaya, 1958.

†18. MAURICE FREEDMAN
   Lineage Organization in Southeastern China, 1958.

†19. FREDERICK BARTH
   Political Leadership among Swat Pathans, 1959.

†20. L. H. PALMIER
Social Status and Power in Java, 1960.
†21. JUDITH DJAMOUR
Malay Kinship and Marriage in Singapore, 1959.
†22. E. R. LEACH
Rethinking Anthropology, 1961.
23. S. M. SALIM
Marsh Dwellers of the Euphrates Delta, 1962.
†24. S. VAN DER SPRENKEL
Legal Institutions in Manchu China, 1962.
25. CHANDRA JAYAWARDENA
Conflict and Solidarity in a Guianese Plantation, 1963.
26. H. IAN HOGBIN
Kinship and Marriage in a New Guinea Village, 1963.
27. JOAN METGE
A New Maori Migration: Rural and Urban Relations in Northern New Zealand, 1964.
‡28. RAYMOND FIRTH
Essays on Social Organization and Values, 1964.
29. M. G. SWIFT
Malay Peasant Society in Jelebu, 1965.
†30. JEREMY BOISSEVAIN
Saints and Fireworks: Religion and Politics in Rural Malta, 1965.
31. JUDITH DJAMOUR
The Muslim Matrimonial Court in Singapore, 1966.
32. CHIE NAKANE
Kinship and Economic Organization in Rural Japan, 1967.
33. MAURICE FREEDMAN
Chinese Lineage and Society: Fukien and Kwantung, 1966.
34. W. H. R. RIVERS
Kinship and Social Organization, reprinted with commentaries by David Schneider and Raymond Firth, 1968.
35. ROBIN FOX
The Keresan Bridge: A Problem in Pueblo Ethnology, 1967.
36. MARSHALL MURPHREE
Christianity and the Shona, 1969.
37. G. K. NUKUNYA
Kinship and Marriage among the Anlo Ewe, 1969.
38. LUCY MAIR
Anthropology and Social Change, 1969.
39. SANDRA WALLMAN
Take Out Hunger: Two Case Studies of Rural Development in Basutoland, 1969.
40. MEYER FORTES
Time and Social Structure and Other Essays, in press.
41. J. D. FREEMAN
Report on the Iban, in press.
42. W. E. WILLMOTT
The Political Structure of the Chinese Community in Cambodia, in press.
43. I. SCHAPERA
Tribal Innovators: Tswana Chiefs and Social Change 1795–1940, in press.